# solva blues

D1387495

an autobiography

meic **STEVENS**

Cover photographs: Gerallt Llywelyn

Thanks also to Gari Melville of Archif Roc a Phop Cymraeg,
and Raymond Daniel for the photographs

ISBN: 0 86243 732 6

Printed and published in Wales
by Y Lolfa Cyf., Talybont, Ceredigion SY24 5AP
*e-mail* ylolfa@ylolfa.com
*website* www.ylolfa.com
*tel.* (01970) 832 304
*fax* 832 782

# Chapter 1

# *Bet*

It was 1941 and the Second World War. The tune was by Fats Waller, and it was picked out by a pretty, dark-haired young woman on the piano in her parents' sitting-room. At the end of the keyboard, within easy reach, lay a packet of Craven A cigarettes and an art deco ashtray. On top of the piano stood a small white marble bust of Mozart. The woman's name was Betty Davies, and she was sitting in that big old house on the beach in the small village of Solva in west Wales.

Harbour House had a bit of a history. It had been built for a Liverpool man called Henry Whiteside. By trade, Whiteside was renowned as a builder of upright spinets and harpsichords. Yet he had come to Solva to build a lighthouse, after submitting a design in response to an advertisement placed in *The Times* by John Phillips, a wealthy Liverpool merchant. Phillips wanted to build a lighthouse on The Smalls, a dangerous rock lying at the mouth of St Brides Bay. It was a perilous spot where too many ships had foundered in those treacherous and often stormy seas. He chose Whiteside for the job, and this may be why Harbour House – such an imaginative name – came to be so much of a musical venue!

Whiteside's lighthouse was prefabricated in Lower Solva and then erected near the foreshore in a field by the river Solva, called the Gamblyn, so that everyone could see it before it was shipped out to The Smalls. It was a wooden structure, resembling a *gazebo* on a pierhead bandstand but on very tall iron stilts. The revolutionary design didn't last long, for it was soon blown to pieces by one of those frequent gales that lurk off this coast. Whiteside and some Trinity House inspectors were on board at the time and, when the storm finally abated after a few days, some men from Solva rowed the twenty-odd miles out to rescue them. Two men died, however, and Whiteside left under a cloud. I've always thought that a lot of strings had to be pulled to make a lighthouse builder out of a harpsichord maker!

"I'm gonna sit right down and write myself a letter, and make believe it came from you," she sang, tickling the ivories. Bet was an accomplished pianist – what they used to call 'a proper pianist' – and she had passed all her LRAM (Licentiate of the Royal Academy of Music) exams. Most of the family were musical too, which is quite common in Wales. Her father, William Henry Davies (who everyone called Dada), was an ex-Royal Navy shipwright turned carpenter, wheelwright and boat builder who sang in the local choir. Her brother Walter, a submariner, played a Soprani Hundred and Twenty bass accordion, which he'd bought in Italy on his travels. Walter and his accordion had recently been lost at sea in a submarine called HMS *Tarpon*. Bet's other brother, Hayden, played the harmonica and spoons, and he too had been part of the same action against a German battle fleet that was invading Norway in 1940. Hayden was lucky to escape on the only surviving submarine out of nine; the others were depth charged and sunk by German warships and rest in what is now an official war grave at the bottom of the Skagerak, the narrow, shallow sea between Denmark and Norway.

Bet played the piano and accordion in some of the swing bands that entertained the thousands of servicemen and women billeted in the area during the war. Swing was the popular music of the day – all D.J.s (dinner jackets), brass and the sounds of big orchestras like Glenn Miller, the Dorsey Brothers, Ted Heath, Duke Ellington and Count

Basie. At the time, swing was young peoples' music, a far cry from punk, rap, grunge, heavy metal or garage! Bet's day job was working as a staff nurse in Pembroke Cottage Hospital, some thirty miles away in the south of the county, and there was plenty to do with a war on.

As she reached for a Craven A, the telephone rang. Quickstepping across the floor, she picked it up. "Solva Two Seven Five, who's calling, please?" The voice of her ward sister calmly told her to get to the hospital fast. There had been an air raid during the night and there was a hell of a mess. They were calling in all available medical staff in the area. "I'll be there *wap!*" she replied, using a local idiom which means faster than fast. She hung up, ran into the kitchen to tell her parents the bad news, then across the road to beg a lift from Sid Gronow, the fishmonger and one of the few people in the village who drove a car.

Soon, Bet was standing on Haverfordwest station, smelling of hake, in a large crowd of people, most of them in military uniform. Eventually a train arrived and the crowd teemed into the carriages until they were like sardines in a can. As the train pulled out, the noise inside was deafening. She felt someone prodding her in the back; it was a young Welsh Guard, whom she recognized as her landlady's son. He was shouting his head off, but she could hardly hear a word. Bet guessed that he was going home on leave; conversation was impossible in a train that was bulging at the seams with soldiers, sailors and airmen along with their kitbags, rifles and cases. Some were even sleeping on the luggage racks in the compartments. I heard at first hand descriptions of these wartime trains from Victor Parker, a guitarist from Tiger Bay in Cardiff, who had played during the war with Edmundo Ross and Felix Mendelssohn's Hawaiian Serenaders. He told me that the trains were so full the passengers would prop each other up in the corridors and go to sleep. It was impossible to fall over; it was such a tight squeeze they just

*Bet aged eighteen*

*Bet and Gerald, Shrewsbury, 1941*

held each other up!

Bet tried to tell the soldier about the air raid – it was the only thing on her mind. She felt very apprehensive but thought that there was a good chance that most of the bombs had fallen on the sea. Then the train pulled into Pembroke Dock, the end of the line, and its occupants tumbled out and poured towards the crowded exit and into the road.

The lodging house stood almost opposite the station – well, it used to. There was no house there now, just a bloody great hole and a pile of rubble where it once stood, a crew of firemen and workers picking over the debris. As Bet turned she saw that the 6-ft guardsman had fainted to the floor. There was no house, no lodgings, no home to go to. Later, she was told that the house had taken a direct hit and that the guardsman's entire family had been blown to bits. The foetus of the child that the soldier's pregnant sister had been carrying was found fifty yards up the street by an air raid warden.

Bet checked into the hospital and got to work. The ward sister hadn't been exaggerating: it *was* a hell of a mess, a far cry from the tranquillity and peace of Solva, her home and piano. There was nothing *pianissimo* here, but there was plenty of work to do, patching up the wounded, comforting the dying and laying out the dead in the mortuary. After many horrific and blood-filled hours she fell asleep in her friend's bed at the nurses' home in that bombed and shattered town. Her last wakeful thoughts were for the poor girl from the lodging house. Bet could sympathize better than most, for she too was pregnant.

The doctors, nurses and auxiliaries worked furiously for days on end, constantly wondering when the next stick of bombs would fall. What could they do about it? Nothing! What did it matter? There was no point in worrying. They were there, they had work to do and, with luck, it might not happen. They could only live in hope.

Bet was engaged to be married to a young airman she'd met a

while ago in a dance at a military base nearby. His name was Gerald Wright, and he came from Shrewsbury. He was a wireless operator-air gunner on the big white Sunderland flying boats, those huge and beautiful sea-planes, whose runway was the River Cleddau at Neyland. Sometimes, when she knew what time he was flying, Bet and her friends would go down to Neyland and Gerald would wave to them from a port hole as the great white bird took off in a huge cloud of spray. They were in love; he was twenty-six and she was twenty-three. The marriage bans had been called out on three of the four consecutive Sundays at St Aidan's church in Solva – one more week to go and they would be married. They were very happy, and Bet once told me that the wartime was the happiest time of her life.

Before the war, Gerry, as everyone called him, had worked in the air ministry in London. He was a clerical sergeant and, like many others, he volunteered for flight training when the war started. Soon he became a flight sergeant and wireless operator in the Sunderlands, before being transferred to Hampden bombers. He was a racy young man who drove a low-slung, yellow Riley sports coupé with running-boards and wire-spoked wheels. But his aeroplane had recently crash landed somewhere in the Midlands. The undercarriage collapsed, the plane caught fire and the whole crew were incinerated. Gerry was an only son and everyone was devastated.

It was even worse for Bet under the circumstances, and so soon after she had lost her elder brother Walter. She was in a real jam and she had no choice but to tell her parents that she was pregnant. To her amazement they took it well; they weren't angry or, if they were, they didn't show it. They simply accepted the reality of the situation and went on to deal with it as best they could. Both were very formal, strict and religious. Bet's grandfather, Walter Davies the elder – a shoemaker who was originally from Llanfyrnach in the Preseli Mountains – had been a head deacon of the Methodist chapel in Solva

*Bet in Shrewsbury, 1941*

*My father Gerald Wright aged five, with his father, Louis Wright*

in the days when the chapels ruled. If a girl had a child out of wedlock, she would usually be thrown out of the chapel by order of the deacons and minister. She would have very few options and would usually be sent out of the way to some farm to skivvy for some old widower and probably to share his bed. Or she'd have to go away, far away up the line, to Cardiff or London. Some girls I know of – like my great-aunt Edith, who was raped by a farm hand – committed suicide.

I think that the deaths of Walter, then Gerry, and Hayden's merciful escape from the jaws of death (he's eighty-eight now and lives in Newcastle, New South Wales, Australia) helped to make the family stronger in those sad times. Such things were happening to just about everyone, and people had to get on with their lives and hope for the best. Bet's father, William Henry, was a very strong and worldly man, who had sailed the seven seas as a shipwright on the ironclads of the Royal Navy throughout the 1914–18 war, and before that on the last of the great men-of-war under sail. He was a realist, and Bet was his only daughter. Dada was a keen boxing fan, and he had a boxing ring in one of his workshops in Lower Solva where he'd train his sons and some of the other young boys to box. Even Bet was taught how to 'duke'.

Time passed, the war dragged on and nearly everyone was involved in it in one way or another. Most of the local boys had gone away and news of them was scarce. By now, the area was full of strange young men from distant places – England and America – all waiting their turn to play a part in the great venture. In the meantime, naturally enough they looked for a social life outside the barracks, some fun and maybe romance. Many of the local girls married and went away to have families with some of these servicemen, and when the local boys came home they brought brides from other places. It was a severe cultural shock to the area and a bitter blow to the Welsh language which at the time went unnoticed; until the outbreak of the Second

World War, Solva had been almost monoglot Welsh. This was soon to change.

Everything was rationed – beer, food, oil, petrol, even clothes, but people got by and the band played on!

Then there was another air raid on Pembroke Dock and Milford, and once again the hospitals were heaving with casualties. One day Bet found herself nursing a young Scottish merchant navy officer from Greenock on the Clyde. His name was James Alexander Erskine. When the bombs fell he'd been in a hotel, waiting to join a ship. One must have exploded on or near the hotel; he'd heard its threatening whistle as it fell through the air. James followed the drill and lay flat on the floor with his arms protecting his head. The blast blew a whole wall out of the building, and he found himself flying through the air still lying on the bedroom floor, which had become an aerofoil! He landed some way up the road, still clutching the floor, unhurt apart from a generous peppering of glass splinters from broken windows. Bet was given the job of picking the glass out of his body – mainly from his back (most of his clothes had also been blown away by the blast) – with a pair of tweezers. It was a strange way to meet her future husband.

Erskine fell for his nurse – which often happens, so I'm told – and he followed her everywhere as soon as he was discharged from the hospital. He pestered her at every opportunity and, after many phone calls and flowers, he finally got to meet her parents in Solva. He told them he wanted to marry her and, for their part, they told him about Gerry, the cancelled wedding and the unborn child. Bet was not in love with Jim Erskine – she was still grieving the deaths of Gerald and Walter. Her parents, however, saw Jim as the saviour of a potentially embarrassing and possibly tragic situation. Furthermore, they were very fond of him; he was a naval officer and they were a Navy family, so things fell into place. This was by far the best option, almost a godsend.

James Erskine was an engineer – a key man on any ship – and he'd sailed for some time on the 'San boats', so called because they all had names like *San Pedro*, *San Antonio* or *San Alberto*. These ships were hastily built in America to ferry war supplies across the Atlantic. They were not riveted in the usual manner of the day; the ship side plates were welded together, thus increasing the speed at which they could be built. They were not expected to last very long!

Soon, orders came for Jim to join a ship, the MV *Adellan*, which was undergoing repairs in the dry dock at Newport, Monmouthshire, having been torpedoed twice. The family decided that the wedding should take place as soon as possible. Jim joined the *Adellan* in the dry dock on the fifteenth of January, while Bet left her job in the hospital, travelled to Newport and booked into the Tredegar Arms hotel opposite the railway station. Just a couple of days later they were married, with Bet's father and her brother Ivor (who was on leave from the army) and some of the officers from the *Adellan* in attendance. They had a small reception in the hotel, stayed there that night and then boarded the ship the next day to take up residence in the quarters of the chief engineer. Bet stayed on the ship until she sailed for America, then went back to Solva.

But before that, she went to see the Wrights in Shrewsbury, not far by train from Newport. They were not very happy that she'd got married so soon after their son's death, and I later found out that they had doubts as to the parentage of the child she was carrying.

The *Adellan* sailed in convoy for the St Lawrence Seaway in North America, a favourite haunt of the German U-boat packs, while Bet waited in Harbour House for the imminent birth of her baby. By now she was tired and a little confused: what could happen next? Anything! Still, at least she didn't have to worry about the legitimacy of her child, or her own future, which as the wife of an officer in the

My mother's wedding at the Tredegar Arms hotel, Newport, 1941. Her father, WH Davies, and her brother Ivor are on her left

Uncle Hayden — one of the few to survive the attacks on the submarines in Skagerak, where his brother Walter died

*Me in 1942*

*Bet at the piano in the late 1980s*

Merchant Navy was secure. That is until the day a telegram arrived saying that the *Adellan* had been torpedoed and sunk off the Greenland coast by a U-boat on the twelfth of February. There were thirteen survivors, but Jim Erskine was not among them. He'd been in the engine room in the bowels of the ship when the torpedoes hit; he didn't stand a chance.

Exactly one month to the day, on the twelfth of March, Bet went into labour. Her son was born at five past one on 13 March 1942, in the throes of a force eight gale and thunderstorm. Doctor Saunders, the local GP, and his district nurse, who was soon to become Mrs Saunders, delivered the child and when it was all over they left Bet to get some sleep in the front bedroom of that storm-buffeted house. Totally exhausted, Bet went out like a light. When she woke it was still dark. First she thought that the thunderstorm had woken her, but soon she had a strange feeling that something was wrong. She rose and went to the baby's crib. "Jesus, he's not breathing!" She unwrapped the crocheted shawl. The baby was blue and cold and his skin was beginning to turn black. He was dead! No heartbeat! Mercifully, her training as a nurse meant that she knew what to do to resuscitate him. She could tell by his colour that he hadn't been dead long. Praying out loud, she took him by his feet, hung him upside down and started punching him in the back as hard as she dared. After a while, he gave a little croak and spluttered back to life. Later when the fuss had died down, her mother Blodwen – a simple, uneducated, but philosophical woman – said quietly, "That boy has died on the day he was born, and was brought back from the dead; this world is not good enough for him!"

They named the boy Louis (after Gerald's father) Michael (Bet's choice) James (after the dead stepfather).

Betty Davies and Gerald Wright were my mother and father!

★ ★ ★

After a while my mother went back to nursing at the County Hospital in Haverfordwest, where she did a lot of work in the operating theatre. It's just as well that she wasn't afraid of the sight of blood. We carried on living with the family in Harbour House, and I'm told that every one was happy again.

My mother and I used to travel a lot during the war – to Shrewsbury to visit the Wrights, and to my great-aunt Marianne at Tufnell Park in north London. I loved the old steam trains. My mother and I were in London on VE Day when the war in Europe came to an end, and she took me down to Buckingham Palace to join in the celebrations outside on Pall Mall. I had my photograph taken in Trafalgar Square – I've still got it! I can't remember that occasion, but I can vaguely remember being woken up in Auntie Marianne's house when my mother came into the bedroom and took me out into the street, which was crowded with people all singing and dancing. There was a huge bonfire in the middle of the road and people were throwing furniture on to it – chairs and tables, and so on. Then, some men dragged a piano out of the pub on the corner, and people sang and danced around it; a very surreal memory.

All was well until I was four and Bet decided to marry another airman. His name was Donald Stevens and he was from Forest Gate in east London. He was stationed in Brawdy, an aerodrome near Solva, and he was a navigator in the Coastal Command. After the war ended and he was demobbed, he got a job with British Overseas Airways and we moved to Harrow in London, near Northolt airport, where he was based at that time. He adopted me, and gave me his name. Later he got a job as a manager in a textile factory in Pembroke, and so we moved back to Pembrokeshire. I don't think my mother was happy with him or with London.

Pembroke town is 'down below', as we Welshies from the north of the county call it. It was once the territory of the Norman Marcher

19

Lords; people from there don't usually speak Welsh and their accent is similar to that of the people of the Welsh borders, Welshpool, Llanidloes, Newtown or Hereford. It was there that the unhappiest period of my life began. I was terrified of this man; he was unpredictable and very violent towards me and my mother, who was well under his thumb. It didn't take much for him to beat me with anything that came to hand – a belt buckle, wooden spoon, saucepan, even the leg of a chair once – before locking me in the coal shed outside the back door. I was hysterical. He used to make me read adult books when I was only five years old: Dickens, R. L. Stevenson, Daniel Defoe, Shakespeare and Mark Twain. Then he'd grill me like the Inquisition, until he was satisfied that I had read them properly. He used to try to drum things into me like "Little boys should be seen and not heard". He had a store of stock sayings, and he was always going on about Mao Tse Tung. I was too young to understand most of it, and my mother couldn't do much because she was scared of him too. The only respite I had was when I was allowed out to play and I used to go off walking in the lanes and fields. I'd stay out as long as I dared. I couldn't stand the stink of the man; he had the smelliest feet I've ever known. My mother had two sons by him when we lived in Pembroke. First Martin, then Irving.

I got in such a state that I couldn't do anything; I was frightened all the time and my nerves were shot to pieces. I was put in a class for mentally retarded children in the East End Boys School; all we did was paint and draw all day, which suited me well. Eventually I fell seriously ill; my mother was afraid I might die and somehow she got in touch with my grandfather. Stevens wouldn't let her get the doctor, because questions would have been asked and he would probably have gone to prison, which would have been the best thing for everyone. My grandfather came and took me home to Solva. I can still remember my mother crying hysterically, but fortunately Stevens would not go against my grandfather. He was scared shitless of him, and of what might happen to him if the police got involved.

I spent most of the year in bed, and Dr Saunders came to see me daily. I was suffering from severe malnutrition, was totally emaciated, and my nervous system was in a sorry state. Gradually I got better, and Dr Saunders allowed me to sit my 11+ preliminary exam in bed! And I passed. Later on, although the doctor was a bit concerned, I was allowed to get up and I was taken to St David's Grammar School to sit the 11+ proper. I was late, and the other children had already sat the exam. So there I was, all alone in that big hall, with the headmaster sitting at the desk in front watching me. Before too long I would get to know both 'Jake', as we called the headmaster, and that hall very well.

During the time we were in Pembroke, my grandparents had moved from Harbour House to my great-grandmother's house in River Street, a narrow alley off the main street in Lower Solva. She had died of old age at ninety-six, and I'm sitting in her chair as I write. It's an old bardic chair, won by a great-uncle at an eisteddfod in Cardiff in 1935. When my great-grandmother Anne (known as Mam Roza), became bedridden and too frail to negotiate the two flights of stairs to the thunderbox in the backyard, Dada converted the honourable chair into a commode. At the time there was no sanitation in Lower Solva, although we were lucky enough to have a sink and a cold tap in the kitchen – other people had to share a tap on the wall outside the alley. Dada had semi-retired and now only did jobs he liked, such as mending boats or making big wooden farm-gates. He used to do work in churches and chapels too, with Uncle Syd who looked after the woodwork in St David's Cathedral.

It was quite primitive living in River Street. In Harbour House we had electricity and a proper bathroom. In River Street we had oil lamps, and Mam would cook on an open range fuelled with coal or

*My grandmother, Blodwen Davies ('Mam'), when she was in service in Mathry, aged 25*

culm – a mixture of river clay and coal dust, which would keep the fire in all night. The fire never went out unless Mam needed to clean the ashes out. That house was always warm. All of the houses in the Cwm were built of locally quarried stone and sea sand. Consequently, they were very damp; the salt in the sand makes the walls weep.

I spent the most memorable and the happiest days of my childhood in River Street. I'd go out lobster fishing with Captain Bill Jenkins, skipper of the *Annie*, the last sailing ship to trade out of Solva. It was with Captain Bill that I went to sea for the first time. He had some lobster pots on Carreg Dilys, a small reef near the harbour entrance. I was quite small, and got seasick on the first trip. There were plenty of rowing boats in the harbour – everybody had at least one – and there is still a rowing tradition in Solva. In 2002 the ladies' team won the Heads of the River race on the Thames, and Solva lads go all over the country to rowing events. I well remember those old wooden longboats – *Laddie, Boy John, Shushima, Suzuki, Saucy Sue* and *Larry Gaines*. Nowadays they row fibreglass longboats, which are much lighter and faster.

Dada made me a Pram dinghy, clinker-built of larch with a transom at both ends, a small one at the bow. I was mad on rowing and fishing and spent a lot of time out in the bay. Late one afternoon, after school, I went out in the *Suzuki* to catch some mackerel with an older boy called Derek John. There was an offshore breeze and we rowed further and further from the coast in pursuit of the shoals. We were only wearing vests and shorts, and as the sun set we began to get cold. By now the wind had freshened and the sea was up and quite choppy. As night fell we couldn't see the harbour mouth, and so we turned straight for the shore and rowed like blazes for about five miles. We were nearly exhausted by the time we could hear the breakers in Porth y Bwch, an inaccessible and dangerous cove near Solva.

By now it was pitch black and it would have been a miracle if we had managed to shoot that surf without wrecking the boat and being drowned. Suddenly, I thought I heard the sound of an outboard engine. Derek was lying knackered in the bottom of the boat; it was my turn to row. So it was I who saw a light flashing as the rescue boat climbed up the wave then fell into the trough. Yorrie Thomas and another man had come out to look for us in a boat from Solva.

It was a close call, and they towed us back to Solva quay where a small crowd had gathered on the slip. Dada was among them, so I feigned unconsciousness. If I'd climbed out of that boat unaided I knew that I'd have received the thrashing of the century. Instead, I was carried to a car and driven home. After being checked over by Doctor Bridges, who was staying with us at the time, I was given hot Bovril and put to bed. They had called the St David's lifeboat out, but Yorrie Thomas had found us, and someone phoned St Justinian just in time to stop the launch.

The next day in school we were famous, lost at sea and intrepid sailors at the mercy of the elements. My luck had held again!

*Mother's wedding to Donald Stevens at the County Hotel, Haverfordwest. My grandfather (Dada), William Henry Davies, is behind the bride's left shoulder. Uncle Hayden, Bett's brother is at the back, 2nd on the right*

# Chapter 2

# The Foreshore

The foreshore was a strip of wasteland between the high water mark and the houses facing the sea at the mouth of the narrow Solva Valley. The sides of the valley are steep and still thickly clad with bracken, gorse, blackthorn and heather. The south side is a long promontory of Pre-Cambrian rock called Y Gribyn (the crest). Below lies the harbour into which the River Solva flows. The north side of the valley is Y Moelfryn – the bare or rocky hill, which it is. Y Moelfryn is lower than Y Gribyn, and it leads to the wonderland of fields, moors and farms that lie between St Brides Bay and the Irish Sea to the north. Ireland is about fifty miles away, closer than Swansea. The main road from Haverfordwest to St David's passes through the Cwm. Lower Solva then cuts into the rocks of Y Moelfryn and snakes up a steep hill to Solfach Uchaf (Upper Solva), which looks down on the harbour and across St Brides Bay to Skomer Island and the south.

When I was a young boy, the foreshore was my backyard, playground and adventure park. It was a wild and derelict place, owned by no one, where sea meets land, where rickety zinc sheds rattled and flapped in the four winds, and in the undergrowth lay the plundered wrecks of old Morris Eights, Austin Sevens, and lorry cabs. There was even an abandoned American Jeep from the Second World War amidst the hulks of broken boats, their ribs and keels slowly rotting away. Still, at least they had flowers at their funeral! The foreshore was also the free range for Mrs Lewis's chickens; clucking around the wrecks, they shat, picked and laid their lives away in shanty rigged nest boxes. There was also a flock of geese belonging to Mother Raggett from the Ship Inn up the main street led by a big white ferocious gander which we would dare each other to bait with sticks until, neck stretched and hissing like a steam engine, he'd chase us laughing and screaming up the street. He was the true king of the foreshore.

Our house was about thirty yards or so from the beach. Next door was an old lime-kiln and a derelict warehouse, later converted by my grandfather and two of his sons, Syd and Ivor, into a dwelling house for the Lewis family. I even helped to mix the cement. The house still stands and is called Felin Gôg, or cuckoo mill.

The foreshore was a botanical wonderland, where a multitude of wild flowers, fruits, edible plants, as well as medicinal and culinary herbs, grew in profusion. Imported by the Romans, there were alexanders (cow parsley), valerian (which the ancient Celts traded with Phoenicians), samphire (food for Vikings), nettles, sorrel, dock, sea pinks, dog daisies, dandelions, coltsfoot, comfrey, lady's lace and belladonna to name but a few. There were all sorts of birds too – wagtails, blackbirds and thrushes, turnstones, oystercatchers, curlews, black-backed and herring gulls, magpies, robins, skylarks, jackdaws, hedge sparrows, yellowhammers, swifts and swallows, all in their season.

The foreshore isn't there any more. It lies smothered by a thick layer of asphalt and is now a car-park. Our old house still stands, but it has been converted into a pub, a tourist trap; our sitting-room and conservatory now a bar, where strangers eat fast food and drink overpriced neo-beer. It stinks of stale ale, chicken and chips, rancid fat and exhaust fumes; it's a good job that carbon monoxide is odourless! At the end of the summer, though, Harbour House returns exhausted to the real inhabitants of Solva, and it's a good place for a chat and a quiet drink. They still have music, too, and quiz nights, darts and pool.

When I was a small boy the foreshore was a powerful place, and it saddens me to see those stinking motorcars parked on it. I can still smell the herbs and flowers, the sump oil, bird shit, tar, hemp, seaweed, fish and rotting wood, the river, the beach and the sea. It is the odour of life, decay, wild nature and loss.

I sometimes compare the Harbour Inn with what it was when I lived there. What a difference! There was the smell of baking bread and scones, Welsh cakes, fruit pies – blackberry, apple, redcurrant and blackcurrant – mince tarts and sponges made with seagulls' eggs around the first of May, with their bright orange colour and subtle fishy taste. Then there was rabbit pie, game of all sorts, crab, lobster, mussels, cockles, winkles, brown trout, salmon, sewin, eels and many other seasonal fish. On Sunday, we'd enjoy the ritual dinner of roast beef, lamb or pork with Yorkshire pudding and fresh vegetables from the garden – runner beans, broad beans, new potatoes all picked by hand. What a chef Mam was! But beyond all that – the quiet rhythm of the house, the carpenter's shop, and the atmosphere of relief everyone felt at the end of the war – lay the foreshore, harbour, bay, Ireland, the Atlantic Ocean and the rest of the big wide world.

Our front door was tall, wide and arched with a glazed light above the lion's-head-shaped iron knocker whose eyes gazed forebodingly on the veldt of the front lawn. In front of the house, there was a small gravelled forecourt, where Maldwyn Vaughne the milkman used to park his pony and trap every morning. It was a real sight to see the pony trotting quickly down the steep hill, crates of bottles rattling loudly in the trap, before he turned the hairpin bend at speed and clattered to a halt at our front gate. What amazing control and rapport between man and horse! Inside the gate was a small lawn surrounded by a low wall and flowerbeds where red roses, daffodils, narcissi and wallflowers grew. In the centre of the lawn, which was always white with daisies, stood a birdbath on a plinth. A famous local fisherman, Kit Phillips from Abereiddi, when asked "Is it time to go fishing yet?" would reply "The fish will be there when your foot can cover five daisies." You could fish all the year round if our lawn was anything to go by!

The narrow main street still stretches from the bottom of the hill, between the houses and the converted store lofts and warehouses of the sailing era, then turns right over a small stone bridge, before going up a very steep hill to the fields of the farms beyond: Penrhiw, Clover Hill, Tregadwgan, Caermedris and on to Haverfordwest, south Wales, England, Europe and the Orient. You can still go by sea if you have a strong boat and a lot of spare time. If you decide not to climb that hill and so carry on past the dilapidated Cambrian Hotel – where the two Miss Pierces from Grangetown, Cardiff held court (I wonder how they came to be in Solva?) – you'll pass an old iron water pump at the foot of a small hill, Cornel Pwmp. Then you'll enter a straight but narrow lane with cottages, gardens and orchards on both sides. This is Prengas, or Prendergast – a name, so I'm told, derived from that of an old aristocratic Basque family. I don't know how they reached Solva either! Nowadays, Prendergast is inhabited in summer by tourists, who rent the pretty, well-kept cottages. It's big business; you can pay £1,000 a week to stay in one of these. In winter, however, there is emptiness but for a handful of locals and the ghosts of a more vibrant age. There is no longer a real community there, and when my old schoolmate Dai the Bomb – lord mayor of Prengas – dies, so too will an era.

Dai's a bit older than me, but we went to St David's Grammar School at the same time and he got me into a lot of trouble. His family used to farm Y Gribyn years ago, and his mother Letty's father was a ship's captain called Protheroe. Dai's father was Jim Evans, Solva's road man, whose job was to keep the hedges, verges and footpaths cut and trimmed and the culverts, drains and ditches clear. It was a big job with plenty of work, and when Jim retired Dai took over from him. Then he retired too, which was a great loss. Nowadays, a gang of strange workmen arrive in vans every now and again; they do with machines the work that one man used to do with a billhook and shovel.

'Dai the Bomb' was not a terrorist or a member of the IRA. He wasn't even a pyromaniac, except on November the fifth, when we all were! When he was young, however, he was a very politically orientated person and a pacifist who went on the early Aldermaston Marches with Bertrand Russell, Michael Foot and Pat Arrowsmith as a paid-up member of the Campaign for Nuclear Disarmament. Dai was a red-hot socialist and a big fan of Aneurin Bevan and Michael Foot.

No cats or dogs sleep in sunlit doorways now, no interesting old characters like Hubert Rees and Willy John walk down the lane with their sailor's roll. No chattering clutches of women, clad in brightly coloured floral-patterned pinafores with their little crocheted hats covering long plaited hair, gossip outside the cottages. And no kids play football in the road in their hobnailed boots – what a racket! Before the war, Prengas could field two football teams, even though there were only about twenty-five cottages in Prengas – my mother and her brothers were in one team, because they were all born there, bar Walter, in Grove House. But saddest of all is the strange and weird absence of the murmur of women speaking their native language or screaming in Welsh, echoing across the valley at us kids, caught once again as we scrumped apples in someone's orchard.

If you entered Harbour House through the front door without being eaten by the lion, you would walk upon a floor of patterned cream and terracotta tiles. Ahead lay a sliding door with a stained-glass window and a broad staircase with another wide, stained glass window at the top. The light in this hallway was wonderful, particularly at sundown when subtle reflections of blue, red and amber would illuminate the house. To the right of the stairs was a large sitting-room and an oak-panelled corridor leading to the kitchen, backyard and, through my grandfather's workshop, to the walled garden.

The backyard had tall wooden gates leading to the foreshore. It was my castle, ordnance depot and barrack square. Dada had a heavy-duty, circular-saw bench there. He would cut and season his own wood, then cut it up into timber as he wanted. I didn't mind the thump of the diesel engine or the black smoke from the stove-pipe exhaust that stuck out of the wall, but the scream of the spinning blade ripping through the log struck terror into me, and I would run and hide behind the back door as if I were about to be struck by lightning. "What's the matter with you, Michael bach?" Mam would tut tut. "Why don't you go out to play?" And off I'd go with my friend Anthony over to the Gamblyn, where years ago the farmers and sailors would gamble on pitch-and-toss whilst waiting for the tides. Mostly we'd go fishing up by the stone bridge, where we'd cast hooks baited with small red wriggly worms into the eddies beneath the arches so they'd float down to the deep brown pool where trout lay in the shade.

The best time to fish was after heavy rain, when the river ran full of mud and the sea turned reddish brown. But we could catch fish anytime we wanted; after all, we knew where they lay. Fly-fishing though was difficult, because the banks are overgrown with blackthorn, willow, rogue sycamore and ash. A blackthorn bush can easily turn a small boy into a pincushion; you have to pick the thorns out straight away or they will fester and hurt. Mam spent a lot of time picking blackthorns out of my body with a darning needle. "You've been dragging in the trash again, you naughty boy," she'd say, but she wasn't angry as it usually meant that we had fresh brown trout for supper.

Dragging in the trash was one of our favourite pastimes. We used to call it 'jungling', and we were the 'Popgun Junglers', small game hunters in the wilds of west Wales. Once we decided to find the source of the River Solva, only to be beaten back after about two miles by bogs, thickets and rapids. So we decided to procure a map. I consulted Dada because he knew everything; he said that the source was somewhere to the north-east of the Gignog bridge. No one had heard of Gignog, but we found it on the ordnance survey map. It was miles away! So one fine morning we made an assault on Solva hill by bicycle. After pedalling for miles through a maze of country lanes, some – the unbelievers and the faint-hearted – turned back. The rest of us made it to Gignog but not much further; once again we were driven back by the *Matto Grosso* and time. Tattered and torn, nettle-stung, insect-bitten, muddy and exhausted, we arrived home late. We hadn't found Atlantis, but we had caught about twenty nice trout and a couple of sewin. So I didn't get a hiding that night.

"Did you see any adders?" Dada asked.

"Yes, Albert killed a couple," I said. "Big ones."

"Good," he said. Dada had a thing about adders, and he used to hunt and kill them on his customary Sunday morning walk over Y Gribyn, while I had to go to chapel. I often wondered why he did it – why did he hate adders so much? To me they were only snakes, and snakes are mysterious creatures which you hardly ever see. Later, however, I found out that after Dada and Mam got married (they met in a hiring fair in St David's) they went to live in a wild place called Kite Mountain up at the back of Roch Mill. It was an old cottage at the end of a long and overgrown path overlooking Newgale Valley. Uncle Walter, their first child, was born there. One day he crawled out of the door and got lost in the undergrowth. When Dada found him, he was playing in a sunlit clearing surrounded by basking adders. Dada killed them all with his walking stick. From then on I knew why he would always tell me to 'cut a stick' before I went dragging up the valley. You don't see many adders nowadays; some say it's something to do with pesticides. One hot afternoon I came across an adder on Caerfarchell moor. I lifted a sheet of rusty corrugated iron and under it lay a female adder who had just given birth to six or seven young. She was startled, but not as much as I was. Her mouth opened wide, and the little snakes wriggled like lightning into it. Then she was gone in a flash, carrying her brood safe within.

The foreshore was also our sports ground. It was there that we'd play tip-and-run cricket against one of the old corrugated iron sheds, the stumps drawn in chalk on the door. We played football too, using the prows of two boats pulled up for the winter as goalposts. Chasing was another favourite. This game often degenerated into violence when some of the catchers became a bit over-zealous, and it could easily end up in a communal wrestling match or fist fight involving fifteen or twenty kids. One kid was nominated as on it, then he or she had to recruit three others by chasing and touching them. This group of four then had to catch the other kids one by one, until there was only one left, usually the most swift and elusive runner. You would do anything to avoid capture – hide even. During one game, a boy went missing. We couldn't find him anywhere, and so we went to fetch his mother. By now it was getting dark, and we finally found him fast asleep in one of the chicken shacks on the foreshore.

Sometimes we'd play football up and down the middle of the main road; easy enough at a time when there were hardly any cars on the roads. Only two or three, the evening bus and maybe a tractor would pass through the village, and we could hear them a long way off as they changed down to low gear on the hill. No one seemed to mind us doing this, and we never were told off unless someone broke a window. We also used to roller skate down the only pavement, which ran from the chemist's shop down to Auntie Mattie's house next door to the Ship Inn. Our heavy steel skates were clamped to our boots with a key. You couldn't wear them with daps, the black canvas sneakers we all wore in summer. We all looked forward to the time when we could discard those heavy hobnailed boots that we had to wear for most of the year. But we loved wearing our hobnail boots, because we could skid down Solva hill, raising showers of sparks from the road.

There were a lot of characters in the Cwm, even amongst the kids, and we all had nicknames – Bici Bo, Panda, Jac Newt, Curlew, Choo Choo, Boberts, Dai Cwm, etc. Mine was Mousie, derived from Harbour House – Michael Mouse. There were two older boys called Pantas and Pedro, real names John and Peter respectively, and a boy who was much younger than me and dubbed Dai Cachu-shit because he swore all the time!

Solva is still a great place for children to grow up – if we ever did! There was no youth club or any formalized recreation for young children, or even teenagers, apart from the Girl Guides. We made our own fun and did so with zest. After school broke up, the summer was one long swim in the coves around the bay, which we would reach in our boats. We did a lot of fishing – for pollack, crab, lobster, mackerel and bass – and it was a huge event when the mackerel shoals swam into the bay. I've crossed shoals miles wide, when the water comes alive with hundreds of thousands of beautiful blue, black and silver fish in a feeding frenzy, chasing shoals of whitebait and in turn being hunted by tope, a kind of shark.

The weather was warmer then, and summers seemed to last much longer. You'd often see paint blistering on the doors of the houses in the Cwm, and the road tar melting. You don't see that nowadays, perhaps they've invented heat-resistant paint! Or maybe the summers are just colder.

When the tide was out, we'd often go down the beach in Solva, where we'd swim and sunbathe on the flat rocks. All of my old schoolfriends would be there, girls and boys together, with pop and sandwiches and flasks of tea and coffee. We'd stay on the beach until the tide turned, then either wade back across the harbour to the quay or swim home. It was such a long time ago – happy days. But things have changed and so did we. Most of us would pass our exams and have to go 'up the line' for further education or to seek work, usually in Cardiff, Swansea, England or some other foreign place.

# Chapter 3

# Early School Days

River Street is a short narrow alley of five cottages and two gardens linking the main street in Lower Solva to the other side of the river. In those days, a *bompren* – a wooden bridge fashioned out of two stout planks with a handrail – led to the Gribyn side and the Gamblyn via a strip of waste ground bounded on one side by a footpath running beneath the sycamore wood on the lower slopes of the Gribyn and then on to the beach. There were two derelict warehouses and a cluster of pink and white cottages on that side of the river, between the *bompren* and the stone bridge at the foot of the hill leading to Haverfordwest. Above two disused lime-kilns stood Johnny Jenkins's blacksmith shop, which was going full swing then. I remember going with Dada to have steel rims fitted on some cart-wheels he'd made. First the rims were laid down flat, and then wood shavings and kindling were put all around them and lit. By the time that the circle of fire had died down, the steel had expanded enough for the smith to drop the big heavy wooden cart-wheel carefully into place precisely.

We often used to play forts in those old warehouses: one gang would be barricaded inside with bows and arrows and catapults, while the others would attack, trying to get 'under the guns' with a battering ram made of a tree trunk. The roofs had fallen in long ago and the floorboards stripped for firewood. There were stone steps leading up the gable ends to empty doorways high above the rubble-strewn floors. Thick wooden beams, green with moss and lichen, were still in place and we would dare each other to impromptu tightrope-walking competitions and other dangerous balancing acts.

Our garden was opposite, by the *bompren*, with three narrow stone steps leading down to the water. The river bank was walled with stone, and there were deep holes below the waist-deep water line, where big river eels lived and where trout and sewin hid. Dada loved a feed of baked eels, and I used to spend hours fishing there with a handline, hoping to catch his supper. The most efficient method of catching those river eels was, first, to catch a rabbit, skin and gut it, then tie the puddings – as we called the intestines – up in the skin like a parcel, with the meaty side out and a stone inside for ballast. It was better if you left the parcel hanging around for a couple of days until it started to stink, before lowering it into the river, upstream of the eel holes, on a strong length of twine. The eels would come out almost immediately to feed on the bait. They'd bite into the rabbit skin and, since they refused to let go, it was easy to pull them out of the water still hanging on to the skin. Dada told me that eels' teeth are hook-shaped and that when they bite into something their jaws lock. One time, I remember a conger eel biting a kid in the harbour. The conger must have been stranded in shallow water after the tide went out, and he trod on it. They had a job to get it off, and when they did it took a big chunk out of his leg. By the way, before using this eel-catching trick, it's a good idea to smash a few rotten eggs on the wall near the holes – eels love smelly things, and they'll come out even quicker.

We lived in 2 River Street in a big old double-fronted, two-storeyed cottage with two large rooms up and down, an attic halfway up the stairs and a *twll dan stâr*, literally a hole under the stairs, which used to flood when the river and the tide were high. The house was converted later into two holiday homes. There had originally been an older house behind, onto which our cottage had been built and

*Bet and her brother Syd outside the Grove Hotel, St Davids, 1963*

*Some of the old fishermen from Prengas, Solva on the ship in Milford Haven. Some of my family are in the back row*

which Dada used as a workshop. One of the kitchen doors connected to the old part of the house and another led into the backyard and the thunderbox. Dada built a loft in the backyard to house my pigeons. I had about a dozen; it was hard to say exactly how many because they were always breeding. They would fly around all day and sometimes they would roost on the roof of the house. They were quite a sight and it was good to hear their sounds during the evening. I didn't have to do much with them except put food out and make sure the loft was kept clean. Most of them I caught on local farms up the country; farmers were glad to see me coming because pigeons eat a lot of corn.

In the old house there was a huge disused inglenook fireplace, and I would climb inside it and get up the chimney onto the roof, just like Tom in *The Water Babies*. There were bread ovens on one side, the hearth stone in the middle and a stone ledge all around to sit on. The building was very old, built in the sixteenth century. Originally, it must have stood alone, since it was the only one in the street. Dada kept a long workbench with a vice and a selection of carpentry tools there. I did a lot of woodwork, learning to measure, plane, chisel, gouge and saw. It was also used as a utility room, where game was plucked and skinned and where any other messy jobs were carried out. It was there that I used to cut the sticks for kindling.

Mam wouldn't allow dogs in the River Street house, even though we'd kept them in Harbour House: a cocker spaniel, a labrador retriever called Spot, and a greyhound called Old Bill. These hounds were all black in colour, although Old Bill had a white star on his breast and a white tip to his long tail which meant that you could spot him in the dark. Old Bill was good at rabbit coursing and the others were used as gun dogs; they were all very well trained. Sometimes my uncles, who were all good shots, would shoot rabbits from the backyard gate with a '22 rifle. The Gribyn was infested with rabbits; if you looked carefully, you could see their ears as they grazed on the young shoots of gorse. As a result, the gorse was kept low and sculpted into strange rounded shapes. Rabbits jump up when shot, and the dogs would run off up the hill and bring them back to the gate for our supper. However, Mam had made a no dogs rule when we moved, and it was strictly adhered to. Once, Uncle Syd gave me a black cocker spaniel puppy, but I had to take it back – she just would not allow dogs into No. 2. I did have a cat called Benjamin though. After he was born he was going to be drowned. That's what they did with unwanted puppies or kittens – put them in a sack with a heavy stone and chuck them in the sea. I thought it was cruel, but there were a lot of things like that then. People were more basic and closer to the earth than nowadays. I thought nothing of catching, killing, skinning and gutting half a dozen rabbits, although the women usually used to do that sort of work, killing geese, ducks and chickens at Christmas, and so on. The men used to kill the calves and pigs though. Dada didn't go out hunting very much when we lived in River Street. The Purdy twelve bore hung neglected from a beam in the kitchen, the cartridges on top of the dresser.

We inherited a lodger when we moved to River Street – Mam's nephew, Uncle Harold Davies. He was Mam Roza's grandson, the son of Mam's youngest sister Roza. Roza had died of cancer some years earlier in London, where she worked as a housemaid for a rich family in Berkeley Square. She was quite young when she died, but she had enjoyed life and was very stylish – she wore ra-ra dresses and looked like a Charleston flapper girl. I've seen photos of her dressed in silk and satin fringed dresses, wearing long beaded necklaces, earrings, a feather boa, funny hats with ostrich feathers, silk stockings and pointed high-heeled shoes. Harold was illegitimate, and I think that's why she went or was sent away by her parents. Nevertheless, she ended up with a good job and was far more sophisticated and better turned out than her local contemporaries who had been good chapel girls and stayed at home. No one ever said who Harold's father was. It had to be a local man, but no one ever talked about it.

Harold fought in the 1914–18 war, when he was only seventeen. He came back, unlike his cousin David Evans and his two uncles, Johnny and Gwilym, who were only boys as well, 20, 19 and 18 respectively. They were all killed in the mud of the Somme. Luckily, old Harold came home safe and went off fishing on the Milford trawlers. Like most of his Solva mates he was a good seaman, and later he sailed afar on big cargo boats and tankers, When the Second World War broke out, he had to join the army again and soon found himself in the British Expeditionary Force, being chased across Belgium and France by the German Panzers. He and two other Solva boys, Jack Evans and Benja Howells, made it to Dunkirk beach, where they were lucky to be evacuated along with several thousand other soldiers. Harold made it home once again, then straight back on the Milford trawlers.

After the Second World War there was a slump, and soon hundreds of thousands were looking for work, many of them refugees, stateless persons and ex-prisoners of war. These foreign refugees were exploited because they would work hard for very low pay. This caused a lot of bad feeling in Milford docks, where the refugees were mainly Polish and most of whom had fought with units of the Allied Forces against the German and Japanese. These men were undercutting the standard wages of local trawlermen, and so the local men's wages were also kept low. Although it was the trawler companies who made the profit out of this bad situation, the violent response was directed at these unfortunate men, who from no fault of their own could not go home to Poland because they had fought for the Allies. They would probably have been shot or imprisoned by the Russian communists who then ruled Poland.

Harold and Jack Evans told me a story once in the Ship Inn about an incident that happened when they were trawling for cod off the coast of Iceland. One of the Poles in the crew, a stoker, became constipated, and the skipper plied him with laxatives but to no avail. After a while the complaints, accompanied by loud moans and groans from the poor man's bunk, were beginning to annoy the members of the crew who were trying to get some sleep. The skipper wouldn't put in to Reykjavik and send him to a doctor; the fishing was good and they had to stay with the shoals and so he'd have to suffer until the holds were full. However, Jack Evans came up with a solution, in the form of a half bucket of soft soap, mixed with a bottle of Black Draft, a sailor's cure-all and something like an incredibly strong version of Friar's Balsam. To this he added a handful of caustic balls. When the solution was well stirred, he loaded it into a grease gun and shot it up the Polish arse! "Did he shit?" I asked with quiet respect. "Shit?" they screamed. "We were up to our knees in fucking shit!" Thus the skipper was forced to put into an Icelandic harbour, where the Pole was taken to hospital. No one seemed to know whether he'd survived the ordeal! Those trawlermen were hard bastards, used to danger in those small coal-fired, steam-driven beam trawlers. They fished from the Irish Sea up to the Faeroe Islands and Iceland, along the west coast of Norway and north to Bear Island, Spitsbergen and the Arctic Sea – they were tough!

Those trawlers were not called 'wet boats' for nothing. Their crews were constantly cold and wet. They lived in wet clothes and slept in wet bunks. The only warm place on those boats was the stoke hole where the boiler and furnace was, and that wasn't all that warm. Sometimes there was so much ice on the rigging, wires and superstructure that the men had to chip it off with axes and hammers to prevent the ship from becoming top heavy and capsizing. But the seas after the war were teeming with fish; there had been little or no fishing for six years and everyone wanted their share of the bonanza. If the fish were once again left alone for say five years, we'd see some decent catches landed, the price of fish would go down and the quality up. Even the grand banks of Canada and Nova Scotia are barren of cod nowadays. Sure it was a dangerous job, but it was better than being stuck in a waterlogged ditch, or a waterless *wadhi* being shelled to bits by German artillery!

The trawlermen kept the pubs of Milford, Pembroke docks and Neyland booming, as well as the Ship and the Cambo in Solva. My great-uncle, Rhys Davies, Mam's brother, kept the Ship between the wars. He'd married the widow of a Captain Davies from Solva, no relation. This woman had sailed all over the globe on her husband's ships, especially to the Far East. When Uncle Rhys fell ill and died suddenly, there was a rumour that he'd died of an 'obscure tropical disease' and that he'd caught it from his wife! Later on his brother Edgar, who was a well-known local poet, married her, and he too died young of a mysterious, undiagnosed sickness. It must have been the curse of Fu Manchu! The thrice-married Mrs Davies lived on to a ripe old age, having sold the Ship Inn and retired on the money. I knew her very well and I used to cut wood for her and a few other old ladies in the Cwm. They used to give me the odd half crown now and again, which I saved on the mantelpiece in a small wooden clog that Harold had brought from Holland. I also used to catch and sell sewin and salmon for half a crown a pound and, by the time the Michaelmas travelling fairs came to the area, I could go with a pocket full of money to squander on the rigged coconut and hoopla stalls and the bent rifle ranges. I won a goldfish once and it actually survived; most of the goldfish from the fair die after a couple of days, but this one lived a couple of years and Dada named him Samson. He met his maker when he disappeared down the plughole one day while I was changing his water.

Harold used to drink every night with his mates who had survived the war. They were nearly all bachelors, and their favourite pastimes were heavy drinking and gambling. Harold was hardly ever in the house; he'd arrive home from work in Trecwn, an admiralty arsenal near Fishguard, eat a cooked dinner, change into a smart jacket, slacks and a clean shirt, then off down the Ship, to play cards and drink all night. They all had the same routine, and we scarcely ever saw him. Sometimes I'd hear him coming home from the pub; they didn't have much respect for the licensing laws and so it could be anytime during the early hours of the morning, especially on weekends. I'd hear the front door rattle, open with a bang, then a curse as Harold fell into the hall. More mumbled curses would follow as he crawled upstairs on his hands and knees, with a final bout of cursing as he tried to get through his bedroom door, and finally a loud clang of bedsprings as he literally hit the sack. A bit more mumbling, then loud snores, and Harold had made it home safe again! I used to pull the bedcovers over my head, I was laughing so much.

I slept in a small bed in the corner of my grandparents' bedroom above the kitchen. It was always warm because the fire in the range below was 'stummed up' with culm and would stay in all night. Mam and Dada slept on a feather mattress on a high old brass bedstead that used to glitter in the lamplight. They had Whitney blankets and a home-made patchwork quilt which had been in the family for donkey's years: in the corner was embroidered a date and name – 'Annie Morse, Felinganol, 1809'. They both had an oil lamp on their bedside table; Dada's had a beautiful blue glass reservoir that glowed like a huge sapphire, Mam's was only brass but it glistened like gold. Dada also had the bible and a couple of his favourite books, *Moby Dick* by Herman Melville and *Sailing Alone Around the World* by Joshua Slocumb, which he would read for a while before turning the lamps down and going to sleep.

One day, returning home from school, I was greeted with great excitement; they had received a letter that new houses were soon to be built in Upper Solva on an existing estate on the St David's road and that some of these houses would be old age pensioners' bungalows. Moreover, they had been allocated one. A brand new house! At first, Mam thought it was too good to be true, but then she became timorous about the idea. She was a quiet, cautious person, and the magnitude of such a change of circumstances was intimidating even though our current house was big, dark and damp. Dada persuaded her that we should take this great opportunity. There would be a proper bathroom, electricity, central heating of sorts and no stairs to climb. And, after all, she was fed up with Harold's drinking; sometimes he'd puke up in his sleep or pee the bed and she had to clean up after him and wash his clothes. Mam was religious and a teetotaller, and Dada only had the odd half if he went up the Cambo to play dominoes on a Saturday night. He smoked though, quite heavily, evil smelling Ringers A.1 dark shag tobacco in an old pipe which always seemed to be sticking out of the side of his mouth even when he was working. In the end, it was agreed that we would move and that we couldn't take Harold because there were only two small bedrooms.

I would miss the Cwm, the river, foreshore, woods, the Gribyn, the harbour and the friendly neighbours, not to mention my loony mates up in Prengas. Upper Solva was a different place, a different planet, and I'd been at war with the Upper Solva gang for years; it was an ongoing war, with religious connotations, a bit like Ulster or the Palestinians! I'd be outnumbered twenty to one and would probably be killed in the first battle. I'd better sharpen my bayonet and oil my pistol, an old 4.5 Webley revolver from the First World War. I had ammo too, shortened four-ten shotgun cartridges, which just about fitted and made a horrible bang. I was the only kid in Solva who had a firearm, and I kept it hidden!

Dada and I got busy making new furniture; our furniture was mostly too big for this small abode and we had far too much anyway. I helped him make a cupboard, kitchen table and a hallstand, although we had to buy beds for ours were much too big. We cleaned up and renovated some other pieces, making sure that there was no woodworm by painting all the furniture with a sticky brown solution. We were all very excited; none of us had ever lived in a brand new house before.

Number 12 Bro Dawel is a small L-shaped bungalow attached to the pine end of a row of two larger houses, and there was another bungalow at the far end. It was tiny compared to the River Street house – two small bedrooms, a bathroom and a tiny back kitchen with a scullery and airing cupboard. The sitting-room, though, was quite big with large wide windows that let in a lot of light, a welcome change from our dark old house in the Cwm. There was a small entrance hall, which gave access to all of the rooms. The fireplace in the sitting-room was nicely tiled, with the fire heating a boiler, a back-to-back Aga in the kitchen and radiators. The garden – a long narrow strip of land, high with weeds – stopped at the hedge of Llanunwas woods behind the houses. We had the added pleasure of a huge rookery, with dozens of noisy nests high up in the huge elm trees. The crows certainly came in handy as an alarm clock in the mornings.

Bro Dawel was basically two rows of pre-cast concrete Wimpy houses, built hastily to house, in the main, the people who had been living in the abandoned US Air Force huts after the war. Later, these huts had been used to house Italian prisoners of war. Many of the Solva men who'd fought in the war had married girls from England and had families whom they'd brought home with them. Apart from these ex-military buildings, there was nowhere else for them to live. A few of Mam's old friends lived on the estate, so she had quite a few people to talk to. Dada still had his workshop down the quay, and most days he'd go there to do a bit of boat repairing or to socialize with the lobster fishermen.

It was 1955. Dada was seventy-four, Mam was seventy and I was thirteen. There were a lot more kids on the estate, and other families besides us had moved there from the Cwm. Some lived in Maes Ewan, the other side of the St David's road. Bro Dawel had originally been called Western Avenue, but the parish council decided they wanted a Welsh name, and one member, a woman with a perverted sense of humour, suggested Bro Dawel (Quiet Country), which it certainly was not. Some of the families seemed to be constantly at war; it was nothing to hear a row reach crescendo and a radio, vacuum cleaner or coffee table fly through the window. It could get rather loud and somewhat dangerous, but we minded our business and got on with our lives.

I was doing well at St David's Grammar school, where I was studying English, Welsh, algebra, geometry, arithmetic, history, geography, general science, Latin, scripture, art and woodwork. I did a lot of sport and was in the school gymnastic and athletics teams. We didn't have a rugby team; there were only ninety-seven pupils, both boys and girls, and we couldn't field a soccer and a rugby team. We had a great cricket team and the girls' hockey team was pretty good too. There were some heavy chicks in that team! It was time for me to start thinking about what I was going to do in life. I was no longer a little boy. There was nothing in the area, unless you wanted to work on a farm, or in a shop or office in Haverfordwest. Of course, there was the Army, Navy and Air Force and the Merchant Navy, but I wouldn't have passed the medical for any of those on account of my blurred myopic vision. And I'd miss conscription or 'the call-up', as it was called, by a few months. As far as Mam and Dada were concerned, the Forces were out of the question anyway. Bad karma! We seldom tempted the Old Nick, as he was known; we'd had enough in the war!

Throughout this time, my mother had been living with Stevens in East Ham, London. She was busy raising my two half-brothers and had just had another baby called Adrian Walter. We hardly ever heard from them – they never sent any money to my grandparents. Perhaps we'd get a Christmas card and I might get a birthday card, but that was it. All the time I was in Solva with Mam and Dada, they only visited twice. I'd been up to London in 1953 at the time of the coronation of Elizabeth II, but had a horrible time because of Stevens. Their house was a dreadfully gloomy and unhappy place, despite the television and other mod cons. He had a good job by then in the City and worked in an office overlooking St Paul's. My mother and my brother Martin were very unhappy, and I couldn't wait to get back to Solva.

I had always been good at drawing and painting, and music too. As a boy soprano, I'd won prizes at local eisteddfodau and taken singing and music lessons with Mrs Beer, who was the organist in one of the chapels in Solva. I was also interested in archaeology and had made friends with Dr Felix Oswald, an eminent expert on the Roman period; his son was the curator of Birmingham museum, where the Oswald Collection is kept. How did he get to Solva, I wonder? I liked English literature and wrote poetry too. I'd always been a big reader – the only good thing Stevens did for me was to give me books.

The early teens is an odd time of life, and I was often confused, unsure which way to go. At least I was well aware of the big wide world beyond little Solva; like an astronaut, I had been there several times. Mam, who had little or no education other than the Baptist Sunday school, couldn't help me much, while Dada was old now, and although extremely knowledgeable he belonged to a bygone age. Things were changing fast. Mam had never been to school; as one of the older sisters in a family of twelve, she had to help her mother with

25.

## ST. DAVIDS GRAMMAR SCHOOL.

Term Ending _December 1955._

Name of Pupil _Michael Stephens._

| FORM | NO OF PUPILS | AGE OF PUPIL LAST BDAY | AVERAGE AGE OF FORM | POSITION AT BEGINNING OF TERM | POSITION AT END OF TERM |
|---|---|---|---|---|---|
| IV | 26 | Y 13 M 9 | Y 13 M 4 | — | 17th (n 77) |

| SUBJECT | Term's work Max. : 100 | Term'l Exam Max. : 100 | Position | REMARKS | Teacher's Initials |
|---|---|---|---|---|---|
| Eng. Gram & Comp. | 62 | 50 | 8 | Generally class good work. | J. ew |
| English Literature | 83 | 79 | 4 | | |
| History | 66 | 83 | 6 | Very good. | |
| Latin | | | | | |
| Welsh | 70 | 54 | 8 | Good. | J.J.E. |
| French | | | | | |
| Arithmetic | 26 | 11 | 24 | Poor work. Does not try. | J.D. |
| Algebra | | | | | |
| Geometry | | | | | |
| Scripture | 70 | 74 | 2 | Very good work. | |
| Chemistry Science | 47 | 20 | 21 | Not his best. | |
| Biology | | | | | |
| Geography | 54 | 46 | 21 | Exam. result disappointing | C.R.R |
| Needlework | | | | | |
| Cookery | | | | | |
| Woodwork | 52/50 | 25/50 | 5 | good | |
| Drawing | 35/50 | 31/50 | 4 | | |
| Music | 4 | — | 27 | M. makes no effort. | |
| Shorthand | 54 | 71 | 2 | Poor exam result. | |
| Typewriting | | | | | |
| Book keeping | 55 | 34 | 8 | Poor exam result | |

No. of times School was open 144        No. of times absent 7

Conduct _Very Good._        _A. Griffiths_        Form Master or Mistress

General Remarks _Some of his work is good, but he must apply himself in arithmetic and Science._

_J. J. Evans_ Headmaster.

Next Term begins _10th January 1956_        Parent's Signature

_School Report, 1955. Bottom of the class in music!_

the babies. Mam Roza, who was an incredibly lazy woman, used to sit on a throne-like chair all day looking like Queen Victoria, literally twiddling her thumbs and ordering people around. She was a tyrant, and everybody was afraid of her. Like the archetypal witch, she sat by the fire in her big dark kitchen, dressed always in long black clothes, a black cat on her lap and a bizarrely patterned Paisley shawl draped around her shoulders, strings of jet beads round her throat and a black croched cap covering her long plaited hair. Mam Roza didn't belong in this modern age; she was from a darker mysterious primeval time that somehow survived the present in her.

Dada was beginning to slow up; the daily climb up the steep footpath from the quay was making him tired. He taught me a lot over the years – about astronomy, navigation, carpentry, boat building and the sea, as well as much about birds and animals. He was a veritable encyclopaedia; he knew something about all of the 'ologies' and he was a knowledgeable historian. As I've already mentioned, he was a keen boxing fan who taught all of his children including my mother to 'duke' in a ring that he'd built in his workshop in the Cwm. But he didn't want me to be a carpenter – even though it was in my blood. He wanted me to pursue an academic career!

★ ★ ★

I have a cousin called Byron, Uncle Ivor's son. They lived over in Maes Ewan, and I used to spend a lot of time there. His mother, Auntie Gwenny, was a very kindly lady who was always giving us golden syrup sandwiches and cups of tea. Byron had three sisters and a younger brother. Rita, his eldest sister, became the headmistress of Solva primary school. She taught there all her life, from the time she left Swansea Training College until she retired, and she, Jean, Gail, Robert and Byron still live in the area. Byron and I had similar interests, although he was a few years older than I was. He left St David's school

*Me, aged nine with Louis Wright, my Shrewsbury grandfather*

*Me and my cousin Byron Davies (Uncle Ivor's son) on the footbridge by River Street, Solva*

at fifteen and went to work as a trainee with an aviation company called Air Work, just up the road on St David's Airfield. This company trained pilots for the fleet air arm who had a base called HMS *Goldcrest* at Brawdy. Air Work had Meteor and Vampire jets and a few Mosquito fighter-bombers from the war. Byron and I used to make a lot of model aircraft, both solid and flying models. We were also budding ornithologists.

Another friend was Al Young, whose family somehow got stranded in Solva after the war ended. There were quite a few other families in the same predicament. They lived at first in the disused military huts, then moved to Western Avenue (Bro Dawel). Al's dad, a Scouser, was in the army, and his mother was a woman from Cork city in Ireland. Al was older than me and soon he was called up and joined the RAF for his national service. He worked at Air Work with Byron and a few other local lads from Solva and St David's. I didn't see much of Al for a long time after he joined up; he was drafted to various air force bases in Norfolk, but he always came home for the summer holidays and we carried on swimming, boating and fishing as usual.

At about this time, more people from England gradually began to drift in to Solva. Some would just come for a holiday, staying with people they already knew. Solva wasn't equipped for tourists then, and there was little or no accommodation. Others bought cottages around the Solva and St David's area, cheap at that time. Solva had never been a tourist place, unlike St David's which had the cathedral and which has been something of a tourist trap since the time of the Normans in the Middle Ages and there have always been a few hotels there. The people who came to Solva in the early 1950s seemed to be educated and interesting, and some had sons and daughters our age who would muck in with us and join in our summer fun. We all had boats and we'd sometimes collect driftwood which would then be dumped in an inaccessible cove where we'd go in a small fleet of boats to swim all day and have a barbecue in the evening. There were some big beach parties in those days, and we'd often stay on the beach all night, drinking cider and flagons of beer, barbecuing sausages and fish, singing and dancing all night. We would haul the boats up and relaunch them in the morning when the tide came in, but sometimes we would row back to Solva in the dark marvelling at the fluorescence in the water where the oars raised ripples. Starry skies, moonlit nights and lots of fun!

There were two boys from the Rhondda who came to Solva every summer. They were related to the Mills family and they used to bring a friend called Clive Williams, whom we called Moose. Clive played the guitar and was studying painting in Cardiff College of Art. He had an old Gibson flat-top guitar – I'd never seen anything like it!

Bici Bo, the other boy, had done very well at school. To everyone's amazement, he'd even been made head boy before going on to study English at Swansea University. He was also the Inter-Collegiate featherweight boxing champion, and his most famous knockout was when he floored Kingsley Amis, one of his tutors who was trying to get off with Bici's girlfriend in the Uplands pub one night! Bici had a good friend from Llansamlet near Swansea called Steve Glass, and there was another boy, who had relatives in Solva, called Alan Roch. Both of these guys played the guitar, and Clive taught me a few chords. I tried hard to master them, but I had great difficulty in holding the strings down, and the horrible buzzing sound that came out of the sound hole could hardly be described as music. These boys were much older than me, and they could go to the pubs. They used to occupy the small back room of the Bay Hotel (now the Royal George) at the top of Solva hill. Years ago the Bay was a bit of a rough-and-tumble, ideal for what we called a *sesh* (session). There was a piano there, but it was the guitars which brought the punters in every night. The room was always packed and I could sneak in unnoticed. After a while Clive used to let me take his guitar home during the day when they were down the beach and I'd forget the swimming and stay at home practising on the guitar – poor old Mam!

On Saturday mornings, there was a radio programme called *Saturday Skiffle Club*. Many of the best amateur skiffle groups would do spots, as would recording artists like Lonnie Donegan, Charles McDevitt, Nancy Whiskey and Johnny Duncan and his Blue Grass Boys. The music they played was based on American folk songs and blues. They would play guitars, banjos, mandolins and home-made basses (tea chests), washboards just like the old jug bands of the 1920s and 30s from Mississippi and Louisiana, mouth organs, even spoons and kazoos. This music was accessible to all, and people quickly learned the words of the most popular songs. Many of the standards were also played: songs by Hank Williams, Woody Guthrie and even old jazz numbers like 'St Louis Blues', Fats Waller songs and Louis Armstrong.

There were a lot of old instruments in people's attics: long-forgotten banjos, mandolins and guitars which sailors had brought from overseas. These were dug out. I had a banjo belonging to old Captain Evans of the Fort and a banjo mandolin from another sailor. A lot of sailors from Brawdy would come to the Bay on pay days, and it used to get so wild that it resembled a low dive in the Gut in Valletta, Malta more than an old forgotten pub in west Wales. There would be heavy drinking of rum and black and Worthington bitter and whisky, gambling on pontoon and blind brag in the bar, while the small back room would be packed out, with guitars going hell for leather and everyone singing their heads off. Those who couldn't get in used to stand outside the window in the garden, and people would hand flagons out to them. The Bay resounded to skiffle music every night, 'Rock Island Line', 'Jessie James', 'Railroad Bill', 'Goodnight Irene' and 'Frankie and Johnny', as well as Buddy Holly, The Everlys, Little Richard, Bill Haley and the Comets, Gene Vincent and Elvis. Rock and roll had arrived in the unlikely and unsuspecting west Wales village of Solva. I was fifteen then, it was my first gig and I was nearly ready to rock.

# Chapter 4

# *Guitar*

I had to get my hands on a guitar; it was the only thing on my mind. I had to get one somehow. The guitar that Lonnie Donegan played was simply beautiful, fantastic; it was a Martin 00028, grand auditorium model, the same instrument that Big Bill Broonzy once played, and Lonnie Johnson too. (I have one now, exactly the same – a dream come true!)

Al Young had brought a Dansette record player home, and when he went back to the RAF at the end of the summer he loaned it to me. You could play the old 78 singles or the new vinyl 45s on that machine, and he also loaned me a bunch of albums and EPs – 45 vinyl records that had usually four tracks on them. Al was into jazz in a big way and was a member of some of the London jazz clubs at that time: Ken Colyer's Studio 51, Cy Laurie's near the Windmill Theatre off Piccadilly and the National Jazz Federation's club at 100 Oxford Street (which is still there). He had started to collect records by some of the hottest New Orleans jazz bands as well as recordings by British revivalist bands, including Colyer, The Crane River Band, Sandy Brown from Scotland, Mick Mulligan, the Merseysippi Jazzmen, Humphrey Lyttleton and of course Chris Barber, whose band included Lonnie Donegan's skiffle group (basically the rhythm section of the band but with Barber replacing Jim Bray on double bass). Barber had recorded a recent album called *New Orleans Joys*, which included two skiffle tracks – 'Rock Island Line' and 'John Henry', two American

Negro worksongs. These recordings became so popular that they were released as a single and topped the pop music charts at the time, giving rise to a huge interest in this type of music and of course the guitar. Soon, Donegan left the Barber band and founded his own band with the two guitars, bass and drums format that more or less invented the rock and roll combo that became the norm in the 1960s (such as the Beatles, Rolling Stones and so on). This was the perfect instrumental formula for the modern sound that would make the guitar, especially the electric guitar, the most important instrument in modern music. Donegan went on to make a lot of hit records, mostly based on American folk music. He made a lot of money too!

Lonnie Donegan came very much from the Variety Theatre and jazz club tradition, as did many of the jazz musicians of the day. Many had played in swing bands like Joe Loss, Ronnie Aldrich and the Squadronaires and even in symphony orchestras such as the LSO. Every little mouth had to be fed, and there was no living to be made this side of the Atlantic playing jazz! But things were changing, and a traditional jazz boom, based on dance music, was on the horizon. The jazz clubs were great places to go for a bop, and you'd be guaranteed to meet some nice people too. Wild young people would go to jazz clubs and freak out jiving. Hardly any of these clubs were licensed to sell alcohol, only coffee or soft drinks. Some of the London clubs stayed open all night and were called 'all-nighters'. The band or bands would play a series of sets from dusk till dawn and Friday and Saturday nights, and young people would hitch-hike from all over Britain to join in the fun and games. From the jazz clubs emerged the Beaulieu jazz festival, which was an annual weekend freak-out organized by Lord Montague, a celebrated jazz fan. This festival was the prototype for all future rock and jazz festivals in Britain.

Al Young also introduced me to Broonzy, Josh White, Leadbelly, Jimmy Rushing, Ella Fitzgerald and Big Joe Williams and many other important architects of modern music. Chris Barber's vocalist at the time was Ottilie Patterson, an Irish girl with a very low soulful voice. Humphrey Lyttleton was a great trumpet player, and Cy Laurie an excellent if eccentric clarinettist who went off to India to study Buddhism. Then there was Sandy Brown, a Scottish clarinet player who always reminded me of the great New Orleans creole jazzman Sidney Bechet. For the purists, Ken Colyer's cornet style was much admired – reminiscent of Joe 'King' Oliver (Satchmo's idol) and Bunk Johnson who all played in the Storyville brothels of New Orleans in the early 1900s. Colyer had a more authentic skiffle group within his band, which included Alexis Korner and Dick Bishop. Colyer refused to have anything to do with pop music, so his skiffle group buzzed with authentic Negro folk music and Mississippi mud! Lyrics were now important; people like Bob Dylan owe everything to the folk music tradition as do the Beatles, Stones et al.

And there was I, stuck in Solva with no bread, no broads, no wheels, no experience, and worst of all no guitar! I had to do something – fast!

On Saturday mornings I used to listen religiously to *Saturday Skiffle Club* hosted by Brian Matthew. Mam was usually doing housework in the kitchen at that time, and so I had the sitting-room and the radio to myself. There I'd be, ear glued to the speaker, with a notepad on the table into which I'd scribble the words of the songs I had not heard before for future reference. This notebook became the basis of my early repertoire and the gig list of the Solva Skiffle Group, alternatively called The Satelites and The Neutrons. Our biggest gig was the interval at the annual Regatta dance in the Solva Memorial Hall, which unfortunately doesn't happen any more (God knows why not. They're so middle class now!). But I still have a *sesh* with some of the local musicians when I go home, Max Cole from Carew and Al Jenkins from Solva – it's still happening!

By now, Clive Williams, Steve Glass and Alan Roch had all gone back to college, autumn leaves were whirling in the wind and we were pulling the boats up on to the foreshore for their winter overhauls and a good rest. It was the soccer season too, when Solva would be peaceful after all the summer fun, games and Shennanekins. My friends and I were all back in St David's Grammar School with the GCE examinations threatening in June! I was fourteen years old and life was beginning to get serious.

My grandparents took the *News of the World* and the *Sunday Pictorial* at weekends; Sunday, not my favourite day to the present, was 'the day of rest' and meant that no one did any work. Peace and quiet reigned supreme – all commercial establishments religiously closed, even Mr Gould's paper shop. Nevertheless, papers could be purchased through the front window of Aunty Mattie's house next door to the Ship Inn. In those days the Sunday papers were quite ordinary, no tits and bums, no G-strings, scandal or lurid tales of corruption, pornography and drug trafficking. The slogan of the *News of the World* was 'All human life is here'. And it's still the same, unchanged, much like human nature! Now though it's more like 'Sex drugs and rock and roll, or the diary of a transvestite bisexual, alcoholic, drug -addicted sex maniac cabinet minister and his orgasmic hooker mates!' I never read the Sunday papers then and I don't read them now. I wouldn't waste my ill-gotten gains. The only paper I get is *The Times*. And needless to say I haven't got a television set – like motor cars I've never felt the need to own one. I've known a few journalists in my time, and let it suffice to say that they are a dubious and motley crew! When we lived in River Street, one of my little tasks was to remove the staples from the *Radio Times*, cut it in half, thread the result onto a piece of string, tie a deft reef knot, and hang the whole lot on a nail in the thunderbox. I've wiped my bum with more than enough famous broadcasters! To a certain extent, when I'm feeling religious, I think of the press and TV as a modern version of *Mal Occio* – the evil eye.

Or perhaps shallow and spineless voyeurism (the *Sun*, the *Mirror*, the soaps). Boring shit for bored and ignorant people.

Various music companies were advertising guitars for sale in Sunday newspapers, along with rupture trusses, bedroom slippers, Durex condoms and greenhouses. The guitar was getting big and loads of entrepreneurs were jumping on the bandwagon. It's called cashing in. I replied to one such ad from a company called Bell's of Surbiton, Surrey, although I had no cash. Eventually, a thin, glossy, black and white catalogue arrived. It was full of photographs of amazing guitars – I was overjoyed and felt like joining my pigeons on the roof! The guitars were mostly cheap imports from Sicily named Catania, Firenze and Etna, but there were also some typewritten pages of pink notepaper advertising Hofner guitars from Germany. These were far superior, much more modern than the Italiano jobs and twice the price! By this time, I had learned more about guitars than I knew about sex – which, since the grand entrance of Empress Guitar, had been forgotten and if the Italian instruments were empress, the German Hofner was God!

I felt much like Francis Drake stranded in the Azores without a ship. Very often I would see pictures of famous guitarists such as Bert Weedon or Tommy Steele playing these Hofner guitars. I had no chance of a Hofner, and so I plumped for a Catania. Named after a town in Sicily, it was priced at fifteen guineas and a fortune to me at that time. I would spend ages ogling its picture covetously, the way some of the boys would look at a nudie mag. I'm sure that Mam thought I was going mad!

It was no good considering Mam and Dada as a source of revenue; they were old age pensioners and had very little money, and there was no way that they would have understood this guitar-mania that was taking over my mind. It was possible to earn fifteen quid picking spuds on the farms around St David's, but that wouldn't happen until the following summer. There was very little seasonal work on the land in the Solva area in winter.

My grandparents in Shrewsbury usually bought me something for my birthday, but that was seven months away. Nevertheless, the master plan was beginning to take shape. The gods must have caught the vibe! I had to have a guitar; I felt like a bitch on heat and it wasn't very pleasant. My only regular source of money was a 5*s*. postal order, which arrived each week in a roll of comics – *Dandy*, *Beano*, *Sun* and *Comet* – from my grandparents in Shrewsbury. This was the first time I'd thought up a business deal. I used to send my granny a thank-you letter each week that also contained news of how we were and how I was getting on in school. I began subtly – or so I thought – to mention guitars and music. I told them I wanted to learn music and that I'd already learned some chords and songs. The only problem was the lack of an instrument to play them on. Later I sent them the catalogue with the Catania subtly underlined in red ink accompanied by the message, "This is the one I'd like to play." The next letter from Shrewsbury said that I'd have to curb my enthusiasm and save up my five bobs until I'd got the magical sum of fifteen quid, and not being Einstein didn't prevent me from working out that this process would take more than fifteen months. I couldn't wait that long, I'd explode with frustration or rob a bank or something! I wrote back suggesting that if they could afford it they might advance me the money for the guitar, and then they needn't send me any more 5*s*. postal orders. This was a long shot – would it work? It's funny how the juvenile mind works. I'd never asked them for anything before and I felt embarrassed. I'd committed myself to a process that I didn't really understand and had little control over – I was at sea! The following week the usual roll of comics arrived on Saturday morning, but inside was a letter in my grandfather's handwriting. Very unusual! The letter contained a lecture on the value of money – how hard it was to earn, how you had to respect your daily bread – and on general things appertaining to money matters. Then at the end of the letter he commended me for doing well at school and for wanting to learn music. I knew he played the piano, but he also told me that he had been a musician and had played the violin in the Liverpool Philharmonic Orchestra. The letter concluded by saying that they would be glad to buy me the guitar as a birthday present in advance. Furthermore, I would not have to forfeit my weekly five bob as I was a growing lad and would need some regular income. Wow! He said that he'd sent an order to Bells in Surrey for the Catania guitar, which should arrive soon.

I was amazed; I'd never been so happy in my life. I was ecstatic, dancing like a dervish around the kitchen whilst waving the letter in my poor old grandma's face. At last she read the letter and commented, "Aren't they good people looking after you like that?" They must have thought the same of her and Dada. I danced off up the road to tell Byron the good news. "I'm having a guitar – it's coming in the post!" The wait was agony. Mam kept telling me to come away from the window and leave the curtains alone. I was getting on her nerves – the excitement was *too much*!

Big parcels usually came on the GWR lorry from Haverfordwest station. That's how my bike had arrived, a lovely bright green Raleigh sports bike standing in the back of the lorry amidst the brown cardboard boxes and sacks. Every afternoon, I'd be first off the school bus. I'd sprint for the door of Number 12 and knock furiously. "Nothing today, Michael bach," Mam would say. "Come and have your tea now." Then, about a week after I'd received the famous letter from Shrewsbury, I was running as usual up to the front door, satchel flying behind me, when the door opened and there stood Mam, a big smile on her face and with a long brown cardboard box in her arms. "Is this it?" she asked. Breathlessly, I took it from her. It was addressed to me: Mr L. M. J. Stevens, 12 Bro Dawel, Solva, Pembs. I took it into the kitchen, put it on the table, got a pair of scissors from the drawer and hurriedly cut the box open. It was like Christmas – there she lay, all shiny and brown and beautiful, black and white purfling round the sound hole and edges, and a white plastic plectrum guard. I took her out; she had a beautifully grained, light mahogany back and sides and slotted machine heads. I took her to my bedroom and began tuning her up. Thus began a love affair, a long musical journey, full of adventure and beautiful times which have lasted till the present. As I write this, I'm looking at this strange magical instrument which for me is a work of art and a companion second to none.

I played that guitar constantly. Mam and Dada were very patient with me, and soon my fingers became grooved by the steel strings and would hurt and sometimes bleed. Yet I couldn't put it down. A tutor book had come with the guitar, *First Steps – Play Guitar in a Day*. I couldn't understand any of it. It was nonsense to me; only the chord symbols above the music were any good and some of those were impossible to fret. I used to listen to Radio Luxembourg a lot, and although reception was very bad in west Wales and the music came and went, ebbing and flowing through clouds of static, we somehow got the message, and that message was 'Heartbreak Hotel' by Elvis and 'Tutti Frutti' by Little Richard, and of course Jerry Lee and Bill Haley's Comets, amidst crap schmaltz pop of the type that still emanates from London radio stations. I'd never heard anything like 'Heartbreak Hotel'. The first time I heard it sung was by some girls on the school bus; they were Presley fans and one was my cousin Jean, who still is and always will be an Elvis fanatic!

I wasn't into the sex thing, not even vaguely interested. It was the sound that got me, especially the sound of the electric guitar. The girls were into that too, although they were also carried away by the sex appeal and of course the dancing – the jiving. Most of my boy friends wouldn't be seen dead dancing; it was sissy and not at all cool. I got Jean to teach me how to jive, aided and abetted by her friends, Marian Cox, Pearl Davies and Nesta Phillips. We used to practice in a field near Bro Dawel, and I would sing rock songs with my guitar while they jived in the hay.

There were regular dances in the City Hall, St David's, most often on Friday nights during the summer. The band would usually be Tony Walsh, a local alto-sax player, with drums, accordion and piano. Walsh died a couple of years ago; one of his sons is Ian Walsh who played soccer for Wales. He had some brothers that were just as good. In fact, there were quite a few boys in the St David's and Solva area who could have become top professional soccer players. Alan Jenkins, who is one of the best *sesh* players of banjo and guitar in St David's, was offered a trial for Swansea, but his father wouldn't let him go. This wouldn't happen nowadays, people are more broad-minded. The league scouts would have had a pleasant surprise if they'd ventured into the Wild West in the old days. But the St David's peninsula was remote and largely unvisited – unknown to England, and thank god for that from a conservationist's point of view on ethnic culture.

Those City Hall dances were quite formal affairs. It was there that my mother Bet used to play in some of the local swing bands, with Joffre Swales, 'The Master' from Haverfordwest (who died in the spring of 2003), and of course Jack Holt who was a postman. There were two dances in Haverfordwest on Saturday nights, one at the Drill Hall and the other in the Masonic Hall. Joffre Swales had a full twelve-piece swing orchestra at the Masonic, the posher of the two gigs, and the Drill Hall had the pleasure of the company of the sailors from Brawdy Fleet Air Arm Base and the Harlequins dance band, a smaller, more jazzy band with a lady on piano. The Drill was where the hot jivers like cousin Jean went, and they almost all ended up married to sailors. Jean's parents, Uncle Ivor and Auntie Gwenny, were quite strict and didn't approve of her going out to late dances in town. She used to tell her father that she was going with me. I was the cover for her jiving and snogging with her boyfriend on the late bus home. That bus was a travelling den of iniquity, bulging with drunken puking sailors singing their heads off and trying to have their evil way up the skirts of the country girls. The St David's dances tended to be more parochial; only local lads and lasses would attend, the older boys in their early twenties looking for a girl to marry. It was like that in those days; many of those who met at a dance and then started courting would end up married, and the local girls who went with the sailors usually vanished up the line never to be seen again. I wonder where they all are now?

That's what happened to the girls I used to jive with in the hops. Maud Mathias was a petite black-haired girl in my class and we loved to dance together, taking over one of the corners of the dance floor next to the bandstand. I really fancied her – a teenage crush I guess – and we used to jive all night until we were sweating buckets. I had other jiving partners too – those secret jiving lessons paid off. Most of the boys used to dance in order to pick up a girl. It was totally legitimate and socially acceptable. Some were far more interested in what went on after the dance up the back lane, and there were liaisons which produced 'love children' who had to be legitimized before the shotguns came out. But for me it was a learning process of a different kind – I was there for the music, believe it or not!

Most of the bands played Glenn Miller-type music, although Joffre Swales led the only proper dance orchestra in the area. All the others were combos of four to six musicians, but they worked well enough for the local hops and they'd picked up on some of the early rock numbers especially Bill Haley songs which they played without vocals. Geoff Swales had two vocalists who sang in the style of the famous big bands like Joe Loss etc. Phrases such as "Take your partners for a general excuse me foxtrot" always raised a laugh among the lads who used to stand in groups around the dance floor, plucking up courage to ask one of the girls they fancied for a dance whilst some of the more anxious parents watched from the balcony.

I remember going with a couple of friends to a dance at Fishguard once. It wasn't very well attended. The Swales band was performing, and I asked him to play a pasadoble, which is a Spanish dance. Little did I know that they'd only just finished rehearsing that number and that Joffre was very pleased with the result. Of course, nobody knew how to dance the pasadoble, not even me. After the number, Joffre leapt angrily off the stage and gave me a huge bollocking: "Who the fuck do you think you are, are you taking the piss or what?" I thought he was going to beat me up. Angry men in evening dress still crack me up! I didn't know at the time that he'd been in the Royal Marines during the war, a bandsman thank god! He wrote a very interesting book about his experiences in the Marines during the war, suitably entitled *We Blew and They Were Shattered*. Read it!

Meanwhile the guitar was still favourite and I practised all the time, learning more songs from the radio and from song books and records. Soon I decided to form a skiffle group. Quite a few of the local boys were interested – they were always into new things – but I was the only person in the area with a guitar. No problem! My cousin Byron and I made a bushbass from an old tea chest into which we cut two F holes, like a real double bass, and then we painted it black and white with 'The Satelites' emblazoned on the front. A broom handle, set in an indentation in the top of the box, served as the neck, and all you had to do to get notes was to tighten or slacken the string by pulling the broom handle. It was a very crude musical instrument, but after much practice we began to achieve quite an authentic jug band sound. The basic ensemble consisted of guitar, bushbass and washboard, with anyone else available playing guitar or banjo. I also had a banjo mandolin, borrowed from a retired merchant seaman. Byron and I spent a lot of time experimenting with various types of strings. Lobster pot stringing twine was good for the tea chest bass, but the best was locking wire, used to secure nuts and bolts on aircraft. There was a readily free supply at Air Work just up the road. This wire gave the bass a good loud and clear sound. Byron was something of a Leonardo de Vinci, and he also played this home-made instrument, while Al Young played a metal washboard with two handfuls of metal thimbles on his fingers, most of which had been pinched from local women's sewing boxes. These were the Solva Skifflers or the Satelites.

Around this time, Bill, Al's brother also joined the RAF, and when he came home on leave he brought a large Sunburst cello guitar with an electric pick-up attached. Byron also bought a guitar in a shop in Haverfordwest. It was a nicer one than mine, with steel strings and a fixed bridge. Things were getting exciting, but we had a problem finding rehearsal space. Originally we'd played in Mam's kitchen at Number 12, but this got far too loud for the old folks, who liked to listen to the radio in the room next door in the evening. Next we started to rehearse in a green corrugated iron bus shelter on the St David's road. Later, we found an old chicken shack practically covered by bracken and foliage on Pen Graig overlooking Solva harbour, so we cleaned it out a bit and cut a path through the trash. It became our rehearsal room and had one of the best views in Britain. On weekends, the people sailing below in their yachts and motor boats would be serenaded by The Satelites and their repertoire of blues and American Negro work songs, all emanating from the balmy undergrowth of Pen Graig. We'd take food and soft drinks with us and stay there for hours. Those sessions were our little musical weekend parties.

Now we had three guitarists and, in summer, three more: Clive, Alan and Steve. Our sound was getting bigger and more sophisticated, and in the summer of 1956 Clive and Steve arrived on holiday with a home-made amplifier. We became so good that we were asked to play the interval at the annual Regatta dance, which must have been my first gig. I think that we even got paid thirty bob as well!

The nightly sessions in the Bay Hotel went from strength to strength. People came from miles around, as did quite a few attractive young girls who were on holiday in the area. Local women were hardly ever seen in pubs in those days, and certainly not young girls. Around the same time a young sailor came to the Bay. They called him Paddy, and he was in the Royal Navy at Brawdy. Paddy had an electric Hofner President guitar and a small commercially manufactured amplifier. He used to come up to Mam's house of an evening and we'd practise together in the kitchen. Paddy taught me some more complicated chord progressions, which helped to speed up my progress.

That summer I made up my mind to study fine art – painting. I was going to be a painter and an art teacher – well, that was the plan. Clive Williams was already studying at Cardiff College of Art, and he gave me some information and encouragement, which no one else did; there was nobody in the area who knew anything about fine art and, as far as I knew, no one from St David's Grammar School had ever been to an art college up to then. I was determined to go to art school, an idea that inspired me just as much if not more than the guitar had. Clive told me that the Slade School of Art in London was one of the finest art schools in the world, so I sent for their prospectus. However, the thought of applying for the Slade was too intimidating – it was said that the best students in Britain went there and I knew that I wasn't that brilliant. I had also sent for the Cardiff College of Art prospectus, and I decided to apply there. The Royal College of Art was another possibility, but I didn't think that I'd have much of a chance. And I thought that it would be far too posh.

Around this time, on the sixteenth of January in the winter of

1957, I suffered one of the most traumatic events of my whole life. I came home from school on the bus as usual around four o'clock but, as I walked the thirty yards or so between the road and our front door, a young boy came running up. "Mike!" he said. "There's something wrong with your Dada. He's been taken ill." I ran for the front door, not the kitchen door round the back, part of my normal routine. Before I could knock, Uncle Syd opened the door, his usually benign face bearing a very troubled look. "Come inside quick," he said. "Dada's had a stroke." My head was wondering what a stroke was; I'd never heard of such a thing before.

I went into the sitting-room to find Mam as I'd never seen her before. She was totally distraught – that lovely pillar of humanity, simplicity, goodness, truth and strength was now a pitiful, weeping woman. She was slumped in an armchair and appeared to have shrunk in size. She was wearing her best clothes, including her black hat with the purple ribbon (her favourite colour), because she'd been to St David's that day to visit family. Mam hardly ever went out, as most of the food and other goods were delivered by grocery vans. Apparently she'd caught an early bus, leaving Dada, who most days went to his workshop on the quay, with money to pay the insurance man who called once a week. Mam always controlled the domestic finances; Dada never touched money. It seemed that he had got bored sitting around the house and had gone out to do some work in the garden. There were a lot of stones and pieces of masonry from the demolished military huts still embedded in the ground, and he'd suffered a massive brain haemorrhage whilst trying to lift a seventy- or eighty-pound rock out of the earth.

When Mam arrived home with Uncle Syd, who had decided to come with her to Solva to see his father, she could see Dada through the window, sitting in his chair. She tapped the window, but there was no response. She knocked it again, and this time he got up, though with obvious difficulty, to open the door. Still holding the insurance book and the change in his hand, he collapsed unconscious on the threshold. It was a good job that Syd was there. Doctor Gillam was called, and Dada was put to bed. The doctor said that it was a massive cerebral haemorrhage. He should have died instantaneously, but he was very strong for a man of seventy-six – as anyone would confirm.

For forty-eight hours he lay dying, with Mam trying to feed him a warm water and honey solution with a silver teaspoon. This was the worst experience of my life; all we could do was stand around the bed and watch him die. He made a strange snoring-like sound as the fluid on his chest bubbled, a noise that could be heard all over the house. On the second night I went to bed, leaving Mam in the sitting-room with my cousin Gerald, Syd's son, who had come over to help out. When I woke early the next morning the house was almost silent; the ominous snore had disappeared and there was only the sound of Mam's grieving. I got up and went into the sitting-room. "He's gone," said Gerald, looking me in the eyes. I'll never forget that moment; it brings tears to my eyes as I write.

We laid him out that morning. He was measured with a carpenter's rule, the measurements were written on a scrap of paper, and off I was sent on the bus to Keyston Hill, nine miles down the road to Uncle Jim Davies, Dada's younger brother, to have the coffin made. Uncle Jim had a carpenter's shop at the back of his house – a corrugated iron shed that stands to this day – and Percy, Uncle Jim's son, and I went there to select some timber for Dada's coffin. I climbed up into the roof joists and found some elm planks of which Percy approved, then when all the necessary wood was found we set to with saw, plane and spokeshave – it was a plain, good job and working the wood helped to take my mind off the shocking event of Dada's demise. Two hours later I was alone in the workshop, finishing off the box with different grades of sandpaper. Finally, it was ready to be wax polished. After tea, I caught the last bus home, carrying a letter from Uncle Jim to Mam; she couldn't read it for the tears in her eyes.

Dada was buried in the graveyard behind Penuel Chapel near Roch Gate, a stone's throw from the now-ruined cottage on the side of the St David's road where he and his brothers and sisters were born. Mama and Bet my mother also lie in the same grave, and the names of Walter and little Stuart, his brother who died only eighteen months old during a diphtheria epidemic in Solva, are on the same stone.

Later, when the GCE results came out, I learned that I had passed in seven subjects. I would have to wait until I was sixteen until I could apply for Cardiff Art College, and so I decided to stay in school for another year. So back to school I went to study A level art (mainly Gothic architecture and calligraphy), as well as a couple of other subjects I wasn't interested in. If the truth be known I was skiving – art came so easily to me. But I had to be careful because J. J. Evans, the headmaster, was a very strict disciplinarian, as were most of the staff, especially Miss C. M. Rees, the geography mistress, who had taught my mother, Hayden and Walter. She used to refer to them as her star pupils.

We kids enjoyed a love-hate relationship with our teachers. There were only ninety-seven or so of us and a dozen of them. Sometimes it could become a running battle or, on second thoughts, guerrilla warfare. We would invent dreadful tricks to play on them. Ronald Searle's *St Trinian's* books were a big hit as well as a source of inspiration, and there was a group of fifth and sixth formers, including prefects, who spent a lot of time winding up and terrorizing the academic staff. This was a relentless ongoing game. Poor Aneurin Griffiths, the science teacher, took the brunt of much mischief; he was literally sitting on a powder keg, his laboratory a pyromaniac's nirvana, but a nightmare for him. Every now and then he'd get so frustrated that he'd go into the small room where the chemicals were stored and weep, but there was still no mercy.

On one occasion, a group of sixth formers were manufacturing gasses using a Kipp's apparatus. They persuaded some junior to wind up Aneurin, and when he went into the store room to have a sob they locked him in and ran a tube from the apparatus, which was busily pumping out hydrogen sulphide gas, into the keyhole of the storeroom door. The bell went for the end of the lesson, and everyone piled out into the playground leaving Mr Griffiths to die in the storeroom. Fortunately, the headmaster was doing his rounds. He smelt the gas and released Mr Griffiths, who was in pretty bad shape and stinking of rotten eggs! No one was caught and no one punished, but this was an extremely dangerous and irresponsible trick to play, and things went quiet for a good while afterwards. At other times, the cricket-pitch roller would appear on the roof of the sanitary block. No one could figure out how it had been hoisted up or who had done it. They'd have to call the local fire brigade to get it down, much to the amusement of the whole school.

One morning we arrived on the Solva bus, having been told by a certain sixth former that something big had happened during the night, to find a real grave in the middle of the lawn in front of the school. The grave had a white headstone and an oblong kerb around a bed of gravel, on which had been placed an urn containing a large bunch of daffodils. I can't remember whether it was St David's Day or not, but I do recall a group of teachers including the headmaster and two of the local policemen standing at the graveside engaged in animated conversation. There was holy hell over this one: some pupils were grilled in the head's office by both the headmaster and the police, and in assembly that morning we were threatened with prosecution if we did not reveal the names of the culprits.

It took a week for the furore to die down. The grave, as it happened, was for the woodwork and sports master, Alun Mathias – God bless him – who was very much alive that day and is to this! Inscribed on the tombstone was the epitaph, 'In memory of Bull who died year dot, waylaid by the great leveller.' The miscreants were never discovered, although most of the school knew who they were, and some of these nocturnal undertakers went on to become teachers, university professors and, in one case, a surgeon.

I still wonder at the lengths we would go to bait the teachers at that school. But, at the time, I couldn't wait to leave and I was only waiting for my sixteenth birthday so that I could go to Art College. I had already sat the entrance exam and been accepted by Cardiff College of Art, but I could not start until September 1957. I still did athletics and played some football; in fact, I kept up the distance running and javelin throwing until I was nearly nineteen. I played my last game of soccer for HTV against the BBC at the age of thirty-six, when I got so badly fouled I couldn't walk properly for a month. It was time to give up. The same guy who kicked me in the knee to prevent me from scoring knocked out the actor John Ogwen and broke the arm of the son of the steward of the BBC club. Clearly not cricket, old chap! But he must have been hit by a bit of instant karma in the end, and a broken leg came with it!

There were a lot of characters in school, and quite a few rock and roll fans. Dai Harries and his sister Rowena had a small but good collection of records by Fats Domino, Little Richard, Bill Haley and Elvis. Their parents – who were also musical people – owned a lovely radiogram which looked like a piece of furniture, a kind of cocktail cabinet. We would go down to Dai's house and sit around for hours listening to these records over and over. I can remember going to Haverfordwest with him, John Lloyd and Dai Lines (who later married Rowena) to see *Rock Around the Clock* at the County cinema. We had read in the paper and heard on the radio news lurid tales of rock fans and Teddy boys wrecking cinemas in big cities. There were a few

Teds around Haverfordwest and Milford at the time, but not enough to wreck a cinema we thought. We felt quite daring and wore black shirts and slim jim ties under our school uniforms. We were 'sympathetic' Teds who couldn't afford drape jackets and brothel creeper shoes. The nearest we got to brothel creepers were Eaton Clubmen suede shoes in brown or black with a thick crêpe sole, the kind you could buy from the Littlewoods catalogue at two bob a week. Fortunately, our double-breasted black school blazer with wide lapels was pretty close to a drape jacket – if you forgot to sew the arms of the Bishop of St David's, which was our school badge, on the breast pocket. Duck's arse haircuts were easy if you could get away with it; you just let it grow pretty long then swept it back over your head and plastered it down with a generous dollop of Brylcreem. And jeans could be easily narrowed.

There was a lot of aggro about haircuts and trousers in those days. The captain of the Brawdy naval base even went as far as to ban the sailors from wearing trousers with under seventeen-inch bottoms. Crazy! As it happened there was a bespoke tailor's shop on the base and most of the younger matelots had beautifully made suits in modern designs and materials with twelve-inch bottoms, some as small as ten inch, and really tight fitting. They'd go to a dance in their uniforms with their suit in a holdall and then change in someone's house or in the toilet of a pub. They also used to smuggle out the Pusser's rum. The young writers and the PO on the grog detail had to ditch what was left of the rum after all the sailors had received their tot. What was left was supposed to be poured down the sink, but they'd temporarily disconnect the plumbing and the rum would be caught in a secret receptacle. I've also heard that the staff on some naval ships would disconnect the plumbing to the royal toilet when the queen or another royal came aboard, catching the turds if she'd used it. In fact, I've seen one in the Chief's mess in Brawdy; it was varnished and mounted with an engraved silver plaque stating what it was!

Going back to Ted suits, I eventually 'encouraged' my benefactors in Shrewsbury to buy me a marvellous purple Edwardian jacket with black velvet collar and cuffs. I was always tapering trousers on my granny's old treadle sewing machine – which I still have here in good working order even though it's an antique.

By the end of another great summer in Solva – spent picking spuds on farms in the area, swimming, fishing, boating and playing most nights in the Bay Hotel – it was time for me to embark on my next big expedition. Not to find the source of the river Solva or a peregrine falcon's nest on St David's head or cormorants' eggs on the Green Scar, but a sortie of far more importance and one which would have a profound influence on my life. I was on my way to Cardiff College of Art. And so, on 16 September 1957, I packed my suitcase and headed for the bus to Haverfordwest and the London train.

# Chapter 5

# Art and Jazz

Travel time again, or maybe time travel! I stood at the bus stop at Maes Ewan clutching my Catania guitar in its soft brown cloth case, and with a big old suitcase borrowed from my runaway mother at my side. I'd just sold my beloved to one of my mother's friends in order to pay my travelling expenses. Neither my mother nor Mam had any money to give me – my mother had just done a runner with her three little boys from her cruel husband in London. Elwyn Griffiths, for it was he who bought the guitar for the princely sum of five pounds (a lot of wonger in those days), had loaned the instrument back to me until I could afford to buy another. What a kind and considerate man; he must have known how I felt about guitars. Never mind, I would get my grant after registering at college and then I'd be able to buy another one. In any case, the Catania by now was looking a bit the worse for wear.

The red Western Welsh bus came rattling round the corner and I climbed aboard with a goodbye wave to cousin Jean the jiver, Elvis and my mother Bet, who had kindly come to see me off. It was a lovely sunny autumn morning as the bus trundled down the hill above the harbour and I bade a sad and silent farewell to Solva and my boyhood. It was full tide, the bright sunlight glinting on a beautiful green sea. A lovely and peaceful scene, which I miss as much now as I did then. The bus stopped opposite the Ship Hotel in Lower Solva, and Mr Willie Thomas, a local farmer, got on and sat beside me. I knew him well – he was one of Dada's friends. In fact, Dada had worked quite recently on a new house called Creiglan that he'd had built. Mr Thomas owned most of the fields in the village. His farm, Panteg, stood right in the middle of Upper Solva, and he kept a small herd of Friesian milking cows as well as the last horse and cart in the village. Dada had made that cart, and I remember it well. Mr Thomas's daughter Linda was both milkmaid and milklady. She used to do her round on a bicycle with small churns hanging from the handlebars. She would knock the door and we'd take out a large jug, which she filled from the churn. There were no bottles. Mr Thomas asked me where I was going and, when I told him, he congratulated me warmly, dug into his pocket and handed me five shillings for luck and to help me on my way.

In those days, it used to take an hour to travel the twelve miles to Haverfordwest along the long, winding and very hilly road. When we arrived at the railway station, that place of many memories, the train was on time. It was an old steam locomotive of the Castle class pulling a coal tender and heavy carriages in the cream and brown livery of the Great Western Railway. The carriages had separate compartments with plush velour seats, net luggage racks, and long sliding windows in the doors which were controlled by a thick leather strap that hooked onto a brass stud. Framed pictures of holiday resorts, such as New Quay, Cornwall, Brighton, Clacton, Bournemouth, Blackpool and Penzance hung on the walls alongside large oblong mirrors. There were also roller blinds over the windows and ornate lamps.

It was a five-hour journey to Cardiff. Soon, the verdant meadows of Pembrokeshire and Carmarthenshire rolled past the windows, the Preseli hills shining on the horizon to the north. After Carmarthen, where you could change for Aberystwyth and north Wales, we entered the south Wales coalfield and the countryside became less green.

Llanelli was fully industrialized then, and the land of 'Sosban' lay under a huge cloud of smog and smoke, as did Swansea, Neath and Port Talbot, which was absolutely filthy. Any air that was left stank of fire, carbon and sulphur from the blast furnaces and the Bessemer converters, and towering palls of smoke and steam rose into an infernal grey-green sky illuminated by showers of sparks and flames. Then onwards through the rolling green countryside of Bridgend, the Vale of Glamorgan and Barry before reaching the sprawling seaport city of Cardiff.

I alighted with my battered suitcase and guitar to be greeted enthusiastically by my mother's brother Rhys, who worked as a draughtsman in a municipal drawing office in Cardiff. He lived in Heol Gabriel, off the Philog, near Whitchurch common where I would lodge temporarily with his family until I found digs. Uncle Rhys's wife was Auntie Nancy McNair, a Scottish lady who was a very good cook. I was looking forward to my sojourn.

The following day I boarded a Number 23 bus and went to the Art College at the Old Friary to register as a student. The college was an old Victorian red brick building that might have been a school at some time in the past. It stood in a yard, surrounded by an ornate wrought iron fence, and had a bicycle shed, two outside toilets and a three-storeyed modern extension at the back. Next to this building, among tall trees and much undergrowth, stood the ruined Gothic pillars and arches of the medieval friary – Cistercian I think – which was demolished years ago to make room for the Pearl Assurance tower. Later the art school building too would be pulled down in the name of progress. It's odd how buildings seem to die and get buried just like people. Nearby is the Civic Centre – law courts, police station, City Hall, the National Museum, Temple of Peace and the Welsh Office with the University behind it.

Opposite was the British Home Stores cafeteria, which was handy for coffee breaks and a cheap lunch of beans on toast or chips and gravy. That's about all we could afford on a grant of five pounds a week, three of which went on lodgings. I had to buy my painting and drawing materials and fund my travelling expenses out of the remaining two pounds, and so there wasn't much left for entertainment. It looked as if my new guitar would be a long time coming and that Elwyn Griffiths would have to wait a while for the return of the Catania! Nevertheless, I was lucky to be having breakfast and a cooked evening meal at Uncle Rhys and Auntie Nancy's. They lived in a comfortable new house on a recently built estate off Whitchurch Common and had a son called David who was then a toddler.

Cardiff seemed huge to me. The buildings were so tall, a mixture of old and new architecture. It was a bustling and affluent place, especially Queen Street, High Street, St Mary's Street and The Hayes in the centre. I'd never seen so many shops, pubs, cafés, restaurants, cinemas and barber shops, not to mention the traffic and crowds of people. I was familiar with the West End and Soho, but Cardiff was different – closer, more intimate, down to earth and homely. Somehow I knew I would fit in, and I felt quite at ease. The people spoke in a peculiar accent that I had never heard before. It certainly didn't sound Welsh to a Welshy from the Wild West, although English people, I'm told, can hear the Welshness in a Cardiff accent. If anything, I can always hear a bit of Liverpool 'Scouser' in it and I always thought the people themselves were similar in attitude, probably because they too are a mix of Welsh, English, Irish and Jock with a bit of the rest of the world thrown in for good measure. Strong parallels can be drawn between Liverpool and Cardiff; it's to do with seafaring and the docks, of course.

I couldn't wait to find Bute Street, the gateway to the world. I was desperate to be in some of those places I'd heard of as a boy, when I eavesdropped on the kitchen conversations of my seafaring family through the lamp-lit cracks in the floor of my bedroom in Solva so long ago.

One remarkable thing about Cardiff that I'd never seen before was the trolley buses. These were double-deckers which were powered by electric motors. Overhead a network of electric cables dissected the city like a horizontal spider's web. You could go almost anywhere on a trolley bus. Their pneumatic tyres meant that they were very quiet, and they caused no pollution. The buses had two long metal arms attached to a pivot on the roof, which hooked up to the power cables. They offered a very smooth and near silent ride. Sometimes, however, a jolt would throw the long terminal shafts off the overhead cables, and the conductors – both men and women who wore uniforms and leather shoulder bags slung low like Western gunfighters – would have to pull a twenty-foot pole from beneath the floor of the bus to reconnect the very long and I suppose extremely heavy arms. This was always a bit of a drama, and occasionally the cause of a good laugh. It was a sight to see a five-foot nothing conductress grappling with a twenty-foot pole in the middle of Queen Street in the rush hour!

I was standing in the Kingsway watching this happen, when I noticed an old pub called the Rose and Crown, and so I decided to call in to see what a Cardiff pub was like. It had a long narrow room with a high ceiling, beneath which lay a mahogany bar that stretched nearly the whole length of the room. Opposite the bar, against the wall, ran a long narrow bench with a few stools and some mahogany-topped, cast-iron Britannia tables. On the bar stood several beer pumps, their wooden handles decorated with enamelled plates reading Brains A.l. Dark, Brains SA and Brains Bitter. I ordered a pint of Bulmers' Woodpecker Cider, which is what I drank in those days, and sat down at the table with a couple of elderly men. Thoughts of Bute Street, James Street, the Custom House and Mountstuart Square were running through my mind as I drank the cider, and, after a while I asked one of the men where Bute Street lay. They gave me the directions and asked me where I came from and what I was doing in Cardiff. I told them I was a student and wanted to see the docks. "People don't go down there a lot," one of them told me, "unless they have business or work there. It's a very rough place. You'd better be on the alert if you go down there." With that, I finished my cider and headed down the Hayes past St John's church towards the docks.

The Hayes is a busy thoroughfare nowadays, but then it was more picturesque with its street vendors and fruit, vegetable and flowers stalls all along the pavements. Delivery boys on bicycles, with the names of their employers – usually butchers or grocers – emblazoned on enamelled metal plates, steel baskets in front of the handlebars filled with produce streamed past, while the Hayes Island snack bar with people drinking coffee and tea at tables beneath the tall trees made me think of Paris. I strolled past the department stores of Howells and David Morgan, past the Duke of Wellington and the King's Cross and on into Hayes Bridge Road, gateway to the docks with its pawn shops, dilapidated flop houses, cafés, curry restaurants, Greek Cypriot barber shops, the Salutation, Fishguard Arms, Glastonbury Arms and the Golden Cross. Then under the Great Western railway bridge with Newtown, the Irish Dockers' quarter round Herbert Street, on the left and the Queen's Head a few steps away, until, on the corner opposite, I saw the famous Custom House Hotel (now demolished; I wonder where all the whores go now!).

And there was Bute Street, over the hump-backed canal feeder bridge. It wasn't as I'd seen it in my mind's eye – some sort of street – but a long wide road with a tall rough-hewn granite railway embankment on the left and lengthy rows of multi-storeyed buildings containing shops, pubs and boarding houses and who knew what else. On the right, the pavement seemed to go on forever. I couldn't see the end of it, and so I strode briskly on heading south, trying to look as if I knew where I was going, and minding my own business. It was half past five by then, and a lovely sunset was beginning to light up the western sky. It made me think of St David's, where I have seen some of the most spectacular sunsets anywhere. On I hurried, past noisy bars and shops with live chickens and rabbits in the windows. The atmosphere was so different. It was like a foreign country – the people dressed in seafaring clothes, boiler suits, saris, Arabian robes and the brightly coloured clothes of Africa and the West Indies. Here were people from everywhere. Little kids, both coloured and white, played loudly in the road, running up the pavement and in and out of side alleys. It was like nothing I'd ever seen before. What a buzz!

The sun was setting fast, so I pressed on towards the pier head, walking down the pavement on the right-hand side of Bute Street, then onwards for about half a mile. The further I went, the busier the street became, with more and more sailors and dockers. I passed West Bute Street, which is a narrower street cutting off the main drag at an angle, before coming to James Street on the right almost opposite the dock gates near the Mountstuart Hotel, a huge Victorian pub near the Shipping Federation offices.

At last I was in sight of the pier head, and the hustle and bustle of one of the world's greatest ports was all around. Across the Bristol Channel, in the misty distance, the Devon coast seemed quite close, stretching as far as the horizons of the east and west, and the sea was dotted with ships of all kinds flying flags of all nations. Here was the berth of the Campbell steamers, the ferries that plied between Cardiff and the Devon ports of Weston and Ilfracombe, and here was one of the steamers with people boarding. There was also a trolley bus terminal at the pier head; it looked like a roundabout, with the overhead cables forming a circle up above so that the buses could turn around. To the east stretched the huge mass of Cardiff docks, where dozens of massive cranes reached for the sky and row upon row of cargo ships, big and small, waited to be serviced by them.

I was amazed and exhilarated. It was so good to breathe sea air again and to feel the prevailing south-west wind in my face, carrying the cries of a thousand seabirds. All docks have a distinctive smell: of smoke, steam, oil, tar, diesel fumes, fish and the aromas of spices, bacon and eggs cooking, Madras curry, chop suey, booze and sweat.

After a while, I turned and headed back north up Bute Street. It must have been about 7.30 and it was starting to get dark; I'd have to get back to my digs in Whitchurch. On Bute Street, the bars were getting noisier and there were a lot more people around. I felt a bit uneasy, as I'd heard some hair-raising tales of skulduggery, violence and whoring whilst eavesdropping on conversations back home in River Street. So I quickened my pace and headed for the comparative safety of the city centre.

When I saw the Custom House Hotel on my left, I knew I was nearly out of Bute Street. I'd heard Uncle Harold and some of his friends talk enthusiastically of this pub. As I approached the door I was amazed to hear the sound of jazz being played on an electric guitar. In I went. Around the large bar lingered a good number of sailors and dockers and a few tartily dressed women wearing too much perfume and make-up. Conversation and laughter filled the place. The guitarist, who was a big coloured man with a moustache and a battered trilby hat, sat in a corner by the door, surrounded by sailors, dockers and some of the painted ladies. They were 'hoying it up', as my mother would say, boozing and generally having a grand old time!

I'd never been in such a place before, and I bought a half pint of beer and stayed about an hour lapping up the music and atmosphere. This guy was good on the guitar, the best I'd ever heard up close, playing live. He was playing on an old Gibson L5 – a pre-war cello guitar – through a small Zenith amplifier. He was a pro all right, and

I found out that his name was Victor Parker. His performance was so casual and understated that he would talk with people whilst playing, even cracking jokes. In their turn, the customers would respond appropriately, shouting requests and offering him drinks. Some would shout greetings as they walked through the door and he'd shout back to them. It was magic!

My first night in Cardiff was incredible. Not only had I 'done' Bute Street, but I'd bumped into this amazing scene to boot.

Soon I had to leave, so I walked up town through the twilight past the closed-up city shops and caught a 23 bus home from the Kingsway. Auntie Nancy gave me a bit of a row for being late for supper, which was still in the oven; it was always a nicely cooked dinner of meat, vegetables and gravy. They asked me where I'd been, and I told them that I'd been for a walk and done some sketching. Few people had telephones in those days, so it was a good excuse. I didn't want them to know where I'd really been. I didn't want to worry them.

Bute Street and the docks became a magnet for me, although I didn't go down there all that often. I was only sixteen, very small and boyish looking. Sometimes when I went to a pub, they'd ask my age. I'd say eighteen and I was never refused a drink. I didn't drink much and I rarely spoke to anyone; I'd just buy a half pint and keep a low profile in a secluded corner. I was more interested in soaking in the atmosphere and the character. I always carried my sketch-book and I used to draw the people who frequented the bars and cafés in Caroline Street, where I'd go for beef curry, rice and chips at the Dorothy, a Greek chippy which is still open today. It was only four shillings for a huge meal!

Art College was another experience. Some of the students were quite eccentric, as were some of the teachers. This was partly expressed in the way they dressed; I'd never seen so many oddly dressed persons under one roof. Some of the students wore formal blazers with the college badge (an adaptation of a famous Leonardo da Vinci anatomical drawing) on the breast pocket, collar, tie and grey trousers – much as they would have dressed in school. Miss Baker, my group teacher, wore her hair in a tight bun, no make-up and a weirdly printed and obviously handmade smock, covered with large Egyptian prints that looked like the wall paintings in the tombs of the Pharaohs. With this she wore a heavy tweed skirt, thick brown herringbone-patterned stockings and brown brogue shoes. Many of the girls wore the latest fashion in coloured tights – black, red, yellow and blue – over which some would wear just a long baggy woollen sweater or a sack dress, which was really no more than a shapeless, sleeveless shift. Skintight jeans made of cotton, denim or corduroy in various bright colours were also in vogue. One of the teachers arrived every morning in a bright red Bentley convertible with black leather upholstery, and dressed like Sherlock Holmes in tweeds, complete with deerstalker hat and curly pipe. The head of fashion was Miss Madalena, an Italian lady who looked and dressed like the actress Gina Lollobrigida. Everyone turned when she passed by, and all the boys said "Wow!" as she flashed a huge bright red Roman smile. Sometimes she'd arrive with Sherlock Holmes, her lipstick a perfect match to his Bentley.

The principal, J. C. Tar, known to us as Jack, arrived every morning on an old Hercules bike, dressed in a beige, belted mackintosh that had seen better days, brown trousers, bicycle clips and a flat tweed cap. He had a Hitler moustache and at first I mistook him for the caretaker – which he was, academically!

There were quite a few students from the southern valleys of Glamorgan and a handful from west Wales, but mostly they seemed to be middle-class kids dressed in expensive clothes with posh accents. It was an interesting gathering and I immediately made friends with an older student named John Murray, who also lived in Whitchurch and played the guitar. He took me to a youth club at Whitchurch secondary school, where one of the staff, a Mr Bowen, gave a guitar class of sorts and where I could also use the sports facilities. John also went to Ararat Baptist Chapel on Sunday evenings, and I used go with him just for a good sing. It reminded me of home. A Welsh-speaking lad from Anglesey came with us too; I got the impression he was a bit homesick. At the time, I knew of only four other students who spoke Welsh.

The college routine was similar to school. I went in every morning on the bus to register at 9.30 a.m. Then we'd join our groups to do a bit of painting or drawing. We also had to choose a craft; I chose etching with John Roberts who later retired to a house on the Cross Square in St David's. John and I became good friends; sadly, he died in the summer of 2003. We also had to do a lot of life drawing. There were two life rooms, and several models who would pose nude in the middle of the room on a dais, mattress or divan. We would sit or stand around at our easels, drawing or painting them in various poses. The importance of life drawing was heavily emphasized and was an important part of the curriculum on which we would eventually be assessed. Some of the first-year students were embarrassed at first, but we soon got used to it and would sit in quite a large group of girls and boys chatting away whilst drawing a naked man or woman. One girl used to eat sandwiches! I was an intermediate student, which meant that I had to follow a two-year course before going on to specialize in painting, pottery, sculpture, lithography etching, calligraphy or dress design. The college building was old and dilapidated, but adequate, and it had character, which was important. We were encouraged to keep sketch-books and to draw in them wherever we went. The importance of sketching was underlined heavily and was part of our assessment. We would draw each other quite often. I don't know what happened to my sketch-books; I wish I still had them.

After a while, John Murray and I started to bring our guitars into college. On the ground floor there was a long corridor with the pottery studio at one end and the etching, lithography and sculpture studios at the other. In between lay a large life-drawing room and a couple of classrooms. The students' lockers stood double banked along this corridor, and between classes Murray and I would sit on them and play our guitars. No one seemed to mind; in fact, sometimes a decent crowd of students would gather below and listen to us.

There was also a scruffy common room, where we sometimes played at lunch-time while others were eating their sandwiches. Occasionally, Clive Williams, who taught me guitar in Solva, would come in and have a jam, even though he didn't like playing pop music much. Clive was into jazz – Charlie Christian, Eddie Lang, Eddie Condon, Kenny Burrell and Wes Montgomery. High-class stuff and way beyond our capabilities in those days!

Pete Colwill, a student from Mountain Ash, was another good singer and a bit of a pop star, and he would take me on Wednesday nights to Nixons Ballroom in Penrhiwceiber. Before the dance, we'd go to the Navigation Hotel to tune up. One of the guys who sang with the band used to lend me a white solid Tuxedo guitar – solid guitars were just coming into the music stores then – and I'd rave up on stage, leaping about the place and even playing while lying on my back. Then I'd beat it to catch the last bus back to Cardiff, just as the ritual fight broke out. Tommy had a great voice and as the fight raged he'd belt out 'The Sea of Love'. That singer was none other than Tom Jones!

# Chapter 6

# *Characters*

Ashcroft was a skinny girl with dead straight, shoulder length, pale blond hair, cut straight all around with a fringe. She still wore the summer uniform of Cardiff High School for girls. This embarrassment, so she told me, was imposed by her stepfather – a nondescript, tunnel-visioned cleric, who was obviously ignorant of both the nature of teenage girls and the fashion consciousness of art college eccentrics. This desk jockey had latterly married Ashcroft's mother, the widow of a sheep farmer from the Australian outback, where Ashcroft had been brought up. Ashcroft's uniform consisted of a red and white gingham summer dress, red cardigan and red tights. She was eighteen, but she looked more like a little girl of twelve. She was a scrawny, speedy and aggressive kid, highly (highly) intelligent and obviously artistic with huge chips on both shoulders, and she must have weighed in at around five stone. I felt sorry for her; she was obviously confused, bitter even, and talked a lot of shit. Her father had died young and her mother, who was Welsh by birth, had decided to sell up and come home. Ashcroft was a virgin, as were most of the girls I knew. The others didn't make a big deal of it, but Ashcroft did, making it clear that she wanted to change her condition at the earliest opportunity. This she soon achieved, though without my help let it be emphasized.

Ashcroft loved music and dancing, which she was very good at.

She wasn't exactly ugly but she suffered from bad acne, and her face and apparently most of the rest of her body was spotted with pus-filled sores. She looked dreadful, and I think that many of the art school boys were more than a little revolted by Ashcroft's complaint, let alone her loud and aggressive personality. To be blunt, Ashcroft was a plain ugly, obnoxious Jane, but that did not seem to inhibit or deter her. Life may have been a bit of an assault course for her, but she was SAS. A force five breeze could have blown her away, spots and all, but she was tough and highly sexed. Pretty soon she ditched the school uniform, appearing one day in the garb of a Beat chick – no underwear, an old sweater pinched from her stepfather and far too big for her, skintight jeans, long strings of beads hanging from her neck and some flat black soft leather shoes. This is how she launched herself. Her self-made, self-sanctioned, unsanctified, unhygienic, unmerciful rave that was a blissful hedonistic blitz! Those who stood in her path were engulfed and devoured as if by a swarm of locusts. Ashcroft was deadly.

Art students used to hang out at the Kardomah coffee house in Queen Street. We would lounge around on the first floor, where large windows afforded a panoramic view of the hustle and bustle of Queen Street down below. This is where we would waste most of our time, along with the multitude of hangers-on whom art students always seem to attract. There were loose schoolgirls looking for sexual adventures, petty thieves, quasi-intellectuals, young guys on the make as well as the hip, cool beatniks. We hung around for hours, yakking over cold coffees and Russian teas, trying to impress each other with our ignorance of fine art and literature and most other things. Some of the thieves and beatniks were on various forms of amphetamine sulphate, such as Drynamyl, which in those days was prescribed for slimming and which was mainly obtained by theft from their fat and unhappy mothers who were too high to notice. Then there was

Benzedrine, burgled from the poison cabinet of chemist shops, and Nostraline inhalers which would be cracked open, their contents soaked in orange juice or coke, then drunk. Speed is a very bad drug, as anyone who has been a speed freak will tell you if they are still around to do so! The favourite pills though were purple hearts – in reality a three-sided, light-blue amphetamine tablet. These too were prescribed for slimming and seemed to be everywhere. You could always tell the speed freaks, because they would talk the hind legs off a donkey, usually with a load of plausible-sounding, quasi-philosophical rubbish that seemed to make a lot of sense at the time but wouldn't be remembered let alone stand up when the speed wore off. They all seemed to carry *Howl,* a pamphlet of bullshit by Allen Ginsberg, the American 'beat' poet.

I used to buy the evening *South Wales Echo,* which is still the main newspaper for Cardiff people. It has an entertainment page and lists all the films that are showing in the cinemas – I've always been a big film fan. Now and again there'd be a gig advertised and I'd go there. These were usually amateur-run dances in various church halls, but they'd have all the latest rock records to dance to and sometimes a live group. Equipment was very crude in those days; amplifiers would be home-made jobs in plain wooden DIY boxes, low powered, only ten or fifteen watts, although they seemed loud enough to me at the time.

There was also a show on Saturday mornings at the Gaumont Theatre in Queen Street. It was called 'The Gaumont Teenage Show' and lots of young people went there, including me. The show consisted of local rock bands and skiffle groups: Tony Cheverton, The Alley Cats, The Solid Six and The Stompers are some I remember. Charlotte Church's grandfather played in The Solid Six. These were very early days for rock music anywhere. The first time that I heard The Stompers I was very impressed. They had a tenor sax in the band

and two brothers who sang and played cello guitars with pick-ups screwed to the base of the necks. One of them had an Epiphone Zenith, which was a very good American guitar. He was a small, blond-haired kid and he could play lead guitar. At the time, lead guitarists were very rare. He was Dave Edmunds, aged fourteen!

The Stompers played a lot of Buddy Holly and Everly Brothers songs. The bass guitar hadn't been invented yet, although, unbeknown to us, Leo Fender was on the case in California. So, at this time, bands would have a typical line-up of two or three guitars and drums, and sometimes piano. The Stompers used to rehearse in one of the dressing rooms behind the stage at the Gaumont, and on Sunday afternoons I'd go and play with them there. Like Shirley Bassey, the Edmunds brothers (Dave and Geoff) came from Splott, near the steelworks. They were fanatical about rock and roll music. Jeff got a baritone sax from somewhere and sometimes he would do instrumentals with the tenor player.

Life was very loose and laid back in Cardiff then. You would often see horse-drawn carts and pony traps driven down the streets, especially in Grangetown where the costermongers, fruit and vegetable vendors, would use them to sell from door to door. The rag and bone men too would have small horse-drawn carts to carry the junk they collected from street to street around Splott, Grangetown, Riverside, Canton and the docks.

During this period, I had become aware of a student called Trev. His full name was Trevor Ford, a name he shared with a famous Welsh football player of the day who played for Swansea City. Trev was one of the up-and-coming abstract painters at the college. He'd been a scholarship boy at a posh boarding school, Christ College, Brecon, but he came from a working-class family who lived in Caerleon. His mother was a piano teacher, and his father either a docker or a steelworker in Newport. Trev was a communist, and he used to cause a lot of arguments wherever he went, though mainly in pubs, and these debates sometimes degenerated into fights. He used to paint huge abstracts in primary colours, all palette-knife stuff. No one else painted like that at the college, which seemed to encourage students to paint industrial scenes and drab-coloured valley landscapes.

I soon found out that Trev was a big blues fan and a bit of an expert on the subject. He was also a blues singer in the style of Jimmy Rushing and Big Joe Williams. He called himself a blues shouter and he would sit in with some of the local jazz bands. In fact, it was Trev who introduced me to the jazz scene in Newport. He seemed to know all the local jazz musicians: Keith Jenkins, a brilliant trumpet and piano player; Brian Keen and Lyn Saunders, top tenor banjo players; Mike Harries, a trombonist, and Tom Rosser, his drummer; Howel Bines, a brilliant honky tonk barrel-house pianist who could play in the style of Jimmy Yancey; Johnny Silva, a double bass player, whose father owned a jazz and booze joint, the Ghana Club, on Bute Street; Pete Chapman, John Scantlebury and Victor Parker, as well as Victor Thornhill, a great older bass player who also built and raced motor bikes. There were some characters on that scene, no mistake about it.

There was a jazz club in the cellar of the Philharmonic, a big old pub near the central station at the bottom of St Mary's Street. Many very good jazzmen used to play there; it was there that I saw Acker Bilk, who was then known as 'that clarinet player from Bristol', and the late Cardiganshire jazz pianist Dill Jones played there too.

Mike Harries had a jazz club in a cellar in High Street on Wednesdays and Saturdays – the rest of the week it was the Mavis June School of Ballroom Dancing. Needless to say, the difference on jazz nights was remarkable. Moia O'Keefe, Mike's wife, was also an art student, and she used to take the money on the door at the foot of a narrow flight of stairs. Admission was half a crown. The Mavis June School of

Dancing was a long, narrow basement room with a low ceiling and a polished wooden floor. There was no furniture, save for a radiogram in a wooden cabinet that resembled a sideboard, and there were some alcoves in the walls with wooden benches. On jazz nights these were usually occupied by young couples snogging passionately in the shadows. Meanwhile, the six-piece New Orleans style band blasted out all the great traditional jazz standards: 'Tiger Rag', 'The Saints', 'Momma Don't Allow', 'St Louis Blues', 'Basin Street', 'St Phillip Street Breakdown', 'Creole Love Call'. The list goes on forever.

The Number Seven club used to heave with jiving people, bopping like dervishes, gallons of sweat pouring off them, their discarded clothing and shoes littering the floor. At eleven o'clock the band would pack up and everyone would slope off home. Sometimes there might be a party afterwards, usually on Saturday nights or at the beginning or the end of terms, and sometimes there'd be flat warming, leaving raves and even rent parties. Some of these *soirees* could get rather wild, especially if there was a live band. The sex maniacs would lock themselves in the bedrooms and sometimes the bathrooms, whilst other revellers danced or played musical instruments. The Beat poets, avant-garde quasi-intellectuals, and philosophers would usually take over the kitchen where the food and booze was normally stashed.

Trev took me to a party in St Mellons once. In those days, St Mellons was no more than a posh little village just outside Cardiff on the road to Newport. The parents of the girl who invited us owned a successful greyhound racing kennels and were well off. They had gone on holiday, which is what had instigated the party, and I think it was also her birthday. We went on a Saturday night, arriving in an old Riley with running-boards which was driven by a friend called James Angove, who was also a guitar player. The Harries band had been invited, and they arrived pissed after the jazz club.

The girl opened the door to welcome us. The house was full of greyhound racing trophies, silver and gold cups and plates, and sculptures of famous dogs. Trev put on a worried look, telling the girl that she'd have to put them all away because he'd heard that some local villains were on their way. So we all started stashing these trophies in bags, then locked them up in the wardrobes in her parents' bedroom before locking the door of the room itself.

There was a huge cauldron of punch, which people kept topping up with whatever they'd brought. You had to be very careful because medical or pharmaceutical students would often pour lab alcohol into the punch on the sly – with devastating and sometimes fatal consequences.

I hadn't seen Trev for a while – he was probably in one of the bedrooms with a chick. The band members were extremely well oiled by now and were playing one of their nasty games. They'd fill the bath tub with cold water and lurk around the bathroom door drinking. When a targeted person went in for a pee, they'd pile in behind and chuck the unsuspecting unfortunate into the bath, with much shouting, cheering and laughter. Someone who'd recently been ducked by these jazz hooligans told me that I was going to be the next human sacrifice. So I kept well away from the bathroom door and went looking for Trev. I'd had enough of the party by now, but I couldn't find Trev anywhere. I tried the kitchen door. It was locked, but I could hear the sound of people inside and so I started knocking. From the other end of the corridor came the racket of loud voices shouting "Where's Stevens?" and "Get the fucker!", prompting me to redouble my attack on the kitchen door. Then, I heard Trev's voice shouting "Fuck off". I screamed at him, "It's Mike! Let me in for Christ's sake!" With that, the door opened and Trev dragged me in by the arm before locking the door in the face of the jazz baptists. "Shut up and give us a hand here!" said Trev. I looked around to see the kitchen window open, Angove's car parked outside, Keith Jenkins calmly finishing off a fry-up of steak, bacon and egg and sausages, and Trev passing the contents of the deep freeze and the food cupboards through the window to Angove who calmly loaded them into the Riley. I was a bit taken aback; they were stealing all the goodies.

We all piled out through the kitchen window and into the Riley, which pulled out from the side of the house and into the drive. At that point, the brother of the lady of the house came rushing across the lawn waving a large torch, and shouting "Stop thieves! Burglars! Call the police!!" He leaped onto the running-board of the moving Riley, and Jimmy Angove, who was at the wheel, snatched the torch from his hand while Trev bashed him in the face with a frozen leg of pork. The car roared off, its occupants howling with laughter. "They're lucky we hid the silver," said Trev. "Billy the Dip and his mates would have had it for sure."

"They weren't Jews either," I said, eyeing the leg of pork still in Trev's hand.

"Jews don't breed greyhounds," says Trev.

"Shalom!" said Angove, while Keith Jenkins just grinned as he bit a chunk out of a huge piece of salami. The car looked and smelt like Wally's delicatessen. It was six in the morning and dawn was breaking behind us over the East Moors.

"Let's go to Geoff's," I said. "I'm hungry."

★ ★ ★

The time had come for me to move out of Uncle Rhys's comfortable home. Most of my friends already had flats or bedsits, and I needed my own space in which to live, paint and practise my music. I started making enquiries. As it happened, Colin Davies, one of the college guitarists, was moving into a flat in Cathedral Road. A sculptor called Dave already lived there, and there was room for one more.

The flat was at 118 Cathedral Road in a house named Preste Gaarden. The landlady lived on the ground floor, and it was made clear from the start that no girls were allowed. That was fine by me; I wasn't particularly interested and I'd never had sex anyway. Dave, who was older than me, had though – in fact he was something of a sex maniac and seemed to spend most of his time screwing chicks! Every time I came home he was in bed with some girl or other, and I was always having to make a tactful withdrawal. Colin hardly ever used the flat and stayed with his parents most of the time. Sometimes I'd come home late at night to find the door locked. I'd go around the back and up the metal stairs to the French windows. Occasionally, they too would be locked and I could hear Dave on the job inside with much heavy breathing, twanging of bedsprings, accompanied by ecstatic howls, squeals and grunts. It wasn't unusual for me to have to sleep in the garden shed.

I had to move. The landlady was aware of what was going on, but she didn't know who was responsible. She accused me a few times and lectured me about promiscuity. It was pointless pleading innocence; she was convinced that it was me who was doing all the screwing. Next stop was Mrs Lashmore's house. Mrs Lashmore was a widow who had been putting up students for years, and she had two beautiful dark-haired daughters, who worked away in London. When I moved in she also had two ex-student lodgers, one of whom was a librarian in the University of Wales and the other a metallurgist at the Guest Keene steelworks. This was great; I had my own small room on the first floor with a view over the park, and Mrs Lashmore cooked a wonderful fried breakfast, which together with an evening meal of meat and vegetables cost me £3 a week. Mrs Lashmore was related to the Mendus family, who ran the chemist's shop on the Cross Square in St David's. She'd even heard of my grandparents, which worked as a sort of reference.

I got by successfully enough at college, and the guitar playing was getting better and better. Trev had found a room in the centre of town in an old cinema called the Queens, and I was allowed to set up an easel there. The Queen's studio, as we called it, was used much more for parties than for the creation of works of art. Upstairs, two other students had a studio, but they were sculptors – and painters and sculptors don't mix. Sculpture studios looked more like building sites than studios, and we painters thought sculptors very low-brow. Fairly soon things degenerated into what could be best described as an orgy; the other students, who were two or three years older than me, and Trevor seemed to be trying to fuck their way through all the girls in Cardiff. It was impossible to go in there at any time of the day or night without finding at least one couple at it, on the floor or on a *chaise longue* that we'd purchased from a second-hand shop, ostensibly for models for our life painting and drawing sessions. There were bottle parties all the time, and everyone was welcome.

Opposite was the office of Leo Abse, the solicitor brother of Dannie Abse the celebrated poet. Leo Abse objected to our presence and was always complaining to Jack Tar, the College principal. Every now and then he'd call us into his office and give us a ticking off, ending with a warning that if we didn't cool our act he'd expel us. What a drag! At the same time, Trevor's behaviour towards the staff was getting worse still, to the point where he would openly take the piss out of them, even threatening them with violence. He was also trying to cop on to Miss Madalena. I don't know if he had any success, but it was a very uncool thing to do and it drew attention to us when we should have been keeping a low profile.

Trev and I were doing a lot of heavy drinking at this time. Where did the money come from? I'll tell you. Trev had his head screwed on and he was streetwise. He was also Irish, and there were a lot of Irish clubs and bars in Cardiff and Newport. We used to trawl these, entertaining the boozers with folk music, jazz and blues. Not only would we get free beer and scrumpy, they'd often put the hat round so we'd even have money left to go to the pub the following day.

The Old Arcade, a Brains pub in Church Street, Cardiff, was very popular with the jazz crowd and the art students. I still go there sometimes, although it's degenerated into a sports bar with televisions all over the place and rugby shirts in glass cases on the walls. The spit and sawdust bar at the front, which was one of the best in Wales, now serves meals. The Greyhound was another favoured watering hole, a scrumpy house in Bridge Street, long gone under the redevelopment. Scrumpy was ten pence a pint in those days and very strong. Newtown, the Irish quarter at the top of the docks, was a good place to go and we also used to tour the pubs of Newport and Swansea. It was great fun, but my academic studies were suffering.

We finally got the push from the Queen's studio, which had died anyway and was now just a crash pad and party venue. People would come there in droves, mostly total strangers, bringing loads of booze, musical instruments, stolen property and girls. Often a whole band would arrive with their hangers-on and crates and sometimes barrels of ale. Trev was really pissed off with Leo Abse across the corridor, and in that final party he decided to use Abse's letter-box as a urinal. Everyone thought it a huge joke, with the result that the letter-box became the public john for the rest of the night. When the post arrived in the morning, it landed in a pool of piss. Abse was not amused and went straight to College to rage at the principal. Naturally enough, Trev and I were called in and grilled, threatened and generally berated. We just claimed that we didn't have anything to do with the affair and were in Newport that night, which we could prove. The principal then told us in no uncertain terms that we were lucky not to have been sued for damages and expelled. We restated our innocence, which they could not disprove. The studio, though, was declared out of bounds and we left under threat of expulsion if we got involved in any more activities that might cause complaint. It had been a close shave, and so we just went down to the Old Arcade and got drunk again!

It was a bank holiday, Easter I think, and for some reason I had stayed in Cardiff, instead of going home to the peace and comparative safety of Solva. I was still lodging at Mrs Lashmore's boarding house, and her beautiful daughters were home on holiday. I had breakfast and went out for the day. When I got home at around seven o'clock, the house was strangely quiet. The Bedlington terrier, which was normally aggressive, was behaving very strangely – quiet, whimpering and running up and down the stairs. I shouted around the house, and when there was no answer I went upstairs. Immediately, I noticed that Mrs Lashmore's bedroom door stood ajar. The doors of all the rooms were usually kept shut and the lodgers' rooms had locks on the doors. I pushed her bedroom door open and looked timorously around the room. And there lay Mrs Lashmore, flat on her back across the bed, fully clothed, with her mouth wide open. She was stone dead. I was told later that she'd had a massive heart attack and had died instantaneously. I didn't touch her and fled into my room, locking the door behind me. I dived under the bedclothes; I felt cold and an increasingly sad and lonely feeling crept over me, then I began to shiver.

After some time, I became aware of the front door opening and of the sound of laughter as the other lodgers and the beautiful daughters came in. I jumped out of bed and ran downstairs. It was hard to summon up the words. I just didn't know what to say, so I led them upstairs and pointed silently at their mother's bedroom door. When they came out they were strangely quiet, but they told me to go back to bed and not to worry. They would take over now. I felt great relief, but I was still worried that I would be implicated somehow. After all, I'd been alone in the house with a dead landlady for more than four hours.

Later, one of the beautiful daughters told me that I'd have to look for other lodgings as they were going to sell the house. I've never had much luck with landladies, and I certainly didn't have much luck with Mrs Lashmore. One day I was telling this tale in college, and a student called Geoff Stevens said I could lodge with his family. They lived in an old farmhouse in Rhiwbina, a once rural area which had been overrun by the city and was now full of newer houses. Thus began my final phase in Cardiff Art School. I had a lot more freedom in my new lodgings and I no longer felt that I was being monitored and watched all the time. Pretty soon I would become financially independent to a larger extent as well.

# Chapter 7

# Jazz

Cardiff has a well-established jazz tradition going back to the 1914–18 war, when United States marines were billeted in the Angel Hotel in Westgate Street, opposite Cardiff Athletic rugby ground. The Angel has a big arched porch, constructed of masonry, which extends over the pavement and the steps of the main entrance. The roof of this porch can be reached through French windows on the first floor, and it's possible that this was the first place in Europe where New Orleans jazz music was played. Some evenings, bandsmen from the Marines would sit up on the roof of the porch and play jazz and other music to crowds of people down below in Westgate Street.

Later, between the wars, jazz was often played by coloured musicians from Tiger Bay, such as the legendary Victor Parker, who played with Django Reinhardt and the Edmundo Ross Orchestra. I knew Vic Parker and learnt a lot of music and guitar techniques from him, as did a lot of aspiring musos over the years. Vic was a sociable and public man, who could be seen in the streets and bars of the docks and the city centre. When I knew him, he lived in a flat in Loudon Square and worked as a locomotive driver in the East Moors steelworks. He was known to real Cardiff people as Narker, and he was an extremely funny man, full of stories anecdotes and jokes. There are too many Vic Parker stories to tell here.

I remember once going to a pub where Vic played his old Hofner

Committee cello electric guitar every night to a sizeable crowd. It was a very ornate instrument, with intricate mother-of-pearl inlays all over the ebony finger-board, an exotic bird's-eye maple back and sides, and a carved head in the shape of a maple leaf. Many musicians including yours truly would go to the Quebec to hear him talk and play, or to jam with him. One night a young kid came in with a brand new Gibson Les Paul, which he took out of its case and handed to Victor for evaluation. Gibson have always made some of the finest guitars known to man, and Victor drooled over it before handing it back.

"Can I play a tune with you?" asked the kid eagerly.

"Yes," said Victor. The kid struck up a tune, and Victor joined in. Unfortunately, even with one of the best guitars that money can buy, this kid was one of the worst guitarists anyone in the room had ever heard. Yet, this did not deter Victor, who backed up as best he could until the song ended. There was a mixed response from the audience and one wag called out "How did you manage to follow that, Vic?" Victor who had a pronounced stutter replied: "Yyyou'd need a bbbloodhound tttoo ffuckin' ffollow tthaat!"

Victor always had a laugh up his sleeve.

Ray Norman was another great guitarist who played in the same sort of jazz-orientated style as Victor. I could hear a lot of Django Reinhardt in their music, and Charlie Christian too. Nevertheless, they also had a style of their own, one which had evolved out of playing all kinds of music to entertain the clientele of the many bars and clubs in the docks and the bay. Vic Parker could play anything from 'Freight Train', which he would finger pick, to 'Stardust' and 'Georgia on my Mind' or any of the Billie Holiday or George Gershwin tunes. It was a treat to hear Parker and Norman playing together.

There were other guitarists too who played the same repertoire.

Gerald Ashton, for example, was another good guitarist who 'knew all the chords', as they'd say. There was also a white guitarist, not from the Bay but from uptown somewhere, called Billy Rowlands. I heard him many times and he taught my late friend Royston Jones, who died very young in a car crash. There were also the Denise brothers who soon took off to London and Paris, Tony Chikaderas and Maurice Ali, jazz accordion players, and Bill Chapman (Dave Edmunds's uncle) who was a jazz mandolinist.

I'd always gravitate towards a bar or club, usually in the docks or the Bay, where these people would be having a jam session. All their talk would be of music, and so for me and my ilk it was inevitably an edifying experience. It was also an education to rub shoulders with the clientele of these joints: sailors, hard men, hoodlums, criminals, hookers and hustlers. We're back to the *News of the World* and its "All of human life is here". You had to be streetwise in those places. There were some who would think nothing of mugging or beating people up, and others would go as far as stabbing, shooting or even chopping their victim up with an axe or a broken bottle. It was rough and tough, but if you were on the ball and knew the rules (of which there weren't many) you'd be alright. I've played around these kinds of joints for years, although nowadays there aren't many left because of the mass entertainment of juke boxes, telesport and karaoke. And, of course, so many of the good musicians have moved on or died. Nevertheless, there are still a lot of musicians who have carried on the jazz tradition in Cardiff and round south Wales: Geoff Palser, the trombone player; Eddie Williams who plays trumpet and tenor banjo; and members of the old Mike Harries trad band; and Wyn Lodwick and his compadres, who are based around Swansea and Llanelli and have connections with surviving members of the Ellington and Basie Bands in New York. Austin Davies and Ted Boyce, very good pianists, and the late Bernard Harding and Dave Gill spring to mind too, as do bands like the Arcadians, the Midnight Special and the Adamant Marching Band, who all play in the New Orleans style. Then there is Andy Maule, a brilliant young guitarist and composer, and Billy Thompson, a great young violinist who plays now with Barbara Thompson and Jon Hiseman; Mario Conway, who was the world champion accordion player; and Pino Palladino, a brilliant bass guitarist, and the bassist Paula Gardiner. They and many more ensure that the ship of jazz will never sink in Cardiff Bay.

★ ★ ★

In 1958, Trev Ford decided to form a blues band, having recently heard Royston Jones – a jazz guitarist who'd been taught by Billy Rowlands, as I've already mentioned. The bones of the band were Royston on lead and me on rhythm guitars. Royston had a Hofner President electric guitar, and by this time I had found a big cello Hoyer onto which I fixed an electric pick-up. Roy had his own amp, and I borrowed a small one from a friend called Pete Mower who was a big jazz fan. We had a couple of bassists and drummers but, mostly, we played as a trio with Trev doing the 'shouting', usually in pubs or jazz clubs in Cardiff and Newport as interval bands and occasionally in college hops.

Around this time we discovered a quiet little pub in Union Street, one of the many narrow side streets off Queen Street. It was called the Moulders Arms and it would become the most popular music pub in Cardiff. The first time we went there, it was being kept by the Gomez sisters from Little Spanish Town around George Street in the docks. Later, Arthur Jenkins and his wife Ada, two well-known Cardiff publicans, took over. There were two rooms in the front, a public bar and a small side room, and down a side corridor was a large back room in which stood an upright piano. The Moulders was to become home from home for the artists, beats, musicians and bums. There would always be a group of bohemians in the Moulders at any time of the day or night; the party went on without respite for years. It was also a haunt of the criminal fraternity, and there was always something going cheap, be it knocked-off goods, contraband or drugs. A lot of coloured and black guys frequented the Moulders – it was something of a league of nations – and the Campaign for Nuclear Disarmament and other more radical left-wing groups held meetings there. There was always an omnipresent clique of scruffy, bearded or unshaven, beatnik, existentialist, druggy quasi-philosophers, shrouded in donkey jackets or duffle coats and huddled in a corner talking to themselves, usually totally out of their heads on speed, weed and booze.

The public bar was loud with the conversation, gossip and jokes of the locals, the residents of the small Georgian terraced houses of Union Street and the surrounding area between Queen Street and Bridge Street. In those days people actually lived as communities in the centre of Cardiff, and the place was alive. Nowadays the city centre is dead after the evening pub crawlers, and night clubbers go home. Arthur Jenkins and his wife Ada were large, well-fed people, friendly, open and sympathetic to their customers, real publicans, in contrast to the managerial types who seem to have taken over the licensed victuallers' trade nowadays. The Moulders was a rough-and-ready but interesting hostelry. For me, the Moulders meant music and there was plenty of it; there were four or five guitars and banjos permanently lodged behind the bar, and if the small side room was overcrowded people would move to the back room where the piano was and start another session there. The pub rocked to the sounds of blues, jazz and all sorts of folk music, not to mention West Indian calypso and Bluebeat. Usually, the quieter guitars played the small side room while the trad jazzers' horns farted jazz in the back. It was loud, wild, interesting and risqué.

A lot of drugs were bought and sold in the Moulders – mainly amphetamines, although some of the West Indians smoked marijuana, 'bush' or 'ganja' as they called it. They would sell tiny parcels of bush, wrapped in brown paper and called 'pound deals'. This marijuana was brown in colour with lots of seeds and twigs. It had a pungent smell and was exceedingly strong. Unfortunately, the dope-dealing attracted the unwelcome attention of the police, who rather spoilt things with their 'surprise' attacks, which involved hauling people off to the slammer at the central police station in the civic centre. Usually, the people who were 'hauled off' were coloured; there was still much overt racial prejudice in Cardiff in those days, and marijuana was always associated with black or coloured people. The powers that be might have thought that only black people smoked it, but they were wrong.

Some spoilsports and party poopers used to sell phoney weed; I've seen sage and onion stuffing mix, dried mixed herbs, even dried parsley, sold as marijuana. Deals were done in such a secretive way that it was easy to slip a phoney parcel to over-eager and inexperienced potential pot-smokers. By the time they'd rolled it up, the culprit had vanished; some of the docks' boys must have made a small fortune doing this. Some people I knew used to cut real marijuana with mixed herbs or even dried leaves, thus doubling or trebling the size of the bag. And their profits! This was harder to detect, because it still smelled right when smoked even though it was considerably weaker. Some bush, though, such as Congo Matadi, Durban Poison or any bush from equatorial regions, was too strong to smoke in any quantity. You could put less in a joint, take just one or two puffs, and that would be enough. Nevertheless, I knew some people who smoked like Nigerian witch doctors; the body just builds up a tolerance. It is commonly said that marijuana is non-addictive, but I disagree; I know many people who can't do without their little smoke of bush. However, I don't believe that marijuana is a big threat to 'civilized' society. Smoking weed tends to be done indoors, amongst friends, and the effects are calming. Some people just go to sleep.

There was very little hashish around in the late 1950s, and not all that many people smoked weed either. It tended to be confined to coloured or black people in whose ethnic societies it was customary, and to some jazz musicians, beatniks and art students. It was far from being a social problem and didn't warrant the hysterical attention which it seemed to attract from the authorities and the police. I had no problems at that time; I didn't smoke it and I wasn't involved in that scene. I was still a virgin who got his kicks out of playing the guitar. But that was soon to change.

One night, I was in the Moulders playing the guitar with a couple of other musicians, when in walked Mike Harries, the leader of the Number Seven Club band, along with two other members of the band. They bought a round and sat down opposite, listening to the music and watching. I knew the banjo player of the band well – a Jew called Lyn Saunders, who sometimes came to the Moulders. After a while, Harries came over and asked me if I could play the banjo.

"Yes," I said. "I've had an old banjo at home in Solva since I was a small boy. My late uncle Walter brought it home from his sea travels, from New Orleans, probably."

"Oh! Have you got it with you?" asked Harries.

"No. It's at home and it needs doing up." This banjo had been stringless and bridgeless and with its tuning pegs missing ever since I'd found it under a pile of junk in the attic of Harbour House. But it was a real banjo nevertheless. Harries told me that Saunders was leaving to go to London to join a professional band. They needed a new banjoist, and Saunders had recommended me.

"Could you come to the Students' Union in the University next Saturday night? We're playing the Medics hop. Come for an audition."

When I told Trev about this, he wasn't too pleased and suggested that I didn't want to get involved with these jazz people – they were a lot of phoney bread heads and snobs. I pointed out that there would be two regular paying gigs, on Wednesdays and Saturdays, plus other gigs as well. I'd be earning £4 10s. a week that I didn't already have, and I could do with the experience of playing with a semi-professional band. I detected an element of sour grapes; although Trev had sold Harries a huge abstract painting for his new house at Wenvoe (Harries had recently graduated in architecture), he'd been banned from the jazz club for unruly behaviour. The Newport boys were forever picking fights – they loved a good scrap, especially Jack and Noel Crofton.

On the Saturday night we went to the gig in the students' union, and I sat in with the band for two or three numbers which I knew well. I played Lyn Saunders's banjo, a beautiful Maybelle made in the 1920s in America, and at the end of the gig Harries told me I'd got the job if I could afford to buy a banjo. There was a second-hand shop called Grimwades in Canton, a dilapidated suburb just a short walk west of the city centre, and I'd often seen musical instruments, including old banjos, in the window there. I told Harries that I could get a banjo by the following Wednesday and that I'd meet him in the jazz club. Fortunately, there was a bloke who'd been pestering me to sell him my Hoyer guitar – my only asset. I found him as usual in the Kardomah coffee bar and struck a bargain for a tenner. Later on in Grimwades of Canton I was shown a selection of old G banjos. What I really needed to play in a New Orleans jazz band was a tenor banjo, but even though I scoured the second-hand shops of the city I couldn't find one. Eventually, I went back to Grimwades and bought an old English Windsor G banjo, made in Birmingham, and costing £7 10s. The banjo's skin was slightly ripped, which meant that it wouldn't be as loud as it should be nor would it ring as all good banjos do. So I bought a new set of strings and a skin from Henderson's, a music shop in the Wyndham Arcade, before heading for the Moulders with change in my pocket.

When I arrived the place was empty; it was only 11.30 and I should have been in college. I asked Arthur for the loan of a washing-up bowl to soak the calfskin banjo head. He obliged willingly. "Anything for the music boys," he said smiling. Off I went to the back room to strip the hoop from the banjo. First I undid the bracket screws with a small spanner and then I removed the torn skin. The new calfskin was soaking nicely in the bowl of water, and I went back to the small side room to finish my beer. A couple of people came in and seemed pleased when I told them that I'd probably got a job with the Harries band. The skin was left to soak for a couple of hours, and then, still wet, I put it in its place, loosely tightening the brackets around the brass hoop which encircles the head of a banjo and holds the calfskin head in place.

When I returned the following day, Tuesday lunch-time, the skin was dry enough to tighten up. I put on the new strings and tuned up. The banjo sounded good, as it should have done; it was an old Windsor, probably made around 1930. Nowadays, a banjo like that would cost a couple of thousand. That night I played with the other session musicians at the Moulders. Everybody thought it was great, but I missed my old guitar; guitars are far more versatile than banjos and I wasn't all that wild about the sound either.

I showed up at the appointed hour in the Number Seven Club. Harries and the band were already there. There was no need for introductions; I knew all of them to talk to as we'd often drunk together in the Old Arcade. I showed Harries the banjo, and he was a bit disappointed that I hadn't got a tenor banjo. I told him the story, and he said that even though he liked the sound I should carry on the search for a tenor because it looked more authentic in a trad jazz line-up – which was fair enough I suppose. The gig went well and I had loads of congratulations and pats on the back from the club members. I was the youngest member of the band by far, only seventeen and looking fifteen. Harries said I'd have to wear the band uniform, namely a black waistcoat and trousers, bow tie and a bowler hat! I must have looked a real sight; I usually wore a scruffy black leather jacket, tight jeans and a t-shirt or woollen jumper. But this was my first taste of showbiz, and I had to play along with the charade.

After the gig, the band all went to the Dorothy restaurant in Caroline Street for a curry. This was part of the Wednesday and Saturday night routine. We would meet at the Old Arcade around seven o'clock, have a few pints of Brains SA, talk about jazz music (what else), do the gig, get paid, then the whole band and anyone else around would walk down St Mary's Street to the Dorothy for a huge curry, which cost four shillings. For me, this was certainly living it up. The only problem was that the buses stopped running quite early in those days and I had to walk three or four miles back to Rhiwbina. I'd just have to find digs closer to the town and so back I went to the accommodation pages in the *South Wales Echo*. Bingo, I found a room in Tewkesbury Street, Cathays for three quid a week, with breakfast and an evening meal thrown in.

The landlord was a crane driver at the East Moors steelworks, and the house was next door to the home of one of Trev's mates, Dennis Cummins, who was also an art student. His mother was a large jolly woman who would load us with huge chunks of delicious fruit cake, at every opportunity. Sometimes she'd even hand it over the garden wall to my landlady, much like the Red Cross ladies feeding starving refugees.

Life went on as usual; an endless parade of half imperial sheets of paper, paints, charcoal, life classes, pencils and zinc etching plates. Playing with the band was good too; the traditional jazz band boom had become the next big thing and we got a lot more bookings. I even had groupies who followed the band from gig to gig and came religiously to the Number Seven Club to bop their nights away. I went out with quite a few girls from the jazz club; I was by far the youngest in the band and all the other musicians were married, so I was more eligible.

The jazzmen smoked pipes and wore corduroy jackets and tweedy trousers with suede shoes, so I stuck out like a sore thumb in my beatnik rags. During my time with the Mike Harries band I got to meet quite a few famous jazzers. We were by far the best known and arguably the best-sounding band in south Wales, and when famous American or English bands came to play in Cardiff we were always the support band. We supported most of the big British bands – Humphrey Lyttleton, Chris Barber, Acker Bilk, Terry Lightfoot etc. – as well as real New Orleans bands like George Lewis (Harries's hero), and Sister Rosetta Tharpe, who autographed my banjo skin and told me that if I didn't stop drinking my liver would explode by the time I was twenty-one! Luckily it didn't, and it was a wonderful experience; I learned a lot of new music and chords, of which there are many if you want to play jazz music.

The Art College used to encourage us to visit as many art galleries as possible, and we were made aware of where the 'big' paintings hung. I enjoyed going to the Tate and National galleries, the Louvre and to galleries in Madrid and Barcelona. I would hitch-hike everywhere; it was so easy in those days. Any of the big old British Leyland road service trucks would pick you up, especially if you wore a college scarf or a military uniform. The trucks usually travelled by night, and so we'd go down to the truck parks and talk to the drivers who would tell us which trucks were going to where we wanted to travel. Often, the drivers were pleased to have somebody to talk to, although those old lorries were incredibly loud with the engine mounted through the cab. By the time you arrived in London you'd be hoarse. We usually took some speed to keep us awake.

There were a hell of a lot of kids on the road at that time. Most of them just hitched for kicks, lusting for travel. They were mostly beatnik and bohemian types who used to go to meet other beats in the jazz clubs around Britain. St Ives was also a magnet for art students and Beats, and a lot of people I knew would go to Devon and Cornwall to work in hotels during the summer. I, of course, would repair to sunny Solva and work on farms, spud picking or on the corn harvest. I also did a lot of fishing and spent much time down at the quay or on the beach. But travelling was most definitely in the air and much in vogue with the young bohemians. Other foreign and far-flung places were calling: Spain, Majorca, Ibiza, Formentera, Greece, Italy and New Orleans.

Trev had been called up for national service, which had been deferred until he'd finished his studies. He was in his final year at Malthouse's painting studio, and he was not getting on with the tutors at all. In fact, he was expelled half way through his final term on a trumped-up charge of stealing a palette knife from the Lithography room. As I've said, Trev painted huge abstracts, and the big broad-bladed palette knifes used in the Litho room for mixing colours would have been ideal for him to spread thick gooey swathes of primary colour on canvas.

The truth was that Trev was an unruly influence, a shit stirrer to put it bluntly, and he'd always come up with some kind of left wing socialist excuse for his antisocial behaviour. Yet, he definitely influenced quite a few students, mainly those from industrial mining backgrounds who were riddled with lefty propaganda anyway. I doubted the relevance of Trev's postulations; I'd been involved in local politics at home in the Solva branch of the Labour League of Youth and I knew roughly how party politics worked on a lower level.

Trev was trouble for the college and, inevitably, the powers that be decided they'd had enough of him. Everyone thought that it was a very cruel move on the part of the principal J. C. Tarr. Without college facilities, Trev would find it very difficult to complete his course; the size of his canvasses meant that studio space was imperative. There was no way that he could paint at home. But, as usual, Trev had another trick up his sleeve; he went over to Newport to the art college and spoke to one of the tutors, Tom Rathmell, who was very much on the side of the students. Rathmell used to drink with us sometimes in the Tredegar Arms and the Murrenger in Newport, and it was he who saved Trev's bacon by giving him space in one of the painting studios in Newport. Still Trev couldn't settle and do things like everybody else, and he found a studio in an old building near the Windsor Castle pub. The building had once been an industrial space, a foundry perhaps, so he moved in with another friend of ours, Ozzy Osmond, who was also in his final year of painting. This studio was to be almost a repeat performance of the Queen's studio in Cardiff.

With Trev in Newport it meant that I too spent a lot of time there, mainly in the Tredegar Arms by the station – the hotel where my mother had married James Erskine some twenty years earlier – and the New Found Out, the worst cider house in the world. This pub also stood near the railway station in Newport, and it had a long narrow room in which stood big old cider barrels. There was no furniture, and if you wanted to sit you'd have to do so on beer crates or planks of wood that were held up by beer crates. The clientele were mainly alcoholic dossers and some senile oldies from the local poor house. Trev, who liked talking to old people, thought it was an interesting place. I thought it was one of the lowest dives I'd ever experienced, but the cider was 10$d$. a pint and strong. We used to play there sometimes, and the old drunks loved it, often dancing, which was hilarious. Those poor old geriatric drunks in their long ragged overcoats and worn-out shoes with no laces were funnier than

Charlie Chaplin could ever be.

The landlord didn't care what went on; there was nothing to wreck and there were no windows to be broken. A padded cell with a bar – that was the New Found Out. It closed years ago, but the premises are still standing and when I was there last it had been turned into a snooty little wine bar. I'll have to wear my 'Leave low dives alone' t-shirt more often! 'Low down divas too!'

Trev and Ozzy were usually in their studio in Newport painting furiously and trying to make up for time wasted getting drunk around south Wales, in the jazz clubs or in bed with some of those lovely young girls who'd been so liberal with their charms. Once again Trev was having problems with his landlord, a Newport heavy from the working class, who was constantly demanding his rent of £2 10s. a week. This had usually been spent on beer and cider. Indeed, no one ever seemed to have money, but especially Trevor who was wont to finance his enjoyment from my jazz band pay.

The blues group wasn't very busy and, for the most part, had regressed to pub sessions only. However, one night Trev had secured a gig at the Newport arts ball, where we were to be the second band supporting Keith Jenkins's Castle City Jazzmen. I turned up with my banjo for the gig – I hadn't been able to purchase another guitar – and found Trev drunk as usual. "Where are the boys?" I said, meaning the rest of the band.

"There's only you and me," says Trev, "We'll split the money – fifteen quid – fifty fifty." And that's how we played that night, with Trev 'shouting' and me trying to sound like a band on a solitary banjo. Everyone was dancing furiously, and no one seemed to notice the stripped-down nature of this band without drums, bass or electric guitar. We were paid though and made off to the studio loaded with flagons and girls. I think that Ozzy Osmond even played the mouth organ that night. It didn't make much difference to the sound, but it looked better. Three piss-artists are more of a crowd than two, I guess.

There was an old piano in the studio, and Trev had often tried to hawk it. Prospective buyers would call to see it, but the general opinion was that it was knackered. One evening, Trev crashed into the Tredegar Arms ('the TA' as we called it) in a bit of a panic. "The bastard's stolen my paintings!" he screamed. When we'd calmed him down it transpired that the landlord had been to the studio looking for his back rent. Unsuccessful in his quest, he'd taken some of Trev's paintings hostage and he'd also tried to remove the piano, which we found at the bottom of the top flight of stairs. This prompted yet another of Trev's 'brilliant ideas'. And so, with Trev acting as foreman and shouting "Mind the fucking veneer", we lugged the poor piano back up to the studio, where Trev produced a hammer and some six-inch nails with which he attached the piano to the floor, thus blocking the door to the stairs. "Don't worry, I've found a secret way out," he shouted, and we left through a window in an adjacent room and then down the fire escape. It slowly dawned on me that Trev had never intended to pay the rent. There must have been fifty quid owing to the landlord; no wonder he was annoyed.

Then, one day, we were passing the front door of the building and there stood the piano, obviously waiting for someone to collect it. "The bastard," said Trev. "Go around the Windsor Castle and fetch some of the boys to give us a hand." And so it was that we lugged, pulled and pushed the piano up the four flights of stairs to the studio, which by now was just an empty shell. The couch had gone, and even an old mattress and a few unfinished and rejected canvases had disappeared. With that Trev vanished, to return with a hammer, some more six-inch nails and five Irish labourers carrying buckets of concrete. Once again, the door was barricaded and the piano nailed to the floor, and this time concrete was ceremoniously poured into it. A good job well done, we went back down the pub.

Finally, Trev was served with a writ to vacate the premises, on pain of being taken to court and sued, and so at long last they had to move out. We were in the New Found Out one day when Trev came in. "Come on, Cuntucks," – one of the titles he'd bestowed on me – "We're getting rid of the piano." I loved pianos, probably because I'd been brought up with one, and I have to say that the way Trevor treated this poor old Joanna was cruel. Outside the pub stood one of those big wooden handcarts which street traders used to push – the kind with large wooden cart-wheels. What next but to the studio with crowbar and pincers, where we removed the six-inch nails and heaved the concrete-filled piano out onto the street where it was loaded onto the cart by the lads from the Rothsay Castle. "Drinks allround for everybody who lends a hand," quoth Trev. Followed by a crowd of onlookers, we pushed the piano through the streets of Newport as far as the bridge over the Usk near the castle. There, with much difficulty and an even greater "Heave!", the poor piano was tipped over the balustrade into the river, hitting the water with a resounding splash. There were mighty cheers, and true to his word, Trevor led us to the New Found Out, where he called a round for everyone. I paid. "God bless jazz" I thought. We were star performers in innumerable scrapes, too numerous to mention here.

Trev was always dragging me to posh parties, before taking over the kitchen in the early hours of the morning and cooking huge meals at the expense of the unsuspecting parents of the girls who were throwing the party. Gallons of vintage port, Cognac, Claret and Burgundy must have been misappropriated. The only wine that was sold in our customary watering holes was V.P. wine – not really wine at all, but a sherry-like concoction, heavily fortified with ethylalcohol that was mainly drunk by dossers or alcoholic housewives. It's full name was B.V.P. – British Vine Products – though I doubt very much if any of the ingredients had ever hung from a vine.

Trev wanted to go to Solva before he was gobbled up by the army, and so we settled on a particular weekend. We'd been invited to a student rent party in Partridge Rd and we thought that we'd hitch down west straight after the party when dawn broke. The party was a typical bring-your-own-bottle-job, and it finished up with everyone pairing off. The booze must have run out early, because we all ended up snogging on the floor of the house; there were people everywhere, a sea of snoggers on the floors of every room, even on the stairs. As the darkness at the windows turned to that lovely light ultramarine that announces dawn, I went looking for Trev and found him in a bedroom with one of the jazz club girls whom I knew was a pupil at Cardiff High School for Girls.

Eventually, we got out on the road to Culverhouse Cross. By now it had begun to rain and we weren't having much luck getting lifts. In fact, it took us five hours to get to Swansea, by which time we were soaked to the skin and extremely fed up. However, we soon found a pub called The Adam and Eve and went into the back room where there was a radiator. We ordered a few drinks and when the landlord spotted my banjo he asked if I'd play a tune. "I'll play if we can dry our clothes on your radiators," I offered. Soon our clothes were off and we were sitting in a corner singing our heads off, draped in towels the landlady had found for us. In the end we stayed there all night and got pretty drunk, mostly on the house.

"We'll have to go to the police station now," stated Trev.

"What for?" I asked.

"For a kip and breakfast," Trev replied. And so before long we were tucked up in a cell at Swansea central police station, which was almost next door to the Art College in those days. We had a mug of tea and beans on toast for breakfast and headed towards West Cross at about six o'clock in the morning. This time we were luckier – perhaps people are more sympathetic on a Sunday – and we arrived in Solva late afternoon.

Trev met Mam and my mother Bet, and we had a few drinks in the Bay and the Ship and played a bit of music. Trev even did some sketches of the harbour. They were all glad to see us; Trev could be a charming bastard.

On the way back we called into Swansea again and decided to go to an art students' pub in the high street called the King's Arms. We were in sight of the pub when Trev pulled me to into a doorway. "Look!" he said. "Those chicks from that party." And sure enough there was the Cardiff High School girl and her friend diving into the King's Arms. Trevor legged it in the opposite direction, and later we arrived in Cardiff and went our separate ways.

When I arrived at college the next day, I was called to the principal's office and told that the police had been looking for me and that I had to report to Clifton Street police station. I couldn't think what this was about – I couldn't remember breaking the law. Maybe I had without knowing it, or it was something else I just didn't know about. What was it?

The police were very tough with me and I couldn't understand why. They wanted to know where I'd been on the weekend, and whom I'd been with. It was obviously something serious; but I had to be innocent since I didn't know what it was. "I'll box clever here," I thought. I told them I'd been in Solva and I didn't mention Trevor. Later it transpired that two underage girls who'd been in the same party as us on the Friday night had run away from home. These were the very two whom we'd avoided in Swansea, and I knew that Trev had spent the night with one of them. At last the police let me go, with a lecture about the penalties for sleeping with girls under sixteen. It turned out that one of the girls had dropped me in it by telling the cops she'd been with me! This wasn't the first time; because I was in the band, some girls would tell their parents – some of whom knew me – that they were going to the jazz club with me. I can only suppose that because I was in the band parents thought it was safe for their daughters to stay out late. One of these girls had done this before, and it was she who had dropped me in the shit. I remember her father, a steelworker from Splott, coming down to the club looking for me and his daughter. I'd never had anything to do with his fucking daughter who was a trainee beatnik and a bit of a wayward lass. *Ta waeth!*

★  ★  ★

I fell in love with a Danish *au pair* girl from Odense. Lise worked for a Jewish family who lived in a big house in Cyncoed. It was a severe case of puppy love and I used to meet her in the British Council in Caroline Street and take her out for drinks and things. Finally, I ended up sleeping with her in her employers' house, where I used to climb up an extension and through her bedroom window. She was a tremendous girl – a huge blonde, but with a perfectly proportioned figure.

When she finished her contract, I decided to go to Denmark. We must have written dozens of letters planning everything, and Lise would include lovely little pencil and pen and ink drawings. I needed money, however, and so I managed to convince my grandmother in Shrewsbury – the source of the original Catania guitar – to finance the trip.

I'd never had so much money in my life, £200, and I hit the road for Harwich via London. I thought that I'd have a weekend around the jazz clubs and Soho before heading on to Denmark. Accommodation was no problem; everyone dossed down in Ken Colyer's Studio 51 in Soho. As it happened, I ended up playing banjo with Colyer in the Saturday night all-nighter; Johnny Bastaple, Colyer's banjo player, used to get so drunk he'd pass out in his chair on stage in the middle of a number. He would always have a bottle of whisky under the chair where it wouldn't be kicked over. I made my way to the front of the club where the band was playing and, when Colyer saw me, he simply shoved the sleeping Bastaple off his chair, grabbed his banjo and swung it one-handed towards me. I caught it, leaped into Bastaple's chair and started playing along with the band. Colyer hadn't lost a note during this little aside, and poor old Bastaple lay oblivious to it all, curled up and snoozing by the side of the stage. After the gig we'd go down to the tea stall on the embankment and watch the mist rising from the Thames as dawn broke.

I had a whale of a time in London that week and visited quite a few jazz and rock venues. I saw Tony Sheridan and Joe Brown at the 2i's in Old Compton Street, and Dave Goldberg – a great jazz guitarist. Sheridan was playing the first Fender Jazzmaster I'd ever seen, Goldberg had a Gibson L5 Charlie Christian model, and Joe Brown a Gibson ES 335. You never saw guitars like those in Cardiff. I did all the galleries too and met a few characters (as you will if you go to the right places). London was pretty harmless in those days, unlike now when you've really got to watch yourself, particularly at night.

I didn't make it to Denmark and, although the letters kept coming, I never saw Lise Hansen again.

My money was running out; I'd spent too much on Bloody Marys. In fact, I lived on a diet of Bloody Marys and spaghetti bolognese – tomato rich with lots of Tabasco chilli sauce. I was fortunate to hitch some good rides back to Solva via Cardiff and Swansea, where I stopped off to catch the action.

By now it was July and the weather was good. As I walked up the hill past St Aidan's church, I met two friends who used to play in the Solva skiffle group. They were all agog and said that there were loads of girls camping on Pen Graig, above the harbour. I demanded that they take me there, so we leaped over the stile and legged it for the

Sabine encampment. At the bottom of the field we saw three tents in a hollow above the Fort. And there were girls alright, sunbathing in bathing costumes on the grass! Nonchalantly, we strolled down and engaged them in conversation. Two were from Ross-on-Wye and the other three were from Brecon. Amazingly, I knew one of them – Veronica Evans was the girlfriend of John Murray, a student in Cardiff College of Art. Bingo! The girls had become friends whilst attending a convent school in Brecon. They wanted to know what I was doing in Solva – at that time something like an unknown place on the map – and were pleased when I said I lived there. They asked if they could come home for a bath. "Of course," I said; anything to oblige ladies in distress and bikinis.

The arrival of these girls really made the rest of the summer holidays. They stayed for a fortnight, and when they reluctantly left I was invited to stay with them at Ross-on-Wye. Lesley Boland and Fiona Young lived in Ross, where Lesley's parents kept a big hotel. By this time I had left the Harries band. Because I was footloose and travelled a lot, I found it cumbersome to have to turn up regularly on Wednesdays and Saturdays in Cardiff. I had also decided that I'd had enough of Art College. I was going to be free, and the world lay waiting for a wayward lad.

# Chapter 8

# Folk Music and Stuff

The summer of 1960 was the best yet. The Bay Hotel in Solva was still rocking, although Clive, Steve and Alan had graduated and moved on to become teachers at home and abroad. Clive Williams emigrated to New Zealand where, sadly, he was killed in a car accident some years later. Steve Glass went to teach in Canada, and Alan Roach stayed in the UK. He now lives in Solva and is a keen yachtsman. By now, I was the hub of the Bay sessions, although there was also an accordion and piano player, Jim McCrossan, who still visits Solva and plays in the Ship Hotel.

The guitar-playing tradition was not completely new to the area. There had been a string band led by Dai'r Felin – the late David Lewis, Lower Mill, St David's – whose members were local seamen who had obtained guitars, mandolins and banjos abroad. This band would play in local concerts and at the City Hotel in St David's. I think they had learned to play whilst aboard ships and then got together whilst on leave. This guitar thing still goes on too. There are many good guitarists, banjo players and other musicians in the Solva area, and good music can often be heard in the local pubs.

The Brecon and Hereford girls were great fun and Veronica Evans had my old mate John Murray in tow, along with his ever-present guitar, paints and brushes. (John died recently, in Kilburn, London, having been an art teacher there for years.) I'd more or less moved into the Hereford girls' camp on Pen Graig; there wasn't much point in staggering home after the all-night parties. I'd become friendly with Fiona and Lesley, who were also art students. Fiona's family originally came from the Scottish Highlands around Inverness, whilst Lesley's parents kept the Royal Hotel in Ross. They too were into jazz, fine art, boozing and dancing – always up for a good time!

When they left Solva at the end of the summer, they left their addresses and an invitation to visit. This was ideal; I wasn't in the mood for staying much longer and I'd already decided not to return to Cardiff. I'd have to find a job, and I wanted to start doing some serious painting, or so I thought at the time. How to go about it, though? I had a lot to learn about life.

The St David's peninsula is a perfect place for landscape painting – the sea, land and above all, the ever changing sky. The light there is unique, and some of the dawns, storms and sunsets are beyond belief. It's not surprising that people think it a magical and sacred place. There is no need to exaggerate when painting there. You just wait for the right day or night and off you go; it's a perfect subject. I've been painting and drawing there as long as I can remember and, during my time at art school, I painted quite a few sea and landscapes, various views of St David's Cathedral and scenes at Solva. These early paintings and drawings now reside in private collections.

My mother had a job in the woollen mill at Felinganol, which was owned by Auntie Betty Griffiths. She wasn't my real aunt, but one of my mother's childhood friends. Auntie Betty bought one of my early pictures of the entrance to Solva harbour, a small oil painting which I'd hung in the college summer work exhibition in 1958. I used to sell quite a few oils and watercolours to tourists in the summer and used to exhibit them in the lounge of the Ship.

From time to time I'd go to Haverfordwest in search of painting materials, which could be bought in the Telegraph office shop in

Market Street. Next door was George's Bar, where a crowd of characters used to hang out. Among them were a group of bohemians, older than myself. Some of them were friends of Dylan and Caitlin Thomas, who lived in Laugharne at the time. They were all mighty boozers and raconteurs. Tiggy and Tony Clavier used to drink there. Tiggy was a cat woman, hence the nickname, and Tony was a member of the Phillips family of Picton Castle. He had been a captain in the Tank Corps and had won the military cross in North Africa in the Second World War. (This was something he found profoundly embarrassing. He used to put his M.C. in the bin before Armistice Day, and Tiggy would have to rummage through the rubbish to find it and clean it up. She would then nag him until he agreed to march in the parade.) Tiggy on the other hand had been one of the Little Venice set in Maida Vale, London, and was an intimate friend of Lucian Freud, Nina Hamnett, Robert Colquhoun and Redvers Grey. She had been a model for Jacob Epstein, Augustus John and Michael Ayrton among others. "Look here, boy," she would say. "You paint pictures, and leave the boozing to Tiggy!"

I met Tiggy in Haverfordwest Rugby Club one drunken night. I'd been to town to buy canvas and some sticks of charcoal, and I made the mistake of calling by at George's Bar, where I soon fell in with the usual crowd of professional drinkers and raconteurs who lay in wait for unsuspecting kids like me trying to take a walk on the wild side. The Rugby Club was in a back alley just around the corner. I had a few drinks and at closing time, which was three o'clock in those days, I was invited to go to the club for more drinks. I soon found out that it was possible to drink around the clock on account of the cattle market and various other legal excuses. I said I had some shopping to do and I'd meet them later on.

Somehow I ended up in the rugby club, very drunk! It was a members' only club, but one of the George's lot signed me in. We went into a small private bar where a group of people were sitting at the bar on high stools talking, cracking jokes, drinking and laughing a lot. My memory of that part of the day is hazy to say the least, but I do remember Tiggy and her friend Brian, who turned out to be a local dentist. Brian always wore smartly tailored suits and elegant silk brocade waistcoats which he had specially made. I'd heard rumours of a jet set in Pembrokeshire from my mother, who had been involved with them from time to time over the years, and I'd heard some lurid tales about their escapades.

I was hanging drunk by this time, still clutching my new canvas and box of charcoal sticks. We must have been talking art, because the gentleman of the flamboyant 'Weskit' demanded that I paint him on my virgin canvas. I was in no fit state to finish my drink let alone do a Van Gogh. I told him I had no paint, only sticks of charcoal. The 'Weskit' vanished and returned after a while with a steaming turd on an ashtray. "Here's your pigment," he roared. "Do me with that!" This was the most bizarre thing I'd done to date, and everyone in the bar took it as a huge joke I had no option but to portray the dentist in brown, black and white! God knows what happened to that masterpiece.

I woke up feeling cold in the back of a van with a sack and the top half of a sailor's uniform thrown over me. I opened the back door to find myself on a natural ledge outside a white cottage, overlooking a narrow valley on fire with autumnal beech trees. The door of the cottage opened as if on demand, and a little girl of about eight, wearing red trousers and a white cardigan and accompanied by two prancing dogs, a white Poodle and a Boxer, ran towards me.

"You can come in now," she called. "Daddy's making tea." I was at Spittal Tucking Mill, Tiggy and Tony Clavier's residence near Treffgarn. The little girl was their daughter Vanessa. Tony Clavier was feathering a brace of pheasants in front of the Aga in a small oak-beamed kitchen. There were Siamese cats everywhere, basking on the shelf above the fire and on various pieces of furniture.

"Hello old boy," he said, smiling, "tea's here."

The cats were all over the place. Another time, I was putting coal on the fire and I failed to notice three Siamese kittens sleeping in the hod on top of the coal. Fortunately they leaped out before I threw the coal on the fire. It was bizarre!

Later, Tiggy appeared and took me to see a purpose-built studio up a ladder and through a trap door at the end of the house. It had a bed and a studio easel and lots of stretched canvasses, paints and brushes, as if waiting for an artist to arrive. "You can use this if you want, but you'll have to help out with the pussies," she said. Tiggy had dozens of cats, mainly Siamese blue and sealpoints but also some Siamese-types that were dark brown all over. She had bred these herself and called them English Chocolate Shorthairs; she had even received a fellowship of the Zoological Society for her work in selective breeding.

Spittal Tucking Mill was a very scenic, beautiful and secluded place, perfect for painters, and I decided to accept her offer. Tiggy had a shop in Haverfordwest and Tony worked for a battery company, so they both left quite early each morning leaving me marooned. It was too far to walk to Haverfordwest – the track to the cottage from the main road must have been three miles long. Just below the house there was a fast-flowing trout stream and there were plenty of fishing rods in the gunroom below the studio. So when I wasn't painting I used to walk in the beech forest, or fish for supper.

Tiggy was a character, full of Soho stories; she seemed to know everyone in the art world. She was also a heavy smoker and whisky drinker, and she died of cancer at the age of forty-seven. Later, the Claviers moved from the mill to Wolfscastle, where they reopened an old pub, which they named the Wolf. Tiggy spent most of her time in the pub anyway, so it was a logical step. It was during their time there that she died. She had been a founder member of the Mandrake Club in Soho; it was originally a chess club, but later a famous hangout for artists, alcoholics and bohemians. She told me that Dylan Thomas had tried to pick her up there one afternoon, and that she had told him to get stuffed, or words to that effect. So off he went before returning in a hired Rolls Royce to take her out on a binge. I could tell a lot of stories about life with Tiggy. Let it suffice to say that we did a lot of talking and drinking and that she taught me more about art and life in the short time I lived with her and Tony than I could ever have hoped for at Cardiff Art School.

Tiggy had a son called Jim, who, she hoped, would become an artist. She insisted that his father was a famous painter, but would never say who. I suspected it was either Lucian Freud or Michael Ayrton. Jim, however, went off to Africa to join the Rhodesian Police; I only met him once when he came home on leave. I left Spittal Tucking Mill soon after. London was calling again.

I'd been corresponding with Fiona Young for quite a while and I'd visited Ross-on-Wye and Hereford a few times. It was time for me to hitch-hike up the A40 again, my lifeline to civilization; after all, Ross was on the way to London. It was easy to get lifts in those days, and, before the first Severn Bridge opened, the A40 was the only way to get from west and south Wales to England. All traffic was routed through Gloucester, and so it was that I arrived late one sunny afternoon at the Royal Hotel, which stood next to a church and some castle ruins on an outcrop overlooking the River Wye. The hotel looked posh and I entered nervously and asked for Lesley Boland. Suddenly there she was – big, blond and bouncy as ever, with a huge welcoming smile. She took me to meet her parents who were having an early evening cocktail in their lounge, and then to the kitchen to be fed. She phoned Fiona who arrived in a black Morris Minor, and they took me on a pub crawl. I was given a room at the hotel and told I could stay as long as I liked. This was living again and very different from the solitude and austerity of Spittal Tucking Mill, or Solva.

Lesley was planning to join Fiona at Hereford College of Art; both wanted to be artists at the time, I guess. Hereford art school seemed to be something of a finishing school for the offspring of the local middle class, but they seemed to be having a load of fun as well as doing the usual pottery, painting and drawing. Parties, jazz, sex, boozing and dancing were high on the agenda – at the time there were no drugs there. In fact, drugs wouldn't have made much of an impression. The local cider was intoxicating enough, hallucinogenic and incredibly cheap at ten pence a pint!

Herefordshire as everybody knows is famous for her apple and pear orchards, and there were a good few of them in that 'quiet' Border county. At the time, there was also a New Orleans jazz boom, with jazz music records getting into the hit parade in the UK. Jazz bands could be found regularly in back rooms of olde worlde pubs all over the border counties, as well as in London and all of the big provincial towns and cities. Fiona's mother's black Morris Minor meant that transport was no problem. It was before the days of drink driving laws; inevitably, we did a lot of drinking and driving and it was a miracle that we had neither accidents nor brushes with the law.

I'd run out of money again and so we went apple picking around Hereford, a delightful if soggy experience. My grandparents lived just up the road in Shrewsbury and, when I called to visit them, they asked me if I'd like to move in with them, and perhaps get a job in Shrewsbury. I went to the labour exchange and found a job as a brewer's assistant in Southams brewery!

Southams was a red brick Victorian building with a tall industrial chimney stack. It lay hard by the railway station in the centre of the town. I worked as the tank man at the top of the building. The beer was pumped up from a lower floor, and part of my job was to keep the pipes, tanks and filters clean. The tanks would be either emptied into barrels, which I had to sterilize with a steam hose, or piped down to the bottling room, a no-go area full of rampant middle-aged harridans. Then I'd have to get inside the tanks with another hose pipe and a yard brush to scrub the inside clean. One day some wag with a macabre sense of humour locked me inside one. It was no joke; I nearly suffocated. It's a good job that someone had a good memory!

I used to sit around a lot in the attic of the brewery, thinking, drinking and reading the bible. There was so much beer there that even I got fed up of drinking the stuff! Nevertheless, I looked forward to the arrival of the Guinness lorry, which came from Dublin via Holyhead in those days before the Park Hall brewery in London, with massive tanks of Irish nectar, which I had to pump up to the tank room. Because of the nature of the brew, it was much harder to clean the pump filters and pipes. Often, I would end up with five buckets of Guinness, which I would bottle and then stack in disused wooden crates.

Another interesting brew was S.O.S. – Southams Old Strong – a winter brew similar to barley wine or Bass No. 1. This extremely alcoholic beverage lay maturing in the tanks for nine months. S.O.S. demanded respect and was only sold in third of a pint bottles. A tank of S.O.S., when ready, was always ceremoniously tapped by the aged brewer, who, looking rather like Albert Einstein, he would always give the galley slaves a tot. There was still a cooper at Southams. He worked down in the arched barrel cellar and was the guardian of the lunch-break keg of mild and bitter. There was also a Geordie fireman who tended the boilers. When I asked him if it was true that there were rats in breweries, he told me that he was always the first in the morning and that it was a bit like going to Newmarket races at that time of day. He also told me that there were rats in the modern breweries in Burton on Trent who could gnaw through stainless steel. "The bastards even ate through that," he said with disgust.

Shrewsbury was a boring little border town, not half as lively as Hereford though with plenty of olde worlde pubs with quaint little names like the Old Post Office, the Three Fishes and the Wheatsheaf. For the most part, these were frequented by older, conservative people. I knew that I wouldn't last long there; I was already making plans for my escape.

My grandfather, Louis Algernon Wright, was a prissy, dapper old Edwardian gentleman, who had seen better days, when he worked for Thomas Cook as one of their first international travel couriers. He was an exceedingly fussy man and meticulous about everything in his life, from his garden to his clothes and to what he ate for breakfast each morning, which was always the same meal of fresh grapefruit, egg, bacon and fried bread, liberally sprinkled with wheatgerm, and a cup of maté tea. The table was perfectly laid, just like in a top hotel. Algy, as my grandmother Gertrude used to call him, was from Cheltenham, where his father was the original stationmaster on Brunel's Great Western Railway. Algy had made some money at an early age, holding the heads of the horses that drew the gentry in their carriages to the marvellous new railway station. (The working classes could not yet afford to travel by train.) He must have been a lad of seven or eight and he was rewarded with a silver threepenny piece or sometimes even a sixpence. Soon he began to cultivate the business sense that helped him eventually succeed as the director of a window cleaning company that cleaned up on government contracts during and after the war. Ironically, of course, his only son was killed in that war.

My father, Gerry, was a good looking chap, who by all accounts was very popular with the girls. This annoyed his father, who was jealous of his son, and that is why they did not get on. Algy would refuse to lend Gerry his flash Riley car to take his girlfriends out for drives in the country, but Gerry would often 'borrow' it with the connivance of his mother. This practice came to a sudden end though. One day he arrived at the garage and was distracted by my mother Bet, who had seen something in the garden. He got out to see what was up, then got back in and drove the car into the garage with one of the doors still open. The doors of that model opened outwards and forwards unlike most cars today, and so one unfortunate door was ripped off its hinges. There was holy hell, but soon he bought an M.G. convertible.

Despite this apparent frivolity, Gerald Wright carried a sadness in his heart. When he was eighteen, he fell in love with an older girl called Evelyn Wood. After a clandestine courtship she became pregnant, and things went awry; she gave birth prematurely to a girl, and both Evelyn and the baby died in childbirth. He took the baby's body home to his parents in a shoe box; she was later buried with her mother in the cemetery near Lucifield Road where they lived. Gerry left home soon after and joined the RAF. Four years later when the Second World War broke out he was a staff sergeant in the Air Ministry in London. Like so many of his contemporaries he volunteered for flight training, eventually finding himself in the Sunderland flying boats of Coastal Command at Pembroke Dock, where he met my mother. Later he was moved to the Midlands where he flew in fighter bombers as a flight sergeant before being killed in an air crash in 1941.

★ ★ ★

By this time I was totally fed up of the brewery work; there were no prospects there. I was not being trained as a brewer; if anything I was little more than a labourer. Later I moved to an even more boring job with the Dunlop Rubber Company, still in Shrewsbury, where I spent all day checking tyres. By now, I'd moved from my grandparents' house to live with an aunt; just like my father I didn't get on with Algy. At least I was earning more money with Dunlop, but it was still a dead-end job in a dead-end town, or so it seemed to me at the time. I saw no future there and so London called once again. When I picked up my second month's pay check, I bade farewell to the old folks at home and hit the road for the metropolis, jazz and fun. My short stay in Shrewsbury was the most boring period of my life to date, but I did learn a lot about my father's family history of which I knew very little before.

First, though, I hitch-hiked down to Hereford to see Fiona, doing the usual round of the scrumpy houses before finding myself on the A40 again. I think Fiona gave me a lift to Gloucester. Soon I was heading in the right direction on a lovely sunny morning with not only a hangover but money in my pocket and, for the first time, in the bank too! We said our farewells outside the greasy spoon by the bridge in Gloucester, and it wasn't long before I was sitting in a scammel truck heading for Covent Garden market and shouting to the driver over the noise of the diesel engine about where I came from, where I was going, and who I was. "I'm going to London to get a job in the music business," I screamed. "You scream everybody loves ice cream, rock my baby roll!"

# Chapter 9

# 'Folk you' –
# Me and the Folk Song Revival

I used to hitch-hike quite a bit, all over Britain and western Europe, and so a great deal of my time was spent travelling in lorries. Hitch-hiking was simply one of the done things. Jack Kerouac was one of our heroes; everyone had a copy of *On the Road*, and *The Dharma Bums*. Very often we would hit the road just for kicks, with no premeditated travel plan, just going wherever the lorries would take us, and if we didn't connect with an interesting scene we'd hitch another lorry.

Mostly though I'd head for the bright lights of London or Paris, where the cost of living was much lower. Hitching was the cheapest way to travel, and it was a bit of an adventure. Seasoned hitchers had tales to tell and would sometimes have competitions and even lay bets on how far they could get within a specified time or how quickly they could travel from A to B. I once hitched from Solva to Cardiff early one morning, minus my guitar. I was in the Moulders when some friends from abroad arrived. A session started, and so at about 3 o'clock I hitched back to Solva to get my guitar. I was back by 9 p.m. I'd hitched three hundred miles in seven hours that day!

There were also tricks of the trade. For example, in the late 1950s almost anyone would pick up a soldier or sailor in uniform; there was conscription, and almost every family had sons in the military. A college scarf worked the same way. Choosing good places to stand, like lay-bys or roundabouts where traffic slows down, was important, as were well-lit spots where drivers could have a good look at you. The best places, however, were lorry parks or transport caffs, greasy spoons, where you could chat up the drivers; if one wasn't going your way, he'd generally introduce you to one of his mates who was. I did a lot of walking too, and I didn't like hitching in built-up areas where police would quite often arrive and ask embarrassing questions like "Who are you?" and "Where are you going?" or "Where do you come from?" Most of us had nothing to hide, but we still tended to keep clear of the police, who didn't have much sympathy for young people with long hair, beards and what they thought were weird clothes. On the whole, though, hitching is an interesting and rewarding experience – it gets you there quickly and for free.

One night I was bound for London, and so I went to a lorry park off Tyndall Street in Cardiff, armed with guitar, college scarf and a handful of amphetamine pills to keep me awake. It was 11 p.m. and I soon got a lift on an Edward England spud lorry bound for Covent Garden. Off we went, shouting our conversation over the roaring diesel engine that bisected the cabin. We arrived at about 5 a.m. in the hustle and bustle of the narrow alleys and dimly lit streets of the biggest fruit and veg market in Europe. The driver went off to dump his load, and I dived into a pub to quench my thirst, my mouth dry as a bone on account of the speed and shouting at the driver for five hours!

The pubs in Covent Garden were open all night for the convenience of market traders and porters, but anyone could get a drink if they behaved themselves; the costermen are no killjoys! At that time of the morning, the Garden pubs were really the domain of market traders, but there were others who drank there too – night people, characters, hoboes, artists, insomniacs, members of the performing arts, theatre people, actors and even the aristocracy and other kinds of prostitutes.

The pub was heaving, loud with the shouts of traders making deals, porters telling jokes and jostling each other; one group was even breaking into song in a corner. Quite a few were obviously whores; who knows why they were in a bar at five in the morning. It could have been lunch-time or a Saturday night, the place was so full. I bought a pint of Fuller's London Pride and retired to a shadowy corner. The speed was working well; I was wide awake and very thirsty. I sat there incognito watching the charade from the depths of my donkey jacket.

From what I could see through the window, it was all go outside too: hundreds of porters, dealers, traders and lorry drivers were shouting their heads off, waving their arms around and pushing handcarts piled high with crates, baskets, boxes and sacks. Fruit and vegetables from all over the world overflowed in the alleys. Engines revved, curses flowed, cart-wheels rattled and heavy loads crashed and thudded as they were thrown around like sacks of feathers, all accompanied by the odours and smells from the damp early morning market in the blue light of dawn.

Some society toffs staggered through the door, dressed for the opera or the Savoy Hotel. They'd obviously been out on the town, then gone slumming round the Soho clubs, hadn't had enough, and ended up in the last oasis. "Let's go down the Garden for a bit of a laugh." The ladies, tall and elegant, wore long evening gowns of silks and satin, mink and silver fox fur stoles, jewels sparkling at their ears and throats. They tottered drunk on high-heeled shoes, while the men in evening dress, crooked bow ties and drooping buttonholes, lurched cackling to the bar. Gesticulating, laughing and pawing each other, they pushed their way to the bar and loudly ordered gins and tonic. One of the barmen, a huge skinhead bouncer, took offence and would not serve them: "This bar's for market workers only mate." An argument ensued and the aristocrats were asked to leave. One of the mink-clad ladies proclaimed loudly in the bouncer's ear, "Dickie's the Marquis of Granby, darling. He always gets served – he owns the area."

"No he ain't," says the bouncer. "The Marquis of Granby's up in Cambridge Circus and he don't open till eleven. You're not Garden workers, so fuck off!" And they were bundled out into the damp dawn protesting loudly: "I say Dickie darling, what a spoilsport, we only want a drinky poo!" I felt quite sorry for them, for they too had briefly illuminated that drab old market tavern with a bright contrast of different colours to that of cabbages, turnips and potatoes. I could still smell the women's expensive perfume. A heavy hand came down on my shoulder, and boldly said in a cockney accent, "You're alright Taffy – you can 'ave another one if you wants. We don't close till eight o'clock!'

Soon the many Italian cafés in the area would open, and the air would fill with the aroma of coffee, bacon, eggs and sausages cooking and the smell of burnt toast. I always had spaghetti Bolognese for breakfast on these occasions; it was only two shillings, a much better deal than the English breakfast! I drank up and made my way to a café I knew near Charing Cross Road. The place was full of porters from the market, early birds who worked in central London, and off-duty Soho whores shagged out and starving. We're back to the good old *News of the World*, I thought. All human life is here, sub-human too!

It was Saturday morning, almost 9 o'clock, and time to slope off up Charing Cross Road to check out the music stores. American guitars were just beginning to come onto the London market via Selmers and Ivor Mairants's shop, then in Wardour Street. Ivor Mairants was also a famous swing guitarist, and he had secured a deal with Martin guitars of Nazareth Pennsylvania. Martins were the most expensive and sought after guitars in the world at that time; the holy grail of boxes, especially for folk and blues singers, as used by Big Bill Broonzy, Lonnie Johnson, Josh White and Lonnie Donegan of course. If only I could get my hands on a 1947 Treble 0 28 with an Adirondac spruce top, Brazilian rosewood body, and herringbone purfling from Germany! The instrument was a geographical symphony before you even took it out of its case. "If wishes were horses, beggars would ride."

The windows of Selmers, which is hard by Denmark Street – Tinpan Alley, the heart of the London music scene – were full of German Hofners, but, to my utmost pleasure, there were a few American Gibsons and Epiphones too; two or three jumbos and a couple of cello jazz guitars, beautiful black and golden sunburst instruments with factory-fitted electric pick-ups. At this time, Fender solid guitars had only just been invented. They were just about unobtainable, only seen on American Rock movies and Buddy Holly album sleeves. I had seen one real one, played by Tony Sheridan in the 2i's coffee bar in Old Compton Street ('the cradle of British Rock' as it was cornily advertised). It was, in fact, a shitty little cellar where you couldn't swing a cat, but now and again good guitarists like Joe Brown and Dave Goldberg would play there. The 2i's was also famous as the home of Tommy Steele, a really useless quasi-rock singer and an even worse guitarist, who quickly went into variety and crap musicals, thank god! I saw Sheridan in the 2i's in 1956. What a revelation! I couldn't believe that I was seeing an electric guitar with horns and all those pick-ups and switches, machine heads all on one side – and horns! I'd also never imagined a guitar made out of a solid plank of wood. No body – what next?

Charing Cross Road was now a teeming river of commuters, most with glazed and sleepy eyes, staring straight ahead, nine to fivers, lambs to the slaughter at the office. Who knows who they were or what they did, and who cared? I was lucky, footloose, and free to go wherever I wanted, young and in my prime! I turned left at Cambridge Circus and walked down Compton Street towards Wardour Street and Ivor Mairants.

Later on I sat in the Gyre and Gimble coffee house (known to us as 'The Two Gees') in Litchfield Street near Colyer's jazz club. I was wondering where I could find a bed, a floor or anywhere to sleep, when I remembered I had an old college friend who'd moved to London to seek his fortune as a painter. His name was Geoff Stevens and he lived with his half-French girlfriend Jeanne in Chalk Farm, which lay between Kentish Town and Hampstead in north London. Geoff agreed to put me up, and so I went looking for work. At the Labour Exchange I was persuaded to join the Civil Service as a clerical officer at the Public Trustees' Office in Holborn Kingsway, Central London.

There is a tube station just round the corner from Queen's Crescent, and it was there that I would catch a train to work every morning if I had any money. If not, I had to walk about five miles to the office and back in the evening. Sometimes I'd jump the tube without paying, and if I got caught I just gave a false address. I didn't like doing this and found it nerve-wracking; I've never been much good at that sort of thing.

I lived on Scott's Porridge Oats made with water instead of milk and extremely strong Turkish coffee which we brewed in a traditional little copper pot with a brass handle. I got paid weekly, and so I ate and drank well at weekends. I earned £8 10s. a week, most of which was spent on booze. Working at the Public Trustees' Office bored me stiff, and I spent most of my time there reading heavy novels in the toilet.

I was always hanging round the jazz clubs, coffee houses and bars of Soho. The Partisan was an extreme left-wing coffee house off Dean

Street in Soho. It had originally been funded by the Labour Party as a place for young socialists to meet, play chess, drink coffee and chew the fat of socialism. Soon it became a hotbed of radical and communist extremism, with all that went with it, namely sex, drugs, blues, anarchy and booze! The Partisan was always full of long haired beatniks, bohemians, dossers, bums and musicians. It was a very interesting place, right in the heart of Soho.

All the avant-garde guitarists and singers hung out at the Partisan. Davy Graham was always playing the guitar there, as did Gerry Lockran, Wizz Jones, Long John Baldry, and folk singers like Alex Campbell, Derrol Adams, Joe Locker, Jack Elliott; it's a long list. There was always someone playing guitar there at any time of day or night. They also had a folk cellar; everywhere there was a 'Folk Cellar', as if the best place for 'Folk' was the cellar! The Malcolm Price Trio, Redd Sullivan, John Baldry, Davy Graham, Shirley Collins, Julie Felix, Gerry Lockran, and Martin Carthy – the whole lot used to play there regularly.

Another Folk Cellar was the Troubadour in Earls Court. It still exists and all the best singers have played there, even Bobby Dylan. In fact this is where I first saw Dylan in 1964. He didn't sing. He was with some American friends and Martin Carthy pissed out of their brains. Very loud, arrogant and full of ego. Years later I saw Davy Graham, a real bigot, throw a very young Roy Harper off the stage because he didn't like his guitar playing. "Fuck off out of here, you cretin," screamed Graham, out of his head on narcotics. Poor young Roy's picking wasn't up to the great man's standard!

The bastion of the British folk revival was The Ballads and Blues Club at 2 Soho Square. This club was held weekly in an unlicensed hired room. It was always packed out and was a singers' club, that is singers just went and were invited up from the floor to perform two or three songs each. I heard the last shanty man, Stan Hugill, for the first time there; later he became the sailing master at the Aberdovey outward bound sea school until he retired – he was a real blast from the past!

I was on the stairs at home one evening trying to play like Big Bill Broonzy, when Syd, our next-door neighbour, came out and just stood watching me. After a while he said "Can you play what you're thinking?" before closing the door and going back to his typewriter. I'd never thought of playing what I was thinking – until then, I always tried to copy other people's music. He made me think differently about music in an instant, and I've been more careful about my music ever since.

★ ★ ★

Geoff was an abstract painter and he use to paint big Jackson Pollock-type paintings. The American action painter was becoming well known and Geoff was doing his version of Taschism, as it was called. He would find old wooden bed frames, which had been thrown out of houses, bring them into his room and stretch canvas on them. Most of the canvas was stolen; the awnings of shop windows were striped canvas in those days. Geoff would steal them in the night, then stitch them together and rack them on a double-bed frame to create a huge space for painting. He had enormous pots of house paint – primary red, yellow, blue, and grey, black and white – which he would hurl at the canvas leaning against the bedroom wall. He would lash the biggest brushes he could find to broomsticks and slash at the canvas with them whilst throwing other materials such as gravel, clay, putty, glue, plaster of Paris and sand or anything else that came to hand into the frame. Jeanne would sit on the bed calmly feeding her baby. It was a bizarre place. Geoff played the artist perfectly, red beard like Vincent, curly pipe in mouth, corduroy suit, beret over one ear, and a running commentary on the great art of existentialism.

On Saturday mornings there was a flea market in Queen's Crescent, and we'd go there to heckle Oswald Moseley's fascists who would turn up every week to harangue the crowd with their ranting and raving from soap boxes – beer crates in fact! The audience would usually shout them down, hurling a few missiles before chasing them down the road. Hyde Park Corner was good for this; I've seen Michael Foot being roughed-up there.

I continued with my job at the office and was given the task of looking after the Duke of Norfolk's stocks and shares; mostly money he'd invested in South American mining companies and railways, and in forestry. But my real interest was hunting down music especially folk, blues and jazz, even though the jazz bug was wearing off. It was hello guitar, bye bye banjo time.

At this time Peggy Seeger and Ewan McColl were living in London. McColl was working with Sydney Carter, a BBC man and a great lyricist. They were co-writing a radio series called *Singing the Fishing*, from which came the famous song 'The Shoals of Herring'. McColl and Seeger were folk snobs, and they ran a select and esoteric club, The Singers' Club, for extreme folkies. This club was Bedouin by nature and moved from pub to pub wherever they could find a suitable room for hire. Little-known traditional songs were sung and musical instruments were all but banished except for Seeger's five-string banjo.

McColl was a real poser – he'd even changed his name. He sang with his hand over one ear and his head cocked on one side with a quasi-intellectual look on his face, or so he thought. Seeger was an accomplished folk musician with a small sweet voice and a huge repertoire of ethnic American songs; her banjo playing made a welcome change from the rest of the 'singing' which was mainly moaning and groaning about wenches and ploughboys and other boring agrarian stuff best left in the farmyard.

I saw Dylan play the Singers' Club once, at a pub in Old Compton Street – the Princess of Bohemia, I think it was called. He was dressed in his folkie cap and sheepskin jacket (just like on the sleeve of *The Freewheeling Bob*), smashed and taking the piss out of the folkies again. Good on you, Bob! He was too much for the Seeger-McColl clan. Not before time, he took folk singing to another level.

One evening I was in the Two Gees, playing blues with Long John Baldry before doing the interval at Colyer's just along the street. There was some shouting from the door, and down the stone stairs came a tall thin bearded guy dressed in a faded blue Levi suit, unobtainable in London at the time, high-heeled western boots and carrying a battered guitar case covered in airline stickers. Baldry looked up, carried on playing and shouted "Piss off Alex." That was my first meeting with Alex Campbell, the true troubadour, and a living dictionary of folk music. Alex, who lived in Paris at the time, was in London to record an album of American songs called *Way Out West* for the Society label.

Alex taught me a lot of songs and influenced my attitude to singing and playing guitar. He also showed me a lot about working an audience. Alex played a beautiful pre-war Gibson J45, "His old Gibson guitar," a mythical thing of magic and wonder. He started a club at the Railway Hotel, Richmond and at the Half Moon in Putney, and he would often call me up from the audience to sing. It was Alex who encouraged me to sing and write songs; he instilled a lot of confidence in me, which was much needed as I was young, shy and very inexperienced.

Alex was a huge boozer, and he showed me a lot about that side of the raconteur. We had many massive drinking sessions, along with his friend the banjo player Derrol Adams and Dominic Behan, Brendan's brother, who was crazy! Jack Elliott would come over, as did an Irish singer called Noel Murphy. As always there was a hell of a lot of boozing going on amongst the folk and jazz crowd, and drugs were beginning to creep on the scene. Drug trafficking was very esoteric then – the weed being controlled and used mainly by West Indians, the opium and smack (heroin) by the Chinese.

I was playing and singing more and more, and I played several folk clubs, just getting up as a floor singer. Most of the people in the folk and jazz clubs knew me and if I turned up at the door of the Troubadour or the Half Moon, or anywhere else, I'd be asked to sing.

Baldry liked playing with me, mainly blues although he had a folk repertoire too. He'd ask me to do the all-nighters on weekends with him, and we'd also do the intervals in most of the jazz clubs. He'd drop me a few bob for that, and we'd play around Soho and other parts of central London from Friday night till Sunday morning, usually ending up in Ken Colyer's where we'd do two spots. I used to play Diz Dizley's Golden Hofner, which he used to leave behind the piano. I'd also play banjo with Colyer's band, when Johnny Bastaple was paralytic drunk. On Sunday mornings we'd end up at dawn at the pie stall on the embankment below Charing Cross Station for a big mug of tea and a hot dog. By then, Baldry usually had a couple of his young male hairdressers in tow and they'd leave me there and slope off to Hampstead for an orgy. I'd go home to Queen's Crescent and sleep on the landing all day recharging. Weekends were hard going.

I hardly ever got paid for singing in London. I was poverty stricken, and so was Geoff my landlord. I couldn't even afford a guitar, and although I tried to buy a Harmony Sovereign from Ivor Mairants I was turned down by the finance company. It was only £45 but that was a fortune to me.

Most of the good folk singers like Wizz Jones, Alex and Derroll would go busking in Paris, usually around the Latin Quarter called St Michel near the Notre Dame de Paris. This area is a warren of narrow streets and alleys on the banks of the Seine. There was a café there called Popov's, kept by a liberal-minded East European who loved music and musicians, and all the folk singers would gather there. You could even sleep there if you'd just arrived and not found a place, but Paris was very cheap then and rooms could be rented for next to nothing, especially in Montparnasse, which was incredibly cheap compared to anywhere in Britain.

The cost of living was much much lower than in London or in any of the provincial cities in England. There were loads of prostitutes round St Michel, and they would buy us drinks and food in the cafés. There were quite a few bordellos in the area; prostitution was legal in Paris then. One young prostitute fancied me; her name was Claire Duval, and she was dark and pretty. I didn't have any kind of sexual affair with her, although she wanted our relationship to go that way. It was easy to avoid having sex with her, because most of the time she was fucking for money and when she was not doing that we would go for walks by the Seine or to Montmartre to watch the street artists at work. They'd do a really good portrait there and then for a few francs, and I paid for her to have hers done once. We would also go to Sacré Coeur, my favourite church; she of course was a Catholic and would light candles and confess. I don't know what happened to her – one time I went to St Michel and she'd disappeared, none of the other girls seemed to know where she had gone. I hope she's still alive – we were the same age. I've never heard from her since, although she did write to my mother in Solva a couple of times. *C'est la vie!*

Living in Paris was cheap and exciting; a bottle of decent wine was 10*d.* and bread, cheese and fruit were a giveaway. You could live like a lord on five shillings a day, and everyone who busked in Paris returned looking much healthier and stronger. The American folk scene was also in its infancy in '60–'61–'62, and many great American folk singers went there to play in the streets and cafés: Richard and Mimi Farina and her sister Joan Baez, Jack Elliott, Phil Ochs, Ian and

Sylvia, Mary Travers, Derrol Adams, Peggy Seeger. I never saw Dylan there – I don't know if he ever played the street – but Wizz Jones and Pete Stanley, an excellent banjo player from England, Davy Graham, Baldry and Alex Campbell all played the cafés of St Michel. Quite often I'd come across a bunch of guys from the Moulders in Cardiff. They were friends of mine – Wally Jones from Llanelli, Robin Grace from Barry, Jimmy Angove from Penarth, and a guy called Mike Bradden who now lives in Australia.

The folk singers were travellers, and they enjoyed every minute of it. There was a network of information a bit like Reuters: information about good places was shared, with distance, money or accommodation no problem. For example, I was in Paris once, when a couple of folkies turned up and we started drinking wine. They told me that the same wine was only a penny a glass in Barcelona. The same time next day, I was drinking it in Barcelona. Luckily, there were two hundred and forty pence to the pound then! That was how we lived – playing, travelling and drinking wine, oh! and eating a healthy diet of bread, cheese, salami, olives and fish. And no chips, which were unheard of outside Britain and America. We sang for our supper.

I used to go home to Solva from time to time, when the *hiraeth* became too much. I liked to see my family and to sit on the quay in Solva. Sometimes I'd get a job on a farm, driving a tractor, cutting hay or picking potatoes, maybe harvesting corn later in the year. They were good times – hard work, but just part of that way of life.

Once I was somewhere in France or Spain and someone asked me how old I was. I realized that I was nearly 21 years old, and so I thought it a good idea to head for home. En route I invited loads of friends to come to Solva to the party. I had little money but great faith, and I arrived eventually after a marathon hitch on the twelfth of March, the day before my birthday. As I opened the side door, which was never locked, I saw my mother washing dishes. She didn't seem at all surprised to see me.

"What are you doing here?" she asked.

"I've come home for my 21st birthday," I said.

"You stupid boy!" she exclaimed. "That was last year, you've missed it!"

I'd lost a year on my travels, and I'd invited dozens of people from all over Europe and from London, Cardiff, Swansea, and many other places! Fortunately, my mother loved parties. "You can have it here, better late than never, but we've no money, no booze and very little food. There's a dance at the Memorial Hall tomorrow night so at least we can have a jig!"

Later, I phoned an old friend, who came down to take me for a drink.

"Great to see you man, where have you been?"

"Long story, John. We've got to organize a party fast!"

And we did just that. First, we stole two barrels of beer from the back of a local pub. "They'll never notice," we thought. Then off we went to the local naval base where John worked in the galley. He had both keys and a pass on his windscreen allowing free access to and from the camp. The galley and store rooms of HMS *Goldcrest* were immediately raided, providing a sumptuous feast of cold meats, steak and kidney pies, cheeses, loaves of bread, pats of butter, condiments and sauces. We borrowed beer pumps and gas cylinders from a local hotel, and we were in business. Instant party!

As people arrived the population of Solva expanded by about a hundred. The Bay Hotel had seen nothing like it since VE Day, and the village hall had never before welcomed such a bunch of international freaks, jazz dancing and snogging all over the floor. We were even asked to play in the interval; our mix of hilly billy jazzy blues folk must have been quite a shock. Back at Betty's house, the place was heaving; there were at least fifty cars parked outside and inside people were eating, dancing, playing all sorts of musical instruments, and drinking from anything that would hold liquid – the ornamental crockery, coronation mugs, saucepans, my rowing trophies, teapots, and even the cat's bowl.

"Michael," my mother said, "half the county's here, and Rowland [a local auctioneer and character] has just given me three hundred pounds."

Hardly anyone went home and the party was still swinging until we went back down the Bay Hotel at midday.

Later we reluctantly left the peace, quiet and tranquil beauty of Solva. The long and winding road was singing arias in our ears.

# Chapter 10

# Manchester

My brother Martin, who was still at St David's school, gave me his old guitar as a birthday present. I was very grateful; I didn't have one of my own. I bade the family farewell and hit the road for Birmingham, where I knew a girl who would put me up for a while. A policeman's daughter, she was a lovely girl who used to visit the Community of St David on the Cross Square in St David's. The Ian Campbell Folk Group had one of the best and biggest folk clubs in Britain, and that's where I was heading.

I ended up at a great session on a Sunday night; it was also New Year's Eve and packed out because the guest singer was Martin Carthy. He played a brilliant set of English folk songs accompanied as usual by his trusty Martin 00018 guitar, and towards the end of the set he was accompanied by Dave Swarbrick, the Ian Campbell Group's fiddler. They went on playing in the backstage room afterwards and decided that night to form the duo, Carthy and Swarbrick, who later recorded some great albums and toured worldwide.

Later still, on the road in the Midlands, I was dropped off at a filling station in Wellington and told that it was a good place to get a lift. I was heading for Cardiff, where Wales were playing Ireland that weekend. A huge sign proclaimed 'Jack Kelly's', and I was greeted by the man himself when I walked in. It was snowing quite heavily outside, and he offered me a cup of tea. Jack Kelly was a big man, dressed in a smart grey double-breasted suit and looking like he'd just had a good day at the races. Curled up on a shelf by the window was a big black cat. As he took a bottle of milk from the fridge, Kelly asked, "Have you ever seen the like of this?" With that, the cat leaped from the shelf and grabbed the bottle with its front paws whilst biting at the lid of the bottle and making a loud snarling sound. The man gently prised the bottle from the cat's embrace and we both laughed.

"No," I said. "Is that how he usually drinks his milk?"

"Yes," said Kelly. "But he can't open the door of the fridge yet, thank god, he's a bit too young. Would you like a drink?" indicating a pub across the road through the driving snow. "I'll be closing up in a minute."

"Off to Cardiff for the rugby is it? Sure Ireland will beat the hell out of youse."

"I'm not so sure about that," I said, knowing that Wales would be fielding a very good team.

He'd been eyeing my guitar for a while, and after a couple of pints I had the whole bar singing. Kelly offered to put me up for the night, saying it was too late to go on and the roads would be blocked with snow, which they were. He had a house full of children around my age and a diminutive wife. Their son Damien, or Ned as he was known, was an art student in Newport. I stayed for a day or so, until the snow melted, and Kelly took me down to the filling station on the A5 where he got me a lift on a lorry to Cardiff. "Call in any time and good luck," he said. I'll never forget his black cat, or his welcome.

Cardiff was jam-packed with rugby supporters as usual, despite the snowy weather. I went to the Tavistock where I knew I could earn a few quid and drink cider for free. I can't remember where I stayed the night of the game, which Wales won, but the next morning I was out on the street early and I went for breakfast in Caroline Street. It was icy cold, and I wondered where to go next. Southern Spain came to mind as I drank another coffee.

When the pubs opened, I went to the Great Western Hotel, just across the road by the railway station. The pub was already full of students from Manchester University, among whom was my old pal Charles Oliver Bethel from the Moulders days. He was now studying English up north. The inevitable singing and drinking session ensued, and, later, now on a bus bound for Manchester, Charlie told me about all the drinking clubs in Manchester and about the fortune I was going to make with him as my manager! Up to a point, Bethel was absolutely right, for Manchester was the city that launched me as a professional folk singer.

Charlie lived in a tower block at Owen's Park, the student village in Withington. He had a small room on the eighth floor, where I slept on the floor most nights. Charlie got the bed, because he paid the rent. Food was no problem. There were two dining rooms with a ticket system, and each student was issued with a book of tickets at the beginning of term. They were entitled to three meals a day, but most students skipped lunch and sometimes breakfast. (The students of the eighth floor common room used to play poker all night and never got up early enough for breakfast.) I would collect all the unused tickets and change the numbers to suit the appropriate meal, which was usually dinner.

At noon every day we went to our HQ at the Union bar, then at 3 o'clock in the afternoon we'd cross the road to a drinking club, before returning to the Union in the evening for a meal and whatever came next. Charlie did get me quite a few gigs in the late-night boozing clubs and we made some money; I was playing strip clubs, gay clubs, folk clubs, gambling clubs; you name it. One lunch-time we were ambling up to the Union when we saw a long powder-blue American car parked in a crowd of people outside. It was a Ford Sunliner. Inside sat a guy with long peroxide blonde hair, wearing a mink coat, Stetson hat, and Texan cowboy boots, and smoking a huge cigar; Jimmy Savile had come to entertain the students at lunchtime in the great hall. Savile was a DJ from Leeds who did *Top of the Pops*, which was recorded just up the road in a BBC studio in a converted church at Rusholm. We weren't interested in Jimmy Savile or pop music, so we just followed our usual routine of boozing and singing in the bar.

In the bar, too, was a guitarist from Edinburgh, Ian Chisholm. He was a very good guitar picker and keen on country blues and traditional folk songs. We would play the folk clubs together, sometimes with an American girl, Eleanor Raskin from New York city. Eleanor had a very powerful voice and was involved in the folk song revival in New York. She was married to Jonah; both were studying for their doctorates after graduating from Colombia University. Eleanor and Jonah were regulars in the folk clubs of Greenwich village and had seen all the up-and-coming singers arrive upon the scene: Joan Baez, Jack Elliott, Phil Ochs, and a young kid they called Bobby Zimmerman.

The session in the union bar was going strong, and the bar was packed. The entertainment secretary was Terry Ellis, and his right-hand man was Chris Wright; they later went on to found Chrysalis records. They had a mate from Hull named Doug D'Arcy, who introduced me to a guy who was with Jimmy Savile, Richard Reese Edwards, a tall, well-dressed, ex-public school boy, now into showbiz and looking for a big act to promote. And he said he'd just found it – me! It's fortunate that I tend to take things with a pinch of salt, and always travel with a guitar and a bottle of chilli sauce. I was even more of a cynic then, and less of a gourmet!

"Can you write songs?"

"Yes."

"Have you heard Donovan?"

"No. Who's that?"

Amazement. "He's got a regular spot on *Ready Steady Go*."

"What's that?"

"Oh my god! Would you like to go on *Top of the Pops*? I might be able to get you on. Have you made any records?"

"No."

"Oh, would you like to make a record?"

"You'd better talk to me," said a pissed-up Charlie. "I'm his manager!"

By this time, Savile had the students in the palm of his hand, even the piss takers. He'd stripped down to a pair of blue-striped boxer shorts and everyone was in stitches.

A few days later, a student I vaguely knew came into the Union refectory where I was with my girlfriend Sue from Liverpool. He told me he'd been sent to bring me to Reese Edwards's office downtown. Later, in a quite well-furnished and professional-looking office near Albert Square, Edwards offered me a contract. The plan was that I'd go off and write some songs, and he played me Donovan's 'Catch the Wind' saying "Can you write like that?"

"Easily," I replied.

The deal was that I'd sign a contract with his company, Anglo-Continental Enterprises. He'd get me work, including all the Mecca dance halls in the north of England, and his company would finance the production of a single written and recorded by me which would be released on a major label. The company would find me a decent flat and pay me a weekly retainer. This was a good deal; I was sleeping on Charlie's floor and only had the clothes I stood up in, which were mostly borrowed. My guitar was cheap and knackered, so they would also buy me a new twelve-string electric acoustic guitar, a Hagstrom. Much to my amazement, all of this actually happened.

By this time I was staying with a drama student, Susan Triesman, from London. She was lovely, highly intelligent and very talented, and I found out later that she was related to the famous actress Sarah Bernhardt. She had a flat near the University, and that is where I started to write songs. I had written 'Walter's Song' – which later became 'Cân Walter' – and 'I saw a field' in Solva some years previously, but I wrote 'Did I Dream', my first single, in Sue's flat in Manchester. I took the lyrics to Reese Edwards's office and played the song for him. A couple of days later we were recording it in Tony Pike's Studio in London, with John Paul Jones (who later became a member of Led Zeppelin) producing. The song was a simple ballad, a love song, to which he added a string ensemble at a later session.

I was taken to sign a contract with Decca, where I met another cigar-smoker, Dick Rowe, who was one of the bosses. "We love your record here at Decca, Mike. You're going a long way in the music business." It seems that he'd recently turned down the Beatles – I was the lucky boy!

Reese Edwards took me to meet Andrew Loog Oldham, manager of the Stones, with whom he'd been at school, and he also arranged for me to audition for Vicky Wickham, the producer of *Ready Steady Go*. He was trying to hype me onto the pop market in a big way. I regarded all of this whimsically, as if it wasn't really happening; the nitty gritty was the slog of travelling almost every day and playing in Mecca dance halls and beat clubs every night, on my own with just an electric twelve-string guitar. I've never driven and so it was mostly trains and buses, and the occasional plane down to London if in a hurry. I did some provincial television – Granada, Tyne Tees, Border, STV – to promote the record, but the big network programmes were unavailable and without these a record single could not take off.

I played all the big R & B clubs in Manchester, Leeds, Sheffield, Liverpool, Hull and Birmingham. This was difficult, because it was the time when the Blues band boom reached its fruition and rapidly

*Playing a Hagstrom 12-string that I bought in Manchester in 1965 after signing to Decca*

turned into a Soul music boom. Tin Pan Alley was cashing in on what had been a much more basic, blues-orientated form of music, and you had bands like The Spencer Davis Group, The Yardbirds, The Stones, Manfred Man and The Animals turning out overt pop chart rubbish. The Brit pop thing was going global in the wake of The Beatles, The Stones and Carnaby Street. The business men had got it all neatly tied up and packaged again, and those who played along couldn't go wrong. Fortunes were rolling in every direction, mainly into the bank accounts of those Jewish business men who have always controlled the music industry and the rag trade which goes hand in glove with it.

Having a single record on the market, even if it didn't chart, was always good for a singer, as the booking agent could use it to con promoters into booking an artist he'd perhaps never heard of. I got a lot of work on the strength of 'Did I Dream', and Reese Edwards got me a lot of publicity in the Manchester press and in provincial rags like the *Western Mail* and *Liverpool Daily Post*.

One day he had a phone call from TWW in Cardiff, who held the commercial broadcasting licence for Wales and the West before HTV. I was in the office at the time.

"Euryn Ogwen Williams? Do you know him?"

"No," I said. "Can't say I do."

"He wants to know if you sing in Welsh."

"Oh, yes, I used to years ago. I can remember some old folk songs, I think."

Before long I found myself on a train to Cardiff, practising some Welsh folk songs I hadn't sung since I was a boy soprano. (You could do that on trains in those days; they had those lovely private compartments that were virtually sound proof.) By the time we pulled into Cardiff General, as it was called then, I'd learnt or remembered five songs. I took a taxi up to Pontcanna fields for my first meeting with Esmé Lewis, whose record of Welsh folk songs I'd listened to so avidly all those years ago as a schoolboy in Solva. She ran through the songs with me, and I can remember singing 'Ar y Bryn roedd Pren' and 'Dau Rosyn Coch', which I later recorded for Warner Brothers, 'Ar Lan y Môr' and two other songs. These were recorded in two sessions and broadcast on an evening programme called *Y Dydd*. I didn't get to see them in Manchester and I didn't get to record any more for the programme. However, they thought it such a good idea to have a bit of music on an evening news and current affairs programme that they got Dafydd Iwan Jones, a young student from the College of Architecture in Cardiff, to take my place. It must have been more economical than to have to pay my larger fee and expenses.

Reese Edwards was always trying to get me publicity by tying me up with people in the public eye, such as Jimmy Savile, an actress from *Coronation Street* called Jennie Moss and Mandy Rice-Davies, who was in cabaret up north fresh from the Profumo scandal. Mandy was from Pont-iets originally, and she'd hired some professional writers in London to put a cabaret together for her, containing semi-blue songs and jokes relating to the Profumo affair. She was doing very well when Richard introduced me to her after one of her shows. She invited me to her hotel in Manchester, and I went up one morning after she'd phoned me. We got on really well, and we used to go out for meals and drinks. Sometimes I'd row her around the boating lake in a Manchester park; she seemed to enjoy the anonymity of being with a scruffy young folk singer and she dressed down as well. She had short hair and usually wore exotic wigs and expensive clothes and jewellery. When she was with me she wore jeans and a zipper jacket and no one seemed to recognize her. This she enjoyed very much.

I had a nervous breakdown at this time. In fact, I thought I'd had a heart attack when I collapsed one afternoon in the Students' Union and had to be taken by ambulance to Manchester Royal Infirmary. Edwards came and told the doctors I'd been on drugs – which I hadn't – and just as they were about to throw me out, Mandy arrived in a Rolls Royce Limo with her uniformed chauffeur.

"This boy's mine!" she said very aggressively. "He's coming with me. Fuck off Richard. You're a little bastard." And to the chauffeur "Pick him up, George, and follow me!"

She took me to a good hotel, booked me in, and then tucked me up in bed. A doctor came and diagnosed a vasivegal attack: a shut down of a very important part of the nervous system. I'd been overworking, drinking too much, and keeping late nights in Mr Smith's club, where George Best, the footballer, would hold court all night surrounded by his harem. Jimmy Savile also hung out there. It was a posh place, and it was only because I knew people that I was allowed in. I never used to dress up – far from it! Mandy sent the doctor every day for two weeks until I recovered and she paid all the bills. I was very grateful to her – she's a great lady. I've never seen her since, but I'd like to repay her kindness someday.

After this breakdown I didn't feel the same. I felt weak and paranoid, worried that it might happen again, and the noise and bustle of the city was too much for me. I didn't go out much – a bit of a problem since I had to make a living. Richard Reese Edwards didn't bother me. I think Mandy had had words with him, possibly threatening him with the Krays! Fortunately, I had some money stashed away and so I was alright for a while. I moved in with Dave, a student, who used to drive me down the M1 to London in his red Triumph Spitfire. Dave had a spare room, and so at least I had a quiet place in a flat in leafy Withington village. There was a popular pub, the Red Lion just round the corner. I was getting stronger and able to eat more normally; the breakdown had ruined my digestive system and I couldn't eat properly for a long time.

One day, I went to the Art College to hear Pete Brown reading poetry. I didn't think much of him or his poetry; he was trying to jump on the bandwagon of the 'Liverpool scene' as exemplified by Roger McGough, Adrian Henri, Brian Patten et al. The college caretaker, who found Brown in a broom cupboard having sex with a girl student, wasn't too keen on him either. This is when I met Tessa Bulman, who was to be the mother of Wizzy and Bethan my eldest daughters. It must have been the hand of fate, because if I hadn't been at the Art College that day we'd probably never have met and our lives would have taken totally different courses.

Tessa was from Carlisle and she was eighteen years old. She was studying sculpture and was one of the best students in the Art School; good enough for Elizabeth Frink, a visiting tutor, to have pinched her flying horses from Tessa. We got on famously, and I soon moved in to her flat on Cheatham Hill. I was beginning to get back into the folk clubs around Manchester, and I soon got a job in the biggest and most popular club in the north of England, the Manchester Sports Guild. I was the host on Sunday nights, when I had to sing a couple of songs, then introduce the main act, which could have been Bill Monroe's Blue Grass Boys, Julie Felix, The McPeake Family, The Dubliners, Ian Campbell, Alex Campbell, Sonny Terry and Brownie McGhee, Lightnin' Hopkins, Ewan McColl and Peggy Seeger, Jesse (San Francisco Bay) Fuller. The list goes on and on! They were great times, and good experience and exposure for me too.

Later, I opened my own clubs, one in Bolton at the Pack Horse on Sunday nights, and the other at the Shakespeare off Piccadilly on Fridays. I was making decent bread at last, and Tessa was pregnant with our first daughter. We moved to a flat next to the J & J club, which was the university's unofficial R & B Club, run by Chris Wright and Terry Ellis. It was a mad house – Geno Washington, Victor Brox Blues Train, Spencer Davis, The Yardbirds, John Mayall (then with

Eric Clapton). Most of the best R & B bands played the J & J and you could get in for five bob!

When Wizz (Isobel Eiliona) was born, I bought a huge wicker basket on the Stockport Road, which Tessa, who is brilliant with a sewing machine, lined with lilac gingham. This was Wizzy's crib. When we went to the J & J club, we simply passed her over the garden wall, and the girls in the cloakroom baby sat while we danced to some of the best music ever played in Britain. Wizz was born in Withington hospital, and when I was visiting Tessa there I went for an eye test. It was discovered that I had photophobia – an eye condition where too much light is let in to the retina. I used to get a lot of headaches, especially in bright sunlight, and ever since I've worn tinted lenses

The presence of a baby had changed our lives considerably and we started to think about moving back to the country, from where we had both originated – Tessa from Cumbria and me from north Pembrokeshire. During this time, I played many of the folk clubs around England; at the time there weren't many in Wales. I also played the second and third Cambridge Folk Festivals. The second was particularly memorable for the presence of Rev. Gary Davis, a Gibson J200-toting ragtime guitar guru. He was a giant of a man, blind, but what a singer, what a presence. He sat in the beer tent all afternoon, showing would-be ragtime guitarists licks and tricks for tots of whisky. I travelled to London on the train the next day to perform with him on Sunday evening at the Marquee Club in Wardour Street. There was only Gary Davis and me on the bill that night, and it was a great gig – even better than the festival. He had two young people acting as his guides – much to my surprise they turned out to be Richard and Linda Thompson.

★ ★ ★

Eleanor and Jonah Raskin had both graduated, she in American Studies and he in English Literature. Ian Chisholm, who had introduced me to the music of Bert Jansch, who was still in Edinburgh then, graduated in Physics and went to work for the BBC in London. The scene had changed, people were moving – so was I but to where? (As far as I know, Ian is a boffin at the BBC in London as far as I know and if you read this Ian please get in touch. Eleanor Raskin is a lawyer in Albany USA, while Jonah is an author of many books and a professor at Sonoma University California.)

The chance meeting with Charlie Bethel on that ice cold morning after a rugby international in Cardiff gave me the wherewithal and opportunity to 'graduate' as a folk singer and guitarist. At the time, Manchester was probably the epicentre of the folk and blues scene; it certainly had more clubs and a bigger audience than anywhere else in Europe. I have to mention some of the best singers that I heard there: the late Harry Boardman, a great traditional singer; Little Tommy Yates; Frank Duffy – also a host at the MSG; and Mary Little from Stockport. Clubs such as the Twisted Wheel, The Oasis, the Yungfrau and the Manchester Cavern were the launching pads for many musicians. It's strange that I had to go to such a dirty old town to bear fruit. Long live Manchester!

# Chapter 11

# Return Journey
## (Back to Solva)

Many thoughts sailed through my head as I walked down Solva hill that day in late spring. I hadn't been home for years, but the same old feeling came over me as I strolled down that green leafy tunnel. The high mossy bank on the Gribyn side was a profusion of wild flowers, fern, blackthorn and whitethorn, red and white campion, lady's lace, elder, forget me not, wild roses and cow parsley; it was all still there, unchanged, the familiar herbaceous scents, the buzz of insects and birdsong. Below on the right side of the valley there was an abundance of wild undergrowth and I could pick out the familiar sound of the rippling river in the bottom. Above hung a cerulean sky, hazed with wood smoke.

I crossed the granite bridge near the ruined smithy and lime kilns where I used to go with Dada to watch Johnny Jenkins *y gof* shoeing horses many years before. As I write today, the smithy has been redeveloped into a large house, one of the many B&Bs in modern Solva. We natives would never have thought to convert that old ruin into anything; strange are the minds of outsiders to the likes of us natives. Tommy Bevan's house on the right of the bridge still stood then, and I turned right up the narrow lane to Cornel Pwmp and Prendergast with its scattered row of cottages nestling under the untamed hillside. Below the road lay orchards and gardens enclosed by high stone walls, with the river running beyond through trees.

I had rented Rose Cottage from an elderly English lady, one of the first colonists. She had become too old to live by herself and had gone to live with her daughter in Haverfordwest. Tessa and our new daughter had travelled from Manchester by train a few days earlier – all our worldly possessions in one bag and Wizzy in her laundry basket. I'd played a gig in London, then another in Swindon folk club the night before. It must have been a Saturday.

Rose Cottage was very small, one up one down, a tiny kitchen at the back, a small flower bed in the front and a rustic arch over the doorway covered in red roses and purple clematis. Opposite, a wooden gate in the wall led to steep steps, an overgrown garden and the river. (Dai the bomb, an old school friend, lived in Chapel House next door. He's one of the last locals in Prendergast.) It was great to see Tessa and Wizz again; we were such a close knit family in those days. This must have been a very different experience for Tessa, who came from Carlisle in Cumbria and had spent most of her life there before going at seventeen to Manchester Art College where she'd studied for two years. Nevertheless, she was a country girl and had been raised with horses and dogs.

I was still weak after the nervous breakdown, and one of the first things I did was visit the doctor, Pat Gillam, who had been in the Royal Navy, and whose father had been a surgeon in Haverfordwest hospital at the same time my mother had nursed there. He examined me, hummed and ha'd and gave me bottle of little white pills called Valium. Later I went to visit one of my mother's old nursing colleagues, Auntie Beryl Vidler, who prescribed a traditional remedy for my condition. She must have concluded that I'd been consuming too much alcohol and gave me a recipe of pearl barley, honey and lemon. It had to be boiled up in a huge cauldron then drunk as hot as possible 'to flush out the system'. I drank a pint of this brew every morning for two years, and it worked. Unfortunately, so did Dr Gillam's prescription; I became a Valium addict for eight years, and it took two years to kick the habit!

Unbelievably, this was to be my most creative period as a songwriter. I had been more interested in playing the guitar and singing collected songs or others from traditional sources, but under the original instigation of Richard Reese Edwards, I involuntarily joined the ranks of singer songwriters (protest) along with Tom Paxton, Phil Ochs, Ewan McColl, Woody Guthrie and Dylan, amongst many others, including the unsung heroes of whom no one's ever heard.

Tessa and I had little money, and so I bought a bow saw with which I walked out every morning up the Felinganol road to the old pine wood. There was a load of timber lying around, blown down by storms, and that became our firewood. This too was therapeutic, helping to build up my muscles whilst the fresh sea air pumped my lungs clean.

We were lucky enough to have a transistor radio, and, to my surprise, one wavelength broadcasted in Welsh – Radio Cymru from Cardiff. From time to time they would play music, really bad music, old American pop songs crudely translated into the Welsh language, and sung by embarrassing lady singers, some of whom I later enjoyed the privilege of meeting.

One morning, I decided to write a song in Welsh, even though I hadn't spoken the language for years. My first attempt was a translation of 'Walter's Song'. I'd heard about a teacher, W. R. Evans, who lived in Fishguard. He was also a poet and he'd written several humorous songs which had been published and broadcasted on the radio. I'd already written a first draft of 'Cân Walter', but I wasn't pleased with it. My poor grasp of the Welsh language and my immaturity as a lyricist meant that it didn't do justice to the original. I went to W.R.'s house one Sunday evening, where he took my words apart and then put them back together, and that was 'Cân Walter'. Not only did W. R. Evans enthuse me, but he was also a source of cultural revelation. Just a few days later I wrote 'Tryweryn': a very simple song in every respect, but a song so strong that it touches people's hearts. And so it should! I had stumbled on a burning issue that had angered the soul of the Welsh nation.

Soon afterwards I found the names of some Welsh record companies – Cambrian, Dryw, and Welsh-Teldisc. I still had an acetate of the session at Tony Pike's with Mike Meeropol, Eleanor Raskin's friend from New York City, and I made an appointment to play it to Mrs Olwen Edwards who ran Teldisc. She wasn't interested, but the BBC was. I'd also phoned their offices in Cardiff and been given an appointment with Meredydd Evans, head of light entertainment. I was met at the General Accident Building, Newport Road, Cardiff, by a lady called Ruth Price who invited me up to her office on the fourth floor where we listened to the songs. "Go and get Hywel," she told her secretary, a sexy chick called Glenys. Into the room strode a very tall young man in a sharp grey suit, pink shirt and floral tie. "This is Hywel Gwynfryn," said Ruth. "He will translate your songs." There stood Gwynfryn, then a virgin to the BBC, with that big, gap-toothed Llangefni smile; we clicked there and then.

The outcome was a TV spot on a music programme, *Hob y Deri Dando*. This show, like most of BBC Cymru's music shows, was recorded in an old chapel that had been converted into a studio on Broadway, in Roath. I sang 'The Vulture and the Dove', retitled 'Yr Eryr a'r Golomen', and 'Love Owed', retitled 'Ond Dof yn Ôl' and later recorded on the Warner Brothers album *Outlander*. Soon afterwards, Dennis Rees of Dryw records in Swansea asked me to record an extended play record of four songs at their studio in Swansea – the very studio where Dylan Thomas had recorded his famous poetry records in the 1950s. The record was an instant and unexpected success, and I received so many requests to perform around Wales that I had to get a telephone. The gigs rolled in – small concerts, television, radio and *Nosweithiau Llawen*. These were exciting times, times of change, and it was now that I really began to learn my craft.

There was a band in Wales called Y Blew who played and sang in the style of The Spencer Davis group, but it was very difficult to record rock music in Wales at that time because there were no multi-track tape records or the mixing desks that go with them. Even at the BBC the studios were only equipped with mono tape recorders and so we didn't have stereo sound. For this reason, I opted for a more simplistic style of music, a 'folky' acoustic sound, which was well suited to recording on the available equipment. In any case, I liked the sound; it suited my style and was easier to reproduce in live performance.

Our life in Solva remained largely unchanged, apart from the telephone. We lived a very simple life, watching Wizzy grow, sawing logs each morning and sitting around the fire at night. We didn't even have a television. Tessa did her sculpture, and I did a lot of painting and drawing when not practising the guitar picking.

That summer of 1967 I decided to form a rock band. My brother, who was studying law at the LSE in London, played bass guitar and we advertised for a drummer in *Melody Maker*. Dougie arrived carrying a small case which contained a pair of socks and underpants, a spare vest and numerous bottles of pills. He'd only just been let out of a mental institution, but that didn't stop him from being a brilliant drummer in the Phil Seaman, Max Roach, modern jazz style. Sometimes he'd sit for hours on the floor in the corner of the sitting-room, and if you said, "OK, Dougie. Are you alright?" He'd say, "Yeah, man – I'm just talking to Lester" (Young, the great be-bop saxophonist), or he'd be having silent conversations with Dizzy

Gillespie or Charlie Parker. His drums followed later by rail; Dougie was a truly great drummer and didn't mind playing Dylan, the Beatles, Otis Redding or Frank Zappa. The band was called The Buzz. It was good fun, but it had little to do with my own music, which we never played. I was in the middle of a creative process, and it was difficult to judge what it really sounded like without a tape recorder. Later I borrowed a Sony quarter-track stereo recorder from a sailor friend who'd bought it in Hong Kong – they weren't on sale here at that time – and I had great fun under a blanket in the bedroom making multi-tracked demos.

I read in *The Melody Maker* that The Beatles had started Apple, and that they had a shop and office in Baker Street. The article said that The Beatles were keen to hear songs by unknowns like me and wanted to help musicians and songwriters. So I edited the demo tapes into two tapes of about ten songs and sent them up to London. For weeks, nothing happened and, eventually, I phoned Apple to be told that they'd received thousands of tapes and they'd try to find mine. They sounded blasé and uninterested. I phoned a week later, and the voice said that although they'd found the tapes they had no means of playing them. I'd double-tracked on the quarter inch and they didn't have a ¼-inch recorder; if you played it on an ordinary machine you would hear two tracks going forward and the other two backwards. It may make a great sound, but the words will be totally incomprehensible! All I could do was to take the machine to Mohamed.

At the time, I had a friend called Giles Chaplin. Giles lived in a derelict mansion in the Preseli hills, and he used to drive us to gigs in the back of a grey open-backed pick-up truck. I happened to meet him at a gig one night, and he told me that he was taking a girlfriend to London. I was welcome to tag along, but I'd have to ride in the back. So in the back I went, all the way from Solva to Baker Street which was more than 300 miles!

By the track above Prengas, Solva
in the late 60s

*Solva, 1968*

I was quite smartly dressed, in my brother's interview suit and a black overcoat. I told my story to the receptionist at Apple and after a while I was directed to a room upstairs where sat a smartly dressed white guy and a flamboyant black chick surrounded by thousands of boxed audio tapes. Cassette players hadn't been invented then. These two characters were typical London show-biz types; some are useful, but most I found are gofers and hangers-on. They couldn't find my tape, and so I got stuck in. After a while I found the boxes and stuck one of the tapes on the quarter track. They seemed amazed that I'd brought the thing all the way from Wales, although they didn't have a clue where Solva was or how far away it was.

"Dylanish," said the limp wrist in a pink paisley shirt.

"Tim Hardin," said the black chick. I found out later that she was Doris Troy, a backing singer for Dusty Springfield.

They were so disinterested that I started to pack up to go. "Don't go," they said in unison, but too late – Stevens was out the door and off towards Soho for a drink. I'd wasted enough time and was very thirsty.

When I got back to Rose Cottage, I still felt disappointed and wondered what I might do next. Once again, I filled my time with cutting wood, a bit of fishing, playing guitar and writing more songs. I was also doing quite a few gigs around rural Wales. The Welsh pop scene seemed to be going from strength to strength in its own parochial way, but we seemed to live in a different world. There was little Welsh spoken openly in Solva, and it showed me that a great change had occurred in my absence.

One day I had to go to Corwen, way up north on the A5. The gig was in the old Eisteddfod pavilion. I'd never been to the area before, and I hitch-hiked with my trusty Harmony Sovereign guitar which I'd got from Pete Townsend of The Who, after he'd smashed it up one night. My Uncle Syd who was a brilliant wood carver patched it up for me.

*Some posters from the booming pop scene in Wales during the late 1960s*

**Cymru'n Canu**

DAFYDD IWAN    HEATHER JONES
MIKE STEVENS    Y BARA MENYN
IRIS WILLIAMS    DEWI MORRIS
CÔR AELWYD TREFORYS    YR AWR
PARTI PENILLION PONTRHYDYFEN

Arweinydd: Parch James Jones, Caerfyrddin;
Llywydd: Gwynfor Evans AS

**Y Tabernacl, Treforys**
**7 pm, Sadwrn**
**Rhagfyr 13, 1969**

Rhaglen - 6ch

PENDRO PENFRO

NOSON FAWR Y FLWYD...

GWALLT YN Y GWYNT

AP 'SACHLIAN A LLUDW'

Neuadd y Farchnad Hwlffordd 9·00
Nos Lun I Nos Iau
wythnos y 'Steddfod
Bwyd ysgafn o 8·30 ymlaen

Meic Stevens
James Hogg
Tebot Piws

Y Diliau
Yr Atgyfodiad
Mici Plwm
a grŵp rhydd newydd danlli

Rhew Poeth

Tocynnau 70c i'w cael ym mhabell
Cwmni Theatr Cymru
ar faes yr Eisteddfod

Prynwch docyn yn ystod y dydd i fod yn siwr o le

The place was packed; I'd never played to such a huge audience in Wales. Everyone spoke Welsh, and I didn't hear a word of English all night until I met a pretty young blonde backstage. I was sure that I'd seen her before and soon realized that it was Heather Jones, even though she'd dyed her hair. I'd come across Heather once before on the *Hob y Deri Dando* show; that time she sat strumming her guitar at the front of an all-girl group that looked and sounded like a school choir. As usual, her father was with her; he always drove her to gigs and was her chaperone. She was also accompanied by a tall, dark, good-looking boy who spoke natural Welsh and was called Geraint Jarman. They were very interested in my music, and asked me a lot of questions about my life, where I lived and so on. Geraint was still in school and said he was going to be a poet. Heather was a first-year student at Caerleon college, where she was studying to become a teacher. I liked them and their youthful enthusiasm, and so I invited them to stay with us at Rose Cottage anytime.

I often went to Cardiff, and a few times I arranged to meet Geraint. Midweek, he would often go to a poetry club run by another would-be poet, Peter Finch, in a pub called the Marchioness of Bute. I went there once with him and sang a couple of songs; it was quite free and easy, a bit like a folk club and full of very hairy people. Heather and Geraint eventually came to Rose Cottage, and, one evening round the fire, the conversation turned to the dearth of new Welsh songs and the general lack of direction and quality. The people at the BBC and HTV in Cardiff were probably trying their best, but it seemed there was no one with the vision, talent, or experience to get a credible music show together. We took the mick out of the amateur girlie groups which the BBC talent scouts would find warbling away in *nosweithiau llawen* in the village halls and vestries of the verdant vales of Carmarthen, Ceredigion, or the rocky mountains of Gwynedd: Y Gemau, Y Perlau, Y Pelydrau and so forth. Not to mention the

'Hogia' (the boys) – Hogia Bryngwran, Hogia'r Wyddfa, Hogia Llandegái – and many others too numerous to count who strummed cheap Japanese guitars and sang Welsh translations of 'She'll be Coming Round the Mountain' and other antiquated Anglo-American popular songs. These groups had been influenced by Triawd y Coleg, a group of students from Bangor University led by Meredydd Evans, who by this time was head of light entertainment at the BBC in Cardiff. We all knew and loved Merêd, who was obviously hell bent on producing some passably good programmes of Welsh music, and we knew others who produced Welsh music shows at HTV. Both Geraint and I were keen to write more songs in Welsh; there was money there for the taking. I was mostly interested in writing in English, but London was going to be a hard nut to crack. One night in Rose Cottage we were sitting round the fire making parodies of the music of these eccentric singing groups, and Geraint came up with a name – Hogia Bryn Sultana. Heather would have to dress up as a boy though. So I suggested Bara Menyn (Bread and Butter), and they agreed with much mirth. The plan was for me to phone up a television producer and say that I'd heard a fantastic new group in Aberystwyth University or somewhere who'd written some great new songs. Then we fell about laughing and went to bed.

Next morning I phoned Euryn Ogwen Williams, a director at HTV, and laid the scam on him. He took it like a 10-pound salmon – hook, line and sinker. Heather and Geraint were a little taken aback when I told them what I'd done, but I said we'd do it anyway. We'd just have to knock some of the parodies we'd created the previous night into shape – a few songs that's all, which would be easy enough. That very morning, we wrote Bara Menyn's first four songs.

"What about the TV show? What will they say when they catch us out and find it's nothing but a joke?"

"Don't worry," I said. "Oggie won't mind, besides the songs are better than most of the shit they broadcast."

A week later we did the show at HTV, all dressed up in unusual clothes. Heather had a huge white wide-brimmed hat and a long dress, Geraint wore a false Zappata moustache and brandished a gun, and I had my hair permed. We must have gone down well, because soon we were receiving letters and phone calls inviting us to perform all over Wales. Dennis Rees of Dryw records whisked us into the studio, and the first Bara Menyn record became a best seller. "What about my poetry?" cried Geraint. "What about my assault on Joan Baez?" wailed Heather. "What the fuck!" said I.

The first record was followed by *Rhagor o'r Bara Menyn* (More Bread and Butter), which also became a best seller. More and more work rolled in, and the fireside joke became one of the most successful singing groups in Wales, all in a matter of two or three months. The Bara Menyn may have been a prank, but big money was landing on us. We did hundreds of concerts and dozens of TV and radio shows while the records, much to our embarrassment, were played constantly on Radio Cymru. I blame it on humour, wine, a couple of joints and the Solva air.

Bara Menyn was fun, fun, fun. Nothing like it had hit Wales before. In our time, we were zany and outrageous, funny and fashionable, young and good looking. People couldn't quite make us out, neither could we, but inadvertently we started up something new in Welsh music that was soon followed by groups like Y Tebot Piws (The purple teapot), and Y Dyniadon Ynfyd Hirfelyn Tesog (the summery sultry mad dwarves).

We were a part of the biggest musical upsurge Wales had seen since the Methodist Revival. Meanwhile, the greatest political movement since Owain Glyndŵr was also breaking. And we all would play our part in it.

*Bara Menyn's first performance at the HTV studios*

# Chapter 12

# 'Take Something With You'

One day in 1967 Kevin Westlake called at Rose Cottage. Kevin was an Irish lad from Haverfordwest who'd played drums with me years ago in the first band at the Trewern Arms in Nevern. I hadn't seen him since, although I'd heard that he'd gone to art college in Cardiff. It seemed that Kevin had soon got tired of college and gone up to London to find work as a drummer. Evidently he'd put himself about the music scene and he'd landed a job in Little Richard's band, which was doing a UK tour at that time. One of the biggest entrepreneurs on the London music scene had seen Kevin playing. Georgio Gomelski was Russian, and he had promoted blues artists like Muddy Waters, Sonny Boy Williamson, Bo Diddley and Howlin' Wolf among a host of other American blues giants. He'd also managed The Rolling Stones, Jeff Beck and Eric Clapton in their early days.

The modern music scene both in America and Britain was changing fast. At the time London was the front runner, due to the influence of the Beatles and Stones. The big record companies had decided that the R & B boom was just about finished and that psychedelic rock was going to be the next big breadwinner. Warner Brothers, CBS, RCA and others were busy setting up subsidiary labels known as 'independents', largely a business ploy to dispel the stodgy, old-fashioned image they had among a young new breed of record buyers. It was also the turn of a new breed of record producer who had emerged on the scene with great success; people like Andrew Loog Oldham the manager of The Stones, who started his Immediate label as a subsidiary of Decca, and who had recently missed signing the Beatles and wanted to get back on track and grab a piece of the action. Also, the hippy thing had just taken off in San Francisco and was gradually catching on here in an esoteric way, mainly amongst London musicians and their friends and lovers. The writing was on the wall, and the big record companies and even the boringly straight merchant bankers who knew little about rock music could read it clearly.

In the States, Georgio Gomelski had unearthed some of the greatest blues singers in history, bringing them on package tours to Europe to the delight of a large audience of young blues fans, myself included, who had never dreamed of seeing them in the flesh. Many of us thought that the originators of modern R & B, Muddy, Howlin' Wolf, Sonny Boy and John Lee Hooker, were long gone, decrepit or dead. Georgio's R & B package tours were original, sensational, beautifully real and sold out! So were his clubs in the London area – The Crawdaddy and Klooks Kleek – which he'd originally used to promote these blues legends and up-and-coming R & B stars like Beck, Clapton and The Stones.

Georgio made a deal with these Mississippi bluesmen; they'd fly over alone and he'd organize 'pick up' bands to back them up on tour. The members of these bands were pulled from a small pool of young London musicians, who were themselves blues fanatics and had heard the original 45 rpm records at that time only sold in the USA. Amongst these musicians were Eric Clapton, Jeff Beck, Charlie Watts, John Mayall, Brian Belshaw, Jim Cregan, Georgie Fame, to name just a few. Georgio had street cred in the music business in London; by cutting a deal with Polydor records (then a subsidiary of the mighty German classical label Deutsche Grammophon) he founded the independent Marmalade label. And Kevin Westlake had been signed to Marmalade.

Another friend from Haverfordwest, Peter Swales (son of Joffre Swales, that well-known local band leader and music teacher) was also working for Marmalade as a production assistant. Georgio had formed a new wave psychedelic band, The Blossom Toes, whose members had worked in The Crawdaddy and had toured as back-up musicians for the American blues giants. Kevin was the drummer, and the rest were Brian Belshaw, bass, with Brian Godding and Jim Cregan on guitars. Marmalade had rented a posh house in Chelsea for the band. No. 6 Holmead Road lay off the Fulham Road right opposite Chelsea football ground, and it was there that The Blossom Toes lived, along with Peter Swales, Jim Cregan, Brian Belshaw and Gary Farr who was also signed to the Marmalade label.

It was becoming obvious that I had to get out of Wales again and up to London where my songs would stand a chance of being heard in the right ears. Kevin impressed upon me that there were all sorts of things going on and that this was an opportune time. There was room for me at Holmead Road, and the other guys who lived there said I could stay rent free. Marmalade was paying anyway. Tessa and I discussed his proposition, and we both agreed it would be for the best – if things went right. A big IF! Sadly and reluctantly, I packed some of the clothes she'd designed and made for me, picked up my Pete Townsend guitar and made that same old bus journey up Solva hill to Haverfordwest railway station, leaving Tessa and Wizz to fend for themselves at Rose Cottage. I can't remember that journey apart from feeling torn between my family in Solva and the prospect of living in London, a dubious and unattractive idea. I felt emotional and exceedingly vulnerable as I rode up that familiar hill once again.

No. 6 Holmead Road was a Georgian terraced house. An arched front door, smart bright red gloss, with a leaded fanlight, led to a long hall, and to the right was a spacious and opulent sitting-room furnished in sage green with a period chaise longue, Queen Anne chairs and a huge sofa. All the fittings and the white marble fireplace were gilded, and there were sage-green ropes with huge gold tassels to pull the thick, floor-length, sage-green velvet curtains back. The hallway led to a spacious and wide-windowed kitchen with a large flagged patio to the rear. Upstairs there were two more floors, each with two large bedrooms and a bathroom.

Kevin was expecting me and he met me at the door as I arrived by black cab from Paddington. "They're all down the pub. Stash your gear in the front bedroom on the first floor and we'll go for a drink." The Rising Sun was conveniently placed a few doors down on the corner of Fulham Road. At the bar stood a crowd of smartly dressed musicians: Big Brian Belshaw; Jim Cregan and his German girlfriend Julia Sachan, who was an artist; and a very good looking and well-built blond guy, Gary Farr – youngest son of Tommy Farr, the famous Welsh boxer of yesteryear who'd gone fifteen rounds with Joe Louis, narrowly missing the world heavyweight title at the Yankee Stadium, New York on 30 August 1937. They all lived at Holmead Road, except for Brian Godding who was married to Angie, the sister of Julie Driscoll who sang with the Brian Auger Trinity, also Marmalade artistes. They were an interesting crowd and they made me feel welcome; I immediately felt at home in their company.

Obviously, a great deal of music was played at the house. The Blossoms had just finished writing their first album *We Are Ever So Clean*, and some close friends, The Action, who were signed to EMI were recording an album at Abbey Road with George Martin. Interestingly, The Action was the only other band he produced at the same time as the Beatles. Reggie King, a miniscule mod who looked a bit like Rod Stewart (one of his arch rivals), was known as the Rodent. He was a brilliant singer and songwriter and he used to bring rough mixes of these sessions to No. 6; they were fantastic and way ahead of anything I'd heard up till then.

Gary Farr was also writing songs for his first Marmalade album. He played a lovely Fender Palomino guitar, which he soon changed for a Martin 12-string better suited to his style, which was aggressive and loud. My finger picking gelled perfectly with his, and we would spend hours sitting cross-legged on the floor working out arrangements on the guitars, Gary with a notebook honing the lyrics, or even writing new songs. Naturally, he asked me to play on *Take Something With You*, the album which gives its title to this chapter. I got the feeling that he'd been looking for a finger-style player and that Kevin had pointed me in his direction. It often works like that in music; one's reputation goes before. The rest of the musicians on the sessions were members of The Action: Ian Whiteman, flute and keyboards; Roger Powell (Quelch), drums; Mike Evans (Ace) on bass; and Reggie King producing, which is what he was good at and had always wanted to do – Georgio and Gary gave him the break. Martin Stone, lead guitarist with The Action, played on one track when I couldn't make it because of a contracted concert at the Brangwyn Hall, Swansea with Bara Menyn (which, once again, was packed out).

The sessions for *Take Something With You* were booked at the Polydor Studio in the Lilly and Skinner building in Oxford Street where Marmalade had their offices. This was a two by four track, Studer-equipped studio. The engineer Klaus was a whizz-kid and he synchronized 2 four tracks, so we had eight tracks and an eight-track mixer, which was very advanced for the time. We recorded half the album there before moving to Advision who had installed a proper eight-track recorder, the first in London.

The sessions were an extension of those held in the sitting-room at Holmead Road; wine, beer, Nepalese black, and the music flowing effortlessly. I'd never played with such good musicians before. This was where modern music should naturally go, waving goodbye to all that sick and hackneyed showbiz pop music. We played great arrangements of wonderful tunes with intelligent and meaningful lyrics – no pretensions, no dots and no bullshit, and all played in the spirit of adventure.

Cat Stevens lived across the Fulham Road from us, and he was recording at the same time. It was all very hush hush; no one knew what they were doing, apart from his own people no one was allowed to go to the studio (Olympic, I think). Anyway, he was a very private and reclusive guy who didn't hang out in the bars, bistros and clubs where the other musicians spent their leisure time – mainly in the wee hours of morning.

We were all friends of Steve Winwood's band, Traffic, who lived in a penthouse apartment near the Cromwell Road air terminal in Earls Court. This was a similar place to Holmead Road, with friends hanging out playing music and smoking hash, drinking and enjoying life, then down to Pye Studios to record all night – another party extension! They also had a place they called The Cottage down in Berkshire. It was supposedly a country retreat, but the parties there were even wilder than anything in London. Traffic were all Brummies or from the Worcester area, and we had a mutual friend who used to come to Rose Cottage in Solva. His name was Gordon Jackson and he too was signed to Marmalade. Gordon made one album on which Traffic played and where most of us made some kind of contribution like backing vocals, rhythm guitar or percussion. These were certainly wild times.

Pete Swales fixed up an appointment for me to see Georgio. I didn't have any demos; I'd foolishly left them in Solva and I had no means of playing them to him, as Nick Golding, the sailor who had loaned me the quarter track Sony, had borrowed it back, got demobbed, and gone to live in Norwich, I knew not where. So nothing came of it. Georgio knew I was an important part of Gary's band and that Gary really didn't want me to leave. So life went on as usual, and the songs remained on a tape in two white boxes on a bookshelf at Rose Cottage.

I did a lot of gigs with Gary, culminating in the Isle of Wight Festival in 1969. Gary's brother Ricky, who was a fly by night of the first water, and the Foulk brothers organized this event. It was the mother and father of every festival in Europe ever since, and of course it was in the same year as Woodstock. The following week, in fact, and loads of freaks who'd been at Woodstock flew over for it. Dylan and The Band were the main attraction, but there were plenty of other major bands there too!

Back at Holmead Road things were changing dramatically. Barry Jenkins, the drummer with The Animals, had moved in drums and all, as well as an American singer-songwriter, Shawn Phillips, who was contracted to RCA. Big stuff! Barry Jenkins had experienced a hard time in California and Australia doing far too much LSD. His head was somewhere else – up his arse probably! He looked like an Indian fakir, a holy man, a mad bedraggled hermit-like character with long straggly hair, a beard and a string of beads around his neck. Barry moved into the same room as Gary, Kevin and me. When he wasn't sleeping, he used to sit cross-legged, carving patterns – psychedelic sort of Celtic curvy whirligigs – on old Gibson SGs. He did one for Eric Clapton and another for Jimi Hendrix amongst others.

Shawn Phillips was a great singer from Fort Worth, Texas. There was no one quite like him except perhaps for Dino Valente, a Californian singer-songwriter. Shawn was an exotic hippy with waist length, dead straight, blond hair, a long green velvet cloak with golden embroidery, and silver and turquoise Navajo jewellery hanging from his neck and wrists. He'd been living in Palermo, Italy, getting his music together and meditating. In fact, he brought his meditation box with him; it was slightly bigger than a tea chest with brightly coloured Tantric and cabalistic symbols painted on the outside. Shawn would sit in this box for hours, chanting and making strange sounds. He was the first person I saw snorting heroin. Most days he'd go down to Kensington Market, which was like a hippy Harrods, full of stalls selling outrageous and beautiful clothes, jewellery, incense, records etc. He would sit on the floor of an oriental clothing stall playing his sitar all day. He told me once that his father had been a heroin addict and as a boy he would often have to tie him to the bed when he was doing cold turkey (withdrawal).

Quite a few Americans were arriving at Holmead Road those days, including a band called Blue Cheer, friends of Kevin from LA who were making an album in London. They had the reputation of being the loudest band on the planet and used to blow people's eardrums if they sat too close to the speaker stacks! Some LA ladies rented the house next door; a vocal group who were trying to get a contract with Apple. They were like the Mamas who'd left the Papas at home. They were way over the top, and you rarely saw them without a big fat joint in their mouths. These girls were really wild, and they all wore beautiful Moroccan gowns of velvet and satin, embroidered with semi-precious stones. They were festooned with oriental jewellery of silver and gold, a sight to behold. Their leader was Karen Harvey-Hammer, a redhead, who had a small boy, her son Justin, in tow. She owned a shop in LA where she sold Colombian artefacts, figurines, beads and pottery smuggled out of Mexico. Another of them, Nicole, eventually married Steve Winwood. She was a heroin addict, and she'd get a load of money from him to go to Greece to get herself cleaned up. A month or so later back she'd come back without a sun tan! These girls were, if anything, super groupies who'd screwed most of the big rock stars in the USA and were now doing the same in London.

Life at Holmead Road was proving to be pretty wild, and the

drugs were getting out of hand. One day somebody spiked my tea with about 1,000 micrograms of acid, which was a heavy trip and I ended up in hospital where I had to be sedated. Our opulent and cosy Georgian house was now nothing but an extension of the recording studio. Polly Palmer, a friend of Traffic, had moved in with a Hammond organ and a huge Mellotron. Barry's drums were set up in the sitting-room with guitars, Marshall stacks and microphones on stands. The floor was festooned with electrical cables and leads while the furniture sat out the back on the patio in the London fog! Reggie King moved in along with a paranoid girl called Suzette, who'd done too much acid and was suffering the consequences. Most of the time she just sat on a mattress staring into space.

We used to play this stupid game. When the telephone rang, everyone would leap to the six extensions and at a signal, sing "Hello, who's there?" in six-part harmony.

"Gary! Where is Gary?" said Georgio's voice one day.

"Wocha want Jorjo man?" says Gary – clearly the only one of us that Georgio considered to have any sense of responsibility.

"Georgio's bringin' down a bunch of Italian TV and film executives. There could be a European tour on here, so he wants us to impress them," said Gary laughing like a fool.

Georgio had already phoned an off licence in Chelsea and ordered a load of flash booze, which we were supposed to pick up later by taxi. He also wanted us to have girls there – the kind of fast chicks who dressed like an advertisement for Carnaby Street. We didn't have any girls, only stoned Suzette and Julia, and the Americans were far too over the top. So off I went to trawl some of the pubs in Fulham Road and Chelsea, where I knew a girl from Cardiff who knew some hippy girls from around and about the area.

Later on two beautiful black Bentley limos drove up to the front door and out got Georgio, that six-foot Russian with black hair and a big black beard – Rasputin comes to mind – followed by six incredibly smart Italian film executives, three impeccably suited men and three Gina Lollobrigida lookalikes dressed in incredibly expensive little black gowns. This was alright; out came the booze in the elegant crystal goblets hired from the off licence, and the party got going. The boys were jamming on their instruments, and the girls were dancing. Instant party, until one of the girls from the King's Road bars suddenly started stripping as she danced with a smart Italian guy. Within seconds she was wearing nothing bar a pair of skimpy black knickers as she gyrated in front of these Italians. Georgio was clearly enjoying this little diversion, but the Italian women took it very badly, the men looked embarrassed and they all wanted to leave. By this time we were all in a similar state of undress as well! Georgio quick to retrieve the situation shouted "Right boys, we all go to the Speakeasy" – a club in the West End for rock musicians and record company executives and their hangers-on. Famous bands used to play there – Eric Clapton, Jimi Hendrix etc. It was a very exclusive and expensive venue. "You boys follow on in taxis," ordered Georgio ushering the Italians into the Bentleys. And this was simply the prologue to yet another wild night!

★ ★ ★

Gary decided to move out to a quiet house in Caterham, Surrey, and he asked me to go with him in order to rehearse for the new album. By now, I wanted to quit and was desperate to return to Solva; the acid trip that landed me in hospital had shocked me and I needed to get my head together. Nevertheless I stayed – I couldn't let him down having gone thus Farr! The final straw came a few days later when Tim Hardin turned up wanting Gary to score heroin for him. Hardin was an addict, and he was in pretty bad shape and really needed a fix. We didn't touch heroin ourselves, but off went Gary, magnanimous as ever, leaving me sitting in the garden trying to humour this guy who was and still is a hero of mine. He was pathetic, shaking and shivering and talking nonsense. Yet, after Gary came back and he'd fixed up, Hardin was a changed man, and we all went to the Rising Sun for a drink and a chat about music as if nothing had happened.

By that time, Mafia-backed gangsters were controlling much of the drug scene in London. It wasn't "Hey, man, we've just come back from Nepal, would you like some of this?" It was getting hairy and I wanted out. I was worried about Tessa and Wizz and I still hadn't got a recording contract; I had just become a session man on other people's records and my music was still in Solva. I had to leave London, which I saw as a gigantic all-powerful whore who demanded your favours completely. If you didn't give them to her, she'd either destroy you, render you impotent, or gobble you up and spit the little pieces into the Thames. I therefore decided to go home to Solva for good, even though I was rehearsing another album, *Strange Fruit*, with Gary. Incidentally, he got Richard Thompson of Fairport Convention to stand in for me.

I found some clothes lying around the house, an old blue cavalry jacket with brass buttons and a pair of Jim Cregan's corduroy trousers with a flap front fly, and my old black hat. I bade adieu to Gary over a couple of pints and a game of darts in a country pub in Surrey, before he drove me in his jeep to Paddington. I felt confused; it was a strange homegoing. I felt I was heading for the unknown, into the darkness beyond. Something was wrong. I could feel the poetry draining away, dissipating into London drizzle, acid flashbacks and loneliness.

# Chapter 13

# Caerforiog

When I travel by train I usually sit next to the dining car and bar. In those days all mainline trains carried dining cars, their tables laid with immaculate white double damask cloths and silver service cutlery for three- and four-course meals, and with a uniformed *maître d'* presiding over a crew of liveried waiters. The journey from Paddington to Haverfordwest took eight hours and seemed to get more boring and tedious the further west we travelled. It's much the same now. After Cardiff the train seems to go slower, and after leaving the 125 at Swansea it's no quicker than a cattle truck and takes an hour and a half to travel sixty miles. Train journeys have always been thought-provoking experiences for me. I usually carry a note pad and pen as well as my guitar, and I've written plenty of songs on trains;

I boarded the midday train at Paddington, after watching Gary zoom off in his battered jeep. My train hummed its way out of the London smog and drizzle, through Reading and Swindon's grey urbanity, and we thundered on along the gleaming tracks of steel towards the wild west, pulling into Haverfordwest at around eight o'clock in the evening. The place was deserted – no bus, no taxis waited outside the station. The next bus wouldn't arrive for an hour, and so I went to the nearest pub, the Milford Arms.

"Anything happening round here tonight?" I asked.

"Folk club up at the Lamb," was the uninterested answer.

I felt spaced out, exhausted and out of place. Was this the result of a four-month stint in London with Gary Farr and the Psychedelics? So I picked up my guitar and trudged off through the gloom up the hill to the Lamb in search of warmth, music and beer.

The folk club was in a small, dimly lit, back room. I've never understood why they turn all the lights off, and it was no different here. One bare, thirty-watt bulb glowed dimly in the corner where the singers performed. I stashed my guitar behind the door in case the organizer thought I might be a singer. There weren't many people there, and I sat unnoticed at the back in a narrow space between a small bar and the wall.

The entertainment started slowly, as a few local singers who were obviously in need of music lessons and inspiration feebly strummed cheap guitars. I was thinking about Tessa and the Solva bus and was drinking up to go when she walked through the door accompanied by two people from Solva – a boy called Dickie and the other a girl I knew. They were in high spirits, laughing a lot and obviously out for a good time. People were turning round and shushing them up, as they did in those days before microphones, calling order for the sacred cow singer.

Tessa didn't notice me, and they all sat down. Dickie came up to the bar to order drinks, and when he saw me sitting in the shadows underneath my black hat his jaw dropped. I knew immediately that something was going on. I didn't say anything; he was a few years younger than me and I didn't know him very well. He went back to the girls with a tray of drinks, and I could see him telling Tessa that I was there. The embarrassment was palpable. "What a weird experience," I thought. I couldn't leave now as I had intended; I'd better play the game.

In the interval, they all went to the bar as did most of the small audience, noisily demanding drinks. Tessa was all coy and said she was surprised to see me and why hadn't I telephoned. The other girl

*Me and Wizz at Caerforiog, 1969*

asked me when I'd arrived, and I told her. Dickie offered to buy me a drink and give me a lift home.

"I was just about to catch the bus," I told them.

"Oh, you may as well stay here now and come home with us," they said.

Tessa hadn't flung herself into my arms or anything romantic; she hadn't even given me a kiss. It was a strange and unsettling experience.

"Did everything go well in London?" she asked.

Suddenly, I was hit by a revelation – the realization of that strange feeling which had come over me in London on the way to the train, a bit like *déjà vu*. In that instant, it was as if I were on a borderline where two distinctly different realities met. Realities meet all the time, but sometimes they cannot gel and only coexist for a while before disappearing, just like the title of one of Gary's love songs, 'Two Separate Paths Together'. Fatigue, flashback, shock; I withdrew into myself. "We'll sort this out in the morning," I said, shaking inside

Rose Cottage was the same warm firelit pink cocoon smelling of wood smoke, incense and *cawl* as always. Tessa produced a half full bottle of whisky. "Strange," I thought. "She never drinks whisky." I just grabbed something to eat, before excusing myself and going up to bed; I could hear them below, laughing and joking and pretty drunk. I must have fallen asleep instantly. When I woke, I had to double check where I was. I could hear the wind outside the window and rain spitting on glass. The morning was cold and grey with waves of sea mist gusting up the Cwm. My head was somewhere else; the sounds and smell of London had not yet died away. I could hear Tessa making tea in the tiny kitchen below and I could smell the toast and marmalade. I dressed and went downstairs, and she came into the sitting-room with a tray. We ate off our laps in the old armchairs.

"Where's Wizz?" I asked.

"Oh, she'll be back lunch-time. She sleeps in Nana Betty's on

Fridays so I can go out for a drink. We usually go to the folk club – there's bugger all happening in Solva these days."

"Was there ever?"

"The singers aren't much good. Why didn't you sing?"

"I'm on holiday," I joked, but she didn't laugh.

"What's with Dickie?"

"Oh, he just drives us in to the club for a drink."

Later I found out that Dickie and Tessa had been seeing each other for quite a while since I'd last been home. Vultures don't take long to arrive after the kill, then the jackals move in. It's a bad move to leave an attractive wife or girlfriend in a place where there aren't many eligible women. She told me that an old retired seaman who lived opposite and who had sailed with my uncle Harold had been visiting her drunk, bearing bottles of whisky and nylon stockings. He was well over seventy.

"The dirty old bastard!" I said. Tessa thought it was hilarious.

"That's the way they are, chancers. And they don't change."

I suddenly realized that I had changed; for once I felt free of the thickly insulated slowness and ominous predictability of that place.

My mother arrived with Wizz at midday. She was surprised and delighted to see me, as was Wizz, who leaped on to my lap screaming, "Dada, Dada!" She was two and a half years old and a beautiful child. Tessa had got herself a smashing horse, an English thoroughbred gelding called Copper Knight who had been raced under National Hunt rules under the name of Piccadilly. He was only fifteen two hands high and a bit too slow for the racetrack, so he'd been sold as a hunter and a point to pointer in south Pembrokeshire. He was a beautiful horse; and you can see him on the cover of *Outlander* with Wizz and me on the back. We became great friends and had many adventures. We also had a black labrador bitch named Nofus (No Fuss), bred by my cousin Gerald from St David's. Often we would go out riding, with Nofus running ahead like an Apache scout.

Later I had a drink with my mother, who was bursting with gossip about Tessa and Dickie. I told her that I didn't want to know about it. You didn't have to be Sherlock Holmes to suss that out. It was up to her; she'd have to make her choice and if the dice didn't roll right for me I'd have to go back to London. My mother still believed in the old fashioned "Is he man enough to fight?" or even shotguns at dawn; it was still somewhat primitive and tribal down there. By now, I'd also been on prescribed valium for over a year, and my calm mood of distraction was probably a result of taking the drug three times a day, with lots of champagne.

Tessa needed a field for the horse, so I made arrangements with Trevor Morris of Llys-y-coed farm on the Felinganol road, who let us use the old Dardanelles field, where my grandfather's greyhound, Old Bill, had massacred rabbits when I was a small boy. Not long afterwards, Tessa was in Croesgoch buying feed for the horse and she met a farmer who had an old farmhouse for rent. It was called Caerforiog and it stood two miles further up the valley from Solva. The next day we followed his directions up the steep hill past the Baptist chapel (where the famous preacher Jiwbili Young had his first ministry) with its overgrown cemetery, and where all my mam's family had been baptised in a pool in the farmyard. They are all buried there too! Then left at the T-junction at the top of the hill and first right. The long driveway led to a large open farmyard, with granite buildings on the right and the old fifteenth-century farmhouse on the left bordered by a semi-circular walled lawn. At the back there was a large garden with apple trees, overlooking fields that swept gently down to the River Solva in the valley bottom. Caerforiog was perfect for us, cheap to rent and just what I'd dreamed of after all those years tramping around English cities and towns as a song and dance man. Inside, on the ground floor, was a huge kitchen with inglenook fireplace, Aga stove and an old skew, while next to the back door there was another kitchen with a deep old-fashioned sink. There were also three other large rooms on the ground floor; the whole place was light and airy on account of it having plenty of windows front and back. Two flights of stairs led to five bedrooms and a landing on the first floor.

Soon we left Rose Cottage and turned to cleaning and painting Caerforiog. Copper was accommodated in a large field behind the garden, and the semi-circular lawn in front became Wizz's playground. Tessa was in her element; at last she had space to do her sculpture and more space to do her clothes designing and sewing. I was still doing gigs round Wales and playing the odd gig in London with Gary Farr. "This is the life," I thought. Total privacy, peace and quiet – *dyma'r ffordd i'r bywyd iach*! No one came to Caerforiog except the postman and the farm hand who tended the pigs and calves in the out-buildings. I opened an account with a wholesale grocer in Haverfordwest, who delivered our order by van each week.

We lived in the big inner kitchen, which had a large farmhouse table, some old chairs and benches. On the wall I pinned a huge poster of Dylan, which Eleanor Raskin, my American friend from the Bronx, had given me. The kitchen floor was of red and brown tiles, very easy to clean. We slept above the kitchen, a room which was always warm because of the heat from the constantly burning Aga stove. We used to bake bread using Allinson's wholemeal flour and we brewed our own beer and wine.

I needed some form of transport other than the horse, and so I bought a second-hand motor scooter from my brother Martin, who sent it down from Gloucestershire on a British Rail lorry. This was real entertainment: Tessa and Wizzy roared as they watched me trying to ride the bloody thing around the stony pot-holed farmyard falling off all the time. Once I went over the handlebars, flat on my face in a huge muddy puddle. It must have looked like a movie stunt and it certainly made them laugh.

When the news about Caerforiog got round our friends, we began to entertain quite a few visitors. Geraint and Heather came down and we held a Bara Menyn photo session courtesy of a local photographer, Denis Larcombe from Newgale. Caerforiog was a great place for creativity – quiet and tranquil with a beautiful view down Solva valley, wild and herbaceous never having been cultivated or lived in by humans, just wild birds and animals, grazing cattle and sheep. Gary and Kevin Westlake came to visit too, and Gary wrote a couple of songs, including one called 'Down in the Mud'. There was a lot of interest in mystical things among hippies those days, and a few friends from London decided that they wanted to visit the place in the Preseli hills where the blue stones at Stonehenge had originated. I knew where this was – a crag called Carreg Meini near Mynachlog-ddu, birthplace of Waldo Williams, the famous Welsh poet and philosopher. One misty morning we found ourselves walking among the stones. There were monoliths lying everywhere; it was as if some violent upheaval had shaken the crag to pieces, or as if it had been struck by a powerful aerial force like a massive lightning strike. I had one of Tessa's carving hammers and when I broke off a piece of the crag you could smell a sulphurous fiery odour. We all brought pieces back with us; some went to London and some are probably still in the yard at Caerforiog. Peter Swales was there and Kevin, Gary and Tessa. By this time, Peter was working for The Rolling Stones at their Maddox Street office in London. He was Mick Jagger's personal assistant.

I was still doing a lot of work for the BBC in Cardiff, when I met Gareth Wyn Jones, a young director who wanted to film a documentary profile of me and my life. The project was approved by the head of programmes as part of a series of five documentaries on contemporary Welshmen, including one on the work of a Newport drum maker. As a result, a film crew came for one week to Caerforiog, Solva and St David's, followed by another week in Cardiff and London. Gareth just filmed our normal day-to-day life. Often I'd open the front door in the morning and there would be a film crew in the yard with camera rolling. They used an Ariflex 16mm camera. The cameramen were Charles Beddows and Robin Rollinson. In one sequence, Gareth, who had been an officer in the Royal Navy, managed to get hold of a Sea King helicopter from HMS *Goldcrest* at Brawdy. We filmed on Whitesands beach, from where it is said that St Patrick departed for Ireland in the Dark Ages. Tessa was filmed galloping Copper through the surf, and I was lifted in a harness at the end of a wire and flown swinging through the air up to the peak of Carn Llidi, a rocky outcrop overlooking the beach, where they dropped me. The helicopter flew around filming, then I hooked up again and was swung back through the clouds to the beach.

In another sequence, my brother Irving and I played an instrumental called 'Hwiangerdd Mihangel'. It was filmed at night and we sat on rocks in the water; the reflections were fantastic. I saw the rushes later in Cardiff. It was excellent stuff! Others who were filmed included Heather and Geraint, Gary Farr and Mighty Baby in London, and Syd Barrett from Pink Floyd who used to visit us at Caerforiog with his girlfriend, Carmel.

Later Gareth fell out with the BBC, and went to work in Singapore, leaving the film unedited. Some time later the BBC gave another director permission to edit a five-minute profile of me from Gareth's film mags. What was left was thrown out, and thus disappeared eight reels of 16mm film and a record of our lives in 1969. Naughty boy, the late Rhydderch Jones!

Gary had been invited to play the Isle of Wight festival on 31 August 1969. Dylan and The Band were top of the bill supported by a host of international stars, including Tom Paxton, Richie Havens,

Pentangle, Emerson, Lake and Palmer, Traffic, Family and others. Tessa came with me; she was a big Dylan fan. On the thirtieth I recorded a *Disc a Dawn* in Cardiff, and one of the technicians, who lived on the south coast, kindly gave us a lift to our hotel in Portsmouth. In the morning, we drank champagne with a smoked haddock breakfast, before boarding the ferry for the Isle of Wight.

The Festival site was massive, enclosed by a tall corrugated iron fence. The backstage area was also huge, with marquees for the artistes and bands. Directly in front of the stage lay a large press enclosure, and a lot of caravans clustered near the stage area. The PA system was said to be the biggest ever assembled. I found the sheer scale of the event daunting, and I was nervous about playing on that stage with just an acoustic guitar. Later we assembled for a sound check – Gary on vocals and twelve string, Andy Lee on bass and Roger Powell on Conga drums. Everything sounded great, and very loud! Gary was on form and singing well. Soon Julie Driscoll arrived, making friends with Tessa instantly; they hung out all day together.

When the crowds started to arrive, the atmosphere changed rapidly; I'd never seen so many people – they were of all nationalities and from all over Europe and America. Many had come straight from the Woodstock festival held in New York State the previous weekend. Bands and artistes were landing in helicopters in the backstage area; I saw The Who arriving in a chopper they'd hired for the day. Later on we went out to the press area to watch Richie Havens perform; he was fantastic, just two acoustic guitars and a man in a purple turban and a flowing Arab robe playing Conga drums, who was introduced by Havens as Daniel Ben Zebulon.

We were on after Tom Paxton, who performed alone with a Martin D28 guitar as usual. I'd been sitting in a marquee backstage with Family and Traffic, having a drink and a smoke, unaware of the magnitude of the audience. A little later, I walked up the ramp at the side of the stage. I soon went back down again. There was a sea of people as far as the eye could see. It was overwhelming. "Can't hack this," I thought.

"OK, we're on now," said Gary. Next thing, Ricky Farr announced our act. I pulled my hat over my eyes so I couldn't see the monster audience and got stuck into the music. "I don't know why you bother, child; this old world won't change because you're tryin'," sang Gary and it was all coming true. At the end of the set we had a great ovation from an audience of a quarter of a million people. It was only 4.30 p.m.

When we came off, Gary gave us new backstage passes; tight security dictated that the passes were changed before Dylan and The Band arrived. Anyone who didn't have a relevant pass was thrown out by bouncers – even some of those who'd already played were bounced. Not fair, I thought! I was told that Dylan didn't want too many people backstage when he arrived. He'd been staying in a mansion down the road, where he'd been giving a party for The Beatles, Stones, Eric Clapton and their hangers-on.

About an hour before The Band played, Gary and I went looking for Ricky to get some money to pay our band. Finally, we found him in a backstage caravan, the floor covered in bundles of money and Dylan and his manager Al Grossman on their knees counting out their share of the cash – £25,000!

The Band finally came on stage, some two hours late. By now it must have been about 10 o'clock and the atmosphere wasn't at all good. The sound wasn't right and they weren't playing well; they looked smashed out of their heads. During the set, security guys chucked people out of the press area to make room for rows of seats in front of the stage for John Lennon, Yoko Ono, the rest of The Beatles, The Rolling Stones, The Who, and their various toadies. The survivors – us among them – were pushed back against the security barrier. Dylan eventually came on in a white suit, stoned out of his mind. I felt sorry for him and let down too; it was a dreadful performance. I'd last seen him two years earlier in Manchester Free

Trade Hall. He was really good, just him, acoustic guitar and harmonica.

There was chaos when Dylan went off stage after a very short and well below par set. The organizers hadn't made adequate arrangements with the ferry companies. We were lucky to get off the island on the last ferry, which was dangerously overcrowded. Hundreds of thousands were left stranded on the island all night. I told Tessa vehemently that I would never go to another rock festival! We then took the train back to Pembrokeshire, pretty spaced out with champagne hangovers. It had been another weirdly memorable trip. We arrived in Caerforiog, to be greeted at the door by Little Wizz and Big Betty who were delighted to see us once again.

Not long afterwards I was back in London and waiting for Gary in the ante room of a music publisher and agent, Bryan Morrison, when a quietly spoken man with curly hair, wearing a Fair Isle short-sleeved pullover and grey corduroy trousers asked me if he could help. He seemed a cool guy, and so I told him I was waiting for Gary Farr to complete his business in the office and that I was in his band. "Do you write songs?" he asked. I told him that I'd written quite a few, and he asked me if I'd like to record some demo tapes. Within an hour, I was in Central Sound Studio in Denmark Street just round the corner, where I put down about eight songs. The man's name was Ian Samwell, and unknown to me he'd written Cliff Richard's first hit record, 'Move It'. He'd also played the bass with the original band, The Drifters, which later became The Shadows. Nor did I know that he was a talent scout and an A&R man for Warner Brothers records.

Later, back at Caerforiog, I came in from riding one day, and Tessa said that there'd been a phone call from London. She said it was somebody we didn't know, the secretary of Ian Ralfini, the chief of Warner Brothers in London. I thought that she must have either got it wrong or that somebody was playing a joke on me. I phoned the number, and a girl's voice answered, "Ian Ralfini's office. Who's speaking, please?" I told her, and she asked if I could come up to London immediately, as they wanted to sign me to Warner Brothers. Just like that, out of the blue. It was too good to be true. I said that I'd only arrived home from London the previous night and could I come up the following day, and that was what I did.

Back on the bloody train again! Back to stinking Paddington. Stuck in a black hackney in the traffic on Hyde Park corner. The taxi found the building in New Oxford Street and I went up in the elevator and presented myself at reception, where a smart and beautiful blonde sat at a desk. I was ushered into a lounge area and offered champagne. Then out came a smartly suited Italian-looking man with two dolly bird assistants. This was Ian Ralfini, the head of Warners in Europe. Ian Samwell was there too, and Ralfini wasted no time in offering me a five-year contract there and then.

"We think the demos you made at Central Sound are great, and we want you to make more if you've got the songs."

"Oh yeah, I've got a load of songs, but I'll have to think about this a bit."

"We'll give you a fifty thousand pound advance on royalties if you sign now."

I looked at Ian Samwell, who for some reason I trusted. He gave a slight nod and I said, "Give me the contract." I signed on the spot, and more champagne was poured.

"Where are you staying?" said Ralfini. "You'll have to be here a few days to tie things up. We'll book you a hotel. Send for a car for Mike, please."

Sammy came down in the lift with me; he wanted a talk. Outside stood a Bentley and chauffeur to drive us to the Savoy Hotel, where Sammy and I went to the grill bar for a drink.

"They're very excited about your songs at Warners," he said. "They're a very big company and expanding, but you'll have to get a publisher if you haven't already got one." I didn't have a publisher –

I didn't have any kind of organization, just me, my voice, guitar, Tessa and Wizzy.

The following day I went to Warners to pick up a cheque for £50,000, before returning to Lupus Music where it all began. There I met Bryan Morrison, who was just as eager to sign me as a writer assigned to his publishing company, Lupus Music. I left his office £10,000 richer by virtue of another cheque in lieu of a publishing advance! I went straight across the road to Morrison's bank (Barclays Bank, Barclay Square), where I opened an account with the sixty grand, before moving on to The Savoy to meet Gary for lunch. I needed a new guitar, and so off we went to Charing Cross Road, where I found a beautiful second-hand Martin 0018 in Selmers and bought it encased for £95. And then on to Paddington station once more, this time with my head in the clouds. I found an empty compartment and played the Martin all the way to Haverfordwest, where I got a cab outside the station. Tessa was still up when I walked into Caerforiog at about 12.30 a.m. "We're going to be rich," I whooped dancing round the kitchen. I've never won the pools or anything like that, but it must be a similar feeling. I knew the songs were good, but it was greatly reassuring and a real boost to know that one of the biggest record companies in the world thought so too.

The next day Sammy phoned to say that he was making arrangements to record more demos at Central Sound and that I'd have to come back to London soon to discuss booking musicians and studio time to record the first album. He said that he thought we had a very strong single, a song on the first demo tape called 'Great Houdini'. He was keen to record 'Houdini' as soon as possible, and that was fine with me.

"Good god," I said to Tessa who was changing Wizzy's nappy. "I think we've hit the big time!"

"And I think I'm pregnant," she announced.

# Chapter 14

# 'Outlander':
# Into the Big Time

Sammy phoned a few days later to say that he'd booked studio time for me at Central Sound. He also said that there were some musicians he'd like me to meet. Sammy had a girlfriend, a singer called Linda Lewis, and these guys were in her band. Sammy and Linda lived in Hampstead in a flat on Haverstock Hill, and from now on it was there that I stayed when I was in London.

I hung around Caerforiog for a few days, cutting wood, tidying up and riding Copper. I'd been booked by the Welsh Arts Council to tour with an experimental music band called Indo Jazz Fusions. The leaders of this group were John Mayer, a classical Indian musician who'd made the crossover to western music, and a famous West Indian jazz saxophonist, Joe Harriott. Mayer had formed a group of classical Indian musicians, and augmented it by adding Harriott and Chris Taylor, one of the leading orchestral flautists in Britain from the LSO. The tour was imminent, so I had to be ready fast.

Rehearsals for my forthcoming Warner Brothers album had been booked in Central Sound and at a club in south London, and the next time I went back to London I met the musicians whom Sammy had found for the recording sessions. Mike Snow, the keyboard player, was from Liverpool and had been in bands there at the same time as

The Beatles. George Ford was a Jamaican bassist, whose brother Emile Ford had enjoyed a hit with a song called 'What do You Want to Make Those Eyes at Me For'. Dennis Elliot, the drummer, though only 20 years old, was one of the best in the world, and Bernie Holland was an amazing guitarist, who played a Fender Strat finger style. Originally, Bernie was from Ystradgynlais in south Wales where his father was a factory manager. We all met at a demo session in Central Sound, and one of the tracks we recorded became the backing track of the well-known song 'Y Brawd Houdini', the third record to be released by Sain records. Around this time, I would sometimes bump into a young man from Cardiff, called Huw Jones. He was a friend of Heather's and a member of the same Urdd Gobaith Cymru *aelwyd* where they used to sing together. Huw wrote songs and was studying at Jesus College, Oxford.

This was a time of great political upheaval in Wales: the Welsh Language Society, which had been founded in 1962 by, among others, Emyr Llywelyn, John Daniel, Hywel Davies, Neil Jenkins and Cynog Davies, was at the centre of a regime of political protest, mainly because of the precarious state of the Welsh language. By and large, people didn't realize that the language was in imminent danger of dying. Dafydd Iwan, who was a friend of Huw's and his co-founder at Sain records, had already been jailed for non-payment of a fine as a political protest. Huw promptly wrote a protest song about him, 'Paid Digalonni'.

I used to go to a Cardiff pub called the New Ely where a crowd of Welsh students would drink, socialize and sing all night. Huw sang 'Paid Digalonni', and I was so impressed that I asked him to come to London the next day to record the song. I always had studio time booked by Warners at Central Sound, and so we recorded it there – I backed him on acoustic guitar. The record was rush released and sold well. Huw asked me to help him and Dafydd set up a Welsh record company, along with a businessman, Brian Morgan Edwards, who was treasurer of Plaid Cymru. Brian lived in Ninian Road, Cardiff, and Sain opened its first office in a large front room there. Brian worked in London selling computers and was often away, leaving his wife Rona in charge. I was given a pleasant room at the top of the house to use when I was in Cardiff.

I went on to produce Sain's first record, written and sung by Huw Jones and recorded in London. The band consisted of myself and members of Mighty Baby. It just so happened that there was a heavy rain storm that day and that the studio sprang a leak – a few in fact. So there we were, pissing ourselves laughing as Huw sang "Dŵr, dŵr, dŵr" (water, water, water) as the rain gushed through the roof into some half a dozen buckets on the floor of the studio. 'Dŵr' was the first Welsh record to be recorded on a multi-track recorder and mixed down in real stereo. It was a real breakthrough in sound recording in the Welsh language and became a best seller.

My next problem was finding a suitable studio to record my Warners album. I liked Central Sound, an old Soho Studio set up a long time before by the owner Freddie Winrose's father, one of the founders of sound recording in London. Central Sound was a four-track studio – very small, scruffy and basic, and reached by a walk down a dark and narrow corridor off Denmark Street. It was sandwiched between the Giaconda, an Italian café, and the Tin Pan Alley Club, a very exclusive showbiz drinking club full of people from the music industry, old lags and Soho crocodiles.

Gary Farr suggested that I try Morgan, a brand new, eight-track studio in central London. Sammy was my fixer at Warner Brothers, and he'd also been asked to produce my first album, which was fine by me. We had a look round Morgan and decided to book some time to record 'Houdini'. We continued to rehearse at Central Sound and another venue. During these rehearsals, a version of 'Great Houdini'

*Experimenting at the end of the 60s*

was recorded, as was a version of 'Old Joe Blind', a new song I'd written in Cardiff. Unfortunately, the Morgan sessions flopped, and the version of 'Old Joe Blind' on the *Outlander* album is a remix of the Central Sound rehearsal demo with John Van Derrick's violin dropped in during the remix. The version of 'Great Houdini' on Sain 3 is the demo version from Central Sound, remixed, and with Welsh vocals added. 'Great Houdini' did not appear on *Outlander*; we could not nail that song down for the single that Warners wanted it to be, although we tried and tried. Consequently, only the Welsh version survived. Later, the original appeared on a re-release of *Outlander* by Rhino Records. I also recorded some songs in Welsh at Central Sound, with Heather, Geraint and Bill Lovelady, a great Liverpudlian guitarist who was living in Llechryd, near Cardigan. These recordings were released on the Newyddion Da label during the Ammanford Eisteddfod in 1970.

We were having no luck in finding a studio to record *Outlander*. Next we went to Glyn Johns's Olympic Studio, where The Stones recorded at the time. I was trying my best to get the music together. Sammy was a big fan of acoustic guitar, harmonica and vocal songs, like 'Love Owed', while I was more into experimenting with other instrumentation. Then I had a great idea. "Why don't I use the Indian musicians?" I put it to Sammy, who didn't really know what I was talking about. I suggested that he listen to the Indo Jazz Fusions album. This music was far removed from the pop and rock and indeed from any other music of the day, and Sammy couldn't quite make the connection between my Aeolian guitar tuning and the classical Indian music. I convinced him in the end, and, in turn, he convinced Warners to extend the budget for the *Outlander* sessions to accommodate John Mayer as arranger, and the other three musicians, Dewan Motihar, sitar, Keshav Sathe, tablas, and Chris Taylor, who was one of the most sought after flautists in Europe.

At the time, Trident Studios was a state-of-the-art studio. It was owned by the Bank of Japan, boasted a custom-made American Neve desk and an eight-track recorder, and was perfectly situated just off Wardour Street in Soho around the corner from the Ship, a main meeting place for rock musicians. Sammy took me to see the place and to meet Malcolm Toft, the chief engineer. Trident felt just right for me. It was extremely expensive, but Warners were paying.

We usually recorded during the night. Some of the sessions would go on until the early hours, even all night long and we'd have breakfast in a Soho café around seven or eight o'clock. By nature I'm a day person, and I found this a bit of a strain. Nevertheless, I was happy and relieved that we'd at last found a studio where we could all get in a groove. I couldn't handle Olympic, which was a huge barn of a place with Marshall stacks, spaghetti wires and overflowing ashtrays all over the place. Syd Barrett came down to Olympic one night: at the time I was alone in this cavern with an acoustic guitar and I was glad when Syd the intruder arrived with his girlfriend, took the guitar, sat on the floor and began playing to himself. I'd recorded a track called 'One night wonder' that night – it's on *Ghost Town* (Tenth Planet Records). Syd nearly always sat on the floor. There was no furniture in his room, just bare floorboards alternately painted orange and blue, a white telephone, and a Fender Telecaster. I was one of the few allowed in; he liked to be on his own a lot. Sometimes he'd play his Telecaster unamplified. Other times he'd just stare out of the window or into space. Syd didn't seem to want much out of life, just to be alone with his thoughts. He was a good looking guy, and when out and about he would always have a beautiful girl on his arm or be driving her mini Cooper. Thin as a rake, he was a dandy: very exotic clothes, skin-tight satin suits, frilled silk shirts, long flowing scarves and snakeskin boots! I wouldn't have thought he had a drug problem, no more than most people on the scene.

The sessions at Trident were progressing well, and we were nailing down basic tracks in one or two takes. 'Yorric' was done in two takes and 'The Sailor and Madonna' in one, with no overdubs. What you hear on the record is a band playing live. Then came the tracks with Linda's band, 'Rowena', 'Left Over Time' (one take) and 'Ghost Town'. They used the Central Sound demo of 'Old Joe Blind' both for the single and the album, and I didn't get a production credit for that or 'Blue Sleep'! All the other tracks I did alone, using two guitars – a Martin 0018 and a Hagstrom jumbo. Later I sold the Hagstrom to Huw Jones and the Martin went to Heather, only to be stolen from her car. (In fact, there were two Hagstroms; I still have the other.)

★ ★ ★

Sammy's next project was a band called America, a one-hit-wonder ('Horse With No Name'). He also had another American band at the time, Daddy Long Legs, and I went to some of their sessions at Trident. By now, everyone was recording at Trident, including The Beatles. Malcolm Toft was one of the best sound engineers in the world at that time.

The usual rounds of clubbing, partying, recording and stoning continued unabated, and it was heaven to get back to Caerforiog to unwind and re-energize. There was a general drift to the country going on amongst London-based musicians, but I was already there and well-established. Tessa and the kids were happy and well-provided for. Wizz had been born on the day England beat West Germany to the World Cup, whilst Bethan was born on the day the Yanks landed on the moon – more coincidence.

The Warner Brothers experience taught me a lot about the process of sound recording and about how to put records together bandwise. I went on to produce quite a few albums; in fact, most of my Welsh records are self-produced. I also set up the photo shoots and designed

most of the sleeves, with the help of an old mate of mine, Eddie
Lloyd Davies from Halkin Mountain, who had a print shop in Rhyl.
Warners found me a manager – I was totally disorganized in that respect.
He was called Alistair Taylor, a Liverpudlian who had come to London
with Brian Epstein and had worked at Nems for years. He had been
John Lennon's personal assistant at Nems and Apple. Despite this,
nothing much happened. All I remember was going to loads of
restaurants and having long business lunches in Soho or Mayfair. We
didn't do much business, and Warners got fed up with me when
*Outlander* didn't sell very well. The single flopped because we couldn't
get BBC airplays. John Peel wouldn't play it, nor would Jimmy Savile,
and a record has little chance if you can't get it on the BBC playlist. I
heard later that Warners were planning to release *Outlander* in America,
which might have been good, but who can tell. You need a massive
publicity campaign to launch an album. I didn't record for Warner
Brothers again. Even though I was writing a lot of songs, they didn't
show much interest. Moreover, Sammy had gone to America, and so
I didn't have a producer any more. Same old story, back on the night
train to Solva.

So I said goodbye to Warners, although I was still under contract
for three years. My last memory of them is quite funny: Ian Ralfini
was rushing up and down the corridor shouting "Somebody get Derek
[Taylor, the Beatles ex-publicist now a special projects manager for
W/B] to stop smoking that effing grass, we're gonna get busted soon!"
I used to sit in Derek's office quite often, drinking champers and
smoking incredibly strong weed and talking nonsense. The late Derek
Taylor, who was from Wrexham, was a case! Everybody loved him.

The Stones were leaving, The Beatles had split, Hendrix was dead;
the London scene would never be the same.

My break with Warners did not, however, signify the end of my
musical ties with London; there was still a hell of a lot to come.

# Chapter 15

# *Carol-Ann and Schizophrenia*

Carol-Ann Maw is a Texan lady from the Austin–Houston–Dallas triangle, and I first met her in Sammy's flat in late 1969. She was a beautiful hippy girl, with a creamy Mexican complexion, lovely slim figure and long dark hair that curled in ringlets down to her waist. Friendly and generous and with a big smile, she was also a stylish dresser.

When I arrived at the flat, there was a bit of a row going on. This was strange – Sammy was a mild-mannered man who hardly ever raised his voice. Carol-Ann was on the phone, and I was introduced to her as she went off to a meeting. Sammy and Linda went into the kitchen, and I could hear them discussing some problem. Weird – I'd never felt any bad vibes around Sammy or Linda before.

When Sammy came back into the living-room I asked him what was wrong. He went to a cupboard fitted in the wall, opened the double doors and revealed several bulging bin bags.

"That's the problem," he said, "acid!"

The bags were full of colour-coded acid trips. Hundreds of thousands of them.

"Are those hers?" I asked, taken aback.

"She brought it here. She's responsible for it. I only offered to put her up for a while, not have the place turned into a dope emporium!"

Sammy was usually very cool; I'd never seen him so agitated, angry too. "The acid belongs to The Grateful Dead. She's got to get rid of it today!"

To make things worse there was a police station bang next door; Sammy was not a happy man.

Later, after a long recording session, we returned to the flat on Haverstock Hill to find Carol-Ann reading on the sofa with James Taylor's *Sweet Baby James* playing on the turntable.

"That'll all be taken care of tomorrow," she assured Sammy. He said that was cool and he left to join Linda in bed. It was around 2.00 a.m., and I was wondering where I was going to sleep now that the woman from Texas had bagged the sofa. I phoned a friend down Baker Street where I sometimes stayed. Carol-Ann was rolling a joint, and I put an acetate of the evening's recordings on the machine. We had a chat about music, smoked another joint and then crashed out – her on the sofa and me on the carpet.

Next morning I could hear them in the kitchen and was hit by the smell of toast and instant coffee that always reminds me of students. Soon they went out, leaving me with this beautiful Texan dope pedlar. We got talking, and it transpired that she'd smuggled the acid through Heathrow airport and that it belonged to Jerry Garcia and The Grateful Dead. She used to go out with Pigpen the keyboard player, who'd recently died, and now she was working for the Dead family as their acid distribution officer.

Her problem wasn't so much getting the acid into Europe but getting rid of it afterwards. She didn't have any heavy contacts in the drug underworld in London and needed some help and introductions. After sampling the acid, which was what we call 'clear', I volunteered to help her. She seemed like a really nice girl, in her early twenties, adrift in London with a mega problem. I told her that she could stash the acid in my flat in Cardiff and I'd get in touch with some people who'd shift it for her. She was overjoyed and said she needed a break from London. So we got some suitcases and took the acid down to Wales on the train from Paddington.

I had a Honda motorcycle outside the flat in Cardiff, and she said that she liked bikes – her previous boyfriend had ridden bikes. I could see that behind the smile she was still stressed – who wouldn't be, sitting on half a million acid hits with nowhere to put them! That evening we mounted the Honda and rode up to Herefordshire to visit some friends I had there.

Carol-Ann and I had a lot in common; she too was a macrobiotic vegetarian and into the study of ancient and modern mysticism and religions. She used to throw the I Ching every day and she carried the Egyptian Book of the Dead around, amongst other ancient spiritual writings. I was a member of the Spiritualist Association of Great Britain and regularly attended meetings, seances and other functions. A lot of people I knew in the late 1960s were studying the Caballa and witchcraft. I was in deep water here, although unaware of how deep that water was.

Carol-Ann became a constant companion; she would come to gigs with me, iron out any problems and liaise with the Warner Brothers people, which was great since I found it difficult to talk to them. She'd had plenty of experience as one of the Dead family – they also recorded for Warners. Carol-Ann fitted in well with the record industry bosses; she was a very worldly and dynamic person. When she was younger she'd been a medical secretary in a research facility at Houston University in Texas. She came from a straight home; apparently, her father was a high-ranking officer in the US Air Force. This didn't surprise me; I met people from all sorts of backgrounds in the hippy movement. The hippy culture was a universal bulldozer of social barriers, prejudices and class systems.

While I was rushing around, doing TV recording and gigs, and helping Carol-Ann offload her drugs, Tessa and the girls were living quietly in Caerforiog with the horses and other animals, Nofus the dog and Bitw the cat. Kevin and Karen from LA were also there, as were a couple of American musicians called Emily Muff. They were friends of The Incredible String Band, Mike Heron and Robin Williamson, and for a time had lived with them in an old house in the Preseli hills. The Pentre Ifan burial chamber was just over the garden wall! Heron and Williamson had opted for California, leaving Cathy and Janet (Emilly Muff) stranded with little money and nowhere to live. Carol-Ann met them at a Family gig in London, and I invited them to stay at Caerforiog. They needed a place to get their music together, and so they moved into two rooms at the quiet far end of the house. They were quiet thoughtful girls with a car load of musical instruments and little else; they lived on a bowl of rice a day with some salad and seemed to make all their clothes out of knitted wool and old curtains. Their time was spent reading, writing and playing their music. You hardly knew they were there, and their music was quiet acoustic stuff, a bit like The Incredible String Band, with Cathy playing wind instruments and Janet the guitar and Indian harmonium. I suppose visitors might have thought that Caerforiog was some kind of commune, but it wasn't. What was Caerforiog really about? Well, it was just a family and some creative friends living a very simple and healthy life, producing a good deal of music, sculpture, painting and poetry. Pity it came to such a sad, tragic, and untimely end!

Inevitably, Tessa found a hotel bill made out to Mr and Mrs Stevens in my coat pocket; my brief affair was discovered. Tessa had a pretty violent temper, but she didn't explode, her usual response when annoyed. Instead, she quietly demanded that I bring Carol-Ann to Wales to meet her. This really took me by surprise, even though our lifestyle, especially our diet, was designed to alleviate stress, decrease the pressure of life and promote a quiet demeanour and lifestyle. I'd never been so calm and healthy; I found that 'what you eat is what you are' is true to a point, but also that where you live is all important. Certainly, I couldn't now handle a stressful job entertaining and with frequent trips to London like I could earlier in the sixties.

A week later, I met Carol-Ann in London. She agreed to come down to Caerforiog to meet Tessa. In the meantime, Carol-Ann had been busy fulfilling her role in Jerry Garcia's plan to turn the whole of the world on to LSD. A lot of the acid had been exchanged for hashish and sent back to the USA by post. Good hash was five times the price over there – Garcia clearly had his head screwed on. I guess Carol-Ann took the money back personally; she was always jetting to and fro. However, there was still an awful lot of dope and money stashed around the place.

We arrived at Haverfordwest on the good ole' midnight train one fine summer's night, and as usual the local taxi was waiting by appointment. The taxi owners, Mr and Mrs Lunn, were quite elderly. Mrs Lunn, a simple matronly woman, was a pretty tough cookie from Haverfordwest. As we sped along the long and winding road to Caerforiog through that deep blue Pembrokian night under overgrown, grassy, wild flower hedges, I wondered what lay ahead.

The driveway into the farm was about a hundred metres long, wide and straight, so that any car arriving after dark immediately illuminated the yard. The taxi turned the corner into the drive and stopped outside the kitchen door. Warm welcoming amber lights shone from the windows, enhancing the perfect ultramarine and starlit night. I paid Mrs Lunn, and we turned towards the door where Tessa stood dressed in a long green robe. She smiled and seemed glad to see us. We entered the warm, subtly lit, low-ceilinged kitchen and silence, perfect peace.

Tessa had been sitting reading in the inglenook fireplace, and she appeared to be happy and calm. For a change, I was lost for words. I felt embarrassed in my own home, and so I played it by ear. We all sat by the fire, and someone made some herbal tea. An old red enamel coffee pot always used to bubble on the Aga stove, but since the Oshawa diet it had permanently retired. That evening seemed no different from any other homecoming; this wasn't the reception I'd expected. There was simply no perceptible change in the atmosphere. Tessa and Carol-Ann were talking away nineteen to the dozen and seemed to be getting on well. The anticipated explosion never came! Carol-Ann produced a joint of grass she said she had grown in the grounds of the state capitol in Austin Texas, and we shared it before we went to bed. Tessa had made up a room for Carol-Ann on the first landing next to ours, and we all retired about half past one. I went straight to sleep, half expecting the storm to break in the morning.

In the early hours of the morning, a storm did indeed break, though not the kind I'd expected or had ever witnessed before. I woke with the dawn to a loud chorus of birdsong. It was about 5 o'clock and I was alone in the bed. Still half awake, I went to the children's room across the landing. Their beds were empty, and I suddenly remembered Tessa saying that they'd gone to Nanna Betty's in Solva the previous day. Then I heard someone laughing below; it seemed to be coming from outside. I checked Carol-Ann's room, but she was still sound asleep. I went downstairs to the kitchen, where the front door was open. The laughter was coming from the yard, and through the kitchen window I could see Tessa standing barefoot in the middle of the yard wearing only her white cotton nightgown. She was laughing hysterically, and her face, translucent like porcelain, was distorted. This was not Tessa's face! It looked as if she was having a conversation with someone I could not see. She'd spout a stream of words, appear to listen to a reply, then burst out laughing. I'd seen hysterical people before, and there certainly was hysteria here, but there was also something more that was way beyond my comprehension. I went out of the door into the yard. Tessa didn't seem to be aware of me, even though I was only ten feet from her. She was looking straight at something else, something invisible to me. I went back into the house and woke Carol-Ann.

"Come down and have a look at this, for Christ's sake," I pleaded in confusion.

We both looked out of the upstairs window to see her talking, listening, then laughing uncontrollably.

"Does she sleep walk?" asked Carol-Ann.

"Never," I said. "I've never seen or heard of it." If she had been sleep walking, the noise she was making would have surely woken her. In fact, it was strange that she hadn't frightened the birds. The dawn chorus was still going strong, and I could see quite a few small birds in the bushes around the yard seemingly unaffected by the pandemonium in the yard.

"We'd better try to get her in the house," said Carol-Ann.

"No," I said. "No one comes here. Let's just watch her for a while. She might snap out of it!"

"But what the fuck is it?" exclaimed Carol-Ann.

Tessa wasn't standing still, she was moving around quite a bit, gesticulating with her hands and arms and sometimes waving her arms over her head. She was obviously sharing an intensely funny conversation with some person or persons that we couldn't see. What could have invoked this kind of hysteria? I was scared and so was my tough Texan friend!

We went down to the kitchen.

"Is she on anything?"

"No," I said emphatically. "Only that joint we had last night."

"No acid here?"

"No – not unless she got some from Kevin."

"I've never seen anyone quite like this on acid," said Carol-Ann.

"It doesn't look like acid," said I, the expert. Tessa didn't even keep aspirin in the house. We were on a strict health food diet and we didn't even drink alcohol those days.

"Can't leave her out there," I said. "She's only wearing that thin nightgown."

I went out again and stood near her, but still she didn't acknowledge my presence. Eventually I extended my hand and touched her on the arm. She recoiled violently, turning to me with vacant eyes.

"Fuck off!" she screamed. "Can't you see I'm talking with God?"

I shot through the door into the kitchen. Carol-Ann had seen and heard it all through the window.

"The frightening thing was," I said, "when she reacted and turned on me, her eyes were blank – it was like she couldn't see me. She certainly didn't know who I was!"

By this point, I'd decided just to monitor the situation and only take action if she was in danger of hurting herself. I must have been a state of shock. Here we were in an isolated farmhouse in north Pembrokeshire, it was about 6.30 in the morning, and this was a frightening experience that I could not handle. Tessa was obviously hysterical, potentially violent and on a plane that neither Carol-Ann nor I could reach. I thought the best thing was to get Pat Gillam the local doctor when the surgery opened at 9.30 a.m. Thank God, the rest of them were in London and the kids weren't there.

Suddenly, she was in the kitchen, not laughing now. She'd slipped in quietly and was standing near the door looking at us with that weird smile, as if from a higher level, like a cat who's just decided to have a game with a mouse.

"You don't know anything," she purred. "You can't see it, can you?"

Carol-Ann said quietly, "What can you see?" The response was violent, her eyes blazed.

"Shut up!" she screamed. "You're not here, you're not real, go away!"

I had to get Gillam. The energy that was coming off her was electric, and a translucent glow like a halo shone around her head. I'd never seen anything remotely like this. Carol-Ann got up quietly and went to the back kitchen to make some tea. When she came back she poured the tea, offering me a cup which I left on the table. I was totally distracted. During the last tirade Tessa had moved deeper into the room, and she now stood near the table. Carol-Ann offered her a mug of tea, which Tessa dashed out of her hand with an incredibly violent swing of the arm. The mug sailed through the air and shattered against the wall. "She's dangerous," said Carol-Ann, as Tessa screamed hysterically at thin air.

"Just don't touch her, don't go near her, I'm getting the doctor now!" I shouted, making for the back door, where the horse was in the field.

I rode hell for leather for Solva, some two miles down the hill from Caerforiog, and arrived at the doctor's too early for surgery. I knew he'd be up and sure enough he invited me into his kitchen, where his wife Rosemary was getting the girls ready for school.

"What's up?" he said. He probably thought I'd run out of Valium and was having a panic attack.

"Something really strange is happening in Caerforiog. I've never seen anything like it — it's Tessa." It was then I realized I was shaking uncontrollably. "She's totally out of control." I couldn't find the words to describe the experience I'd been having since five that morning!

"Go home," he said. "I'll be up straight after surgery."

I felt confused, tired and embarrassed. I went up to Bet's to see how the girls were. It was about 9 o'clock by now and I asked mother to hang on to the kids. I just said that Tessa had been ill in the night. I didn't say more than that, then back on the horse and away home. It was a beautiful day – sunshine, blue sky, very little wind. I couldn't help but enjoy the ride as it helped to blow the cobwebs away. I stopped to pick up the milk from Mrs Lloyd's in Felinganol. Apart from the nightmare up the road, it could have been a normal summer's day when we would have taken the kids down the beach.

"She's upstairs," said Carol-Ann. I went up to the bedroom, where Tessa was sitting on the bed facing the front window and writing furiously in a sketch-book. I went behind the bed and looked over her shoulder. The writing was tiny, not her own hand, and interrupted by doodles. This was unlike anything I'd seen her do before. She was a trained draughtswoman and sculptor – one of the best students in her year at Manchester Art school – and these were the doodles of a 5-year-old kid!

The morning went on, and on, and Tessa's behaviour became increasingly bizarre. Frantic bouts of writing and drawing would suddenly change to manic conversations with the unseen and inaudible, followed by frantic rushing around the house and yard. Carol-Ann and I kept close, but at a safe distance, in case she tripped or something. It was as if she was cocooned in some other reality.

Finally Dr Gillam arrived at about 11.30 a.m. Tessa heard the car before we did. In fact, we could neither see nor hear the car until it turned into the drive. Tessa, however, went running up the drive, shouting "Pat! Pat! Pat! I'm coming, I'm coming!" As Gillam's old black Morris Minor rattled down the track, Tessa danced around in her nightgown. "How the fuck did she know?" I thought. As Gillam climbed out of the car, his face turned white. We went into the kitchen with Tessa dancing around like a little kid.

"I think it's hypermania," he said. "I'll have to give her a shot of largactyl. Has she had anything?"

"Nothing," I said. Wearily he opened his bag and charged up a hypodermic. Tessa didn't even notice the shot going in.

He told me he'd come back when he'd finished his rounds and that the injection would make her sleep. However, the injection had no visible effect on her – if anything she was getting worse! Poor old Tessa, and poor old Carol-Ann; she'd only just met Tessa – she must have been really freaked out.

Gillam came back about two hours later, to be faced by the same uncontrolled laughing and screaming. He looked tired, worried and emotional – he thought a lot of Tessa, I knew that. He said that she'd have to go to hospital, but, in the meantime, he'd try one more injection of largactyl. I was to phone him in a couple of hours. He said he couldn't give her any more largactyl after this second dose; she'd had enough by then to put a horse to sleep. Gillam left, and the raving continued – singing, laughing, talking, writing. There was no oxygen in the air; it was as if she'd burned it all up like a powerful electric charge. I was amazed that the drug hadn't put her to sleep or at least sedated her. Carol-Ann and I were now totally exhausted and needed a break. I phoned Gillam, who suggested that Tessa might have to be sectioned and sent to Carmarthen mental hospital for a diagnosis and more appropriate treatment. He said that he'd come straight back and do what he could that night. On his return, he administered a large shot of morphine, then left saying that he'd be back in the morning. The morphine worked, although it only sedated Tessa enough for us to put her to bed. She'd had nothing to eat or drink for around thirty-six hours, and we tried to get some water into her as she drifted in and out of an opiate sleep. We both sat up with her, dozing in turn. Tessa was obviously very ill.

Next morning she was up again, raving and talking, dancing and laughing and writing, I'd hoped somehow that the narcotics and the sleep might have brought her down from her previous psychotic level.

No such luck! Whatever this was, it was too strong, more powerful than the sedatives and the morphine. I phoned Pat Gillam, and he told me that hospital was the only choice. With much regret he arrived later that morning and arranged for her to go to St David's hospital, Carmarthen.

# Chapter 16

# *Low*

Tessa was diagnosed as a chronic schizophrenic, with the added complication that she would not respond to drug therapy. Not that they had any drugs with which to treat schizophrenia at the time anyway! She ended up like most mentally ill people in those days, strapped to a bench with a piece of rubber stuffed between her teeth and high voltage electrical current passing though her brain until she convulsed and passed out.

I remembered her telling me that one of her family's best friends was a consultant psychiatrist at a hospital called Garlands, near Carlisle. I went to Dr Gillam and asked him if it was possible to have Tessa transferred there. Gillam went out of his way to help, and very soon Tessa was released from St David's, Carmarthen, and on her way to Carlisle. I was still shocked at the way she had flipped out of sanity overnight, with no perceptible warning signs.

Because we lived outside the village in a country farmhouse, only visited by friends, no one in the village, apart from the Gillams and my mother, knew anything of this affair. Much later I did tell some close family members and years later the girls. Naturally, Tessa's parents knew, but her mother as usual absolved herself of all responsibility – "Tessa's always been a problem child". Her parents had sent Jolyon, Tessa's younger brother, along with Tessa to a boys' boarding school on the Cumbrian coast. Tessa was staying with the headmaster's daughter in a cottage in the grounds of the school. The headmaster's daughter was a nymphomaniac whose husband was at sea most of the time. This woman used to have affairs with the sixth-form boys who would climb through a window, Tessa's bedroom window as it happened, to fuck their teacher. One night Tessa was assaulted by one of the boys. This resulted in a breakdown and she was confined to a room in a wing of the school. The headmaster and his wife who owned the school never reported this for obvious reasons. While Tessa was in this room recuperating, a young English teacher crept into her bed in the nude and tried to have sex with her. Tessa went berserk, hysterical, although she could remember the headmistress dragging her downstairs by her hair. She was thrown out of the school, and her parents blamed it all on Tessa.

I found out many years later that Tessa's grandmother, who was from Doncaster, used to go drinking and whoring at the races, leaving Ruth, Tessa's mother, with anyone who would have her. It was rumoured that Tessa's grandmother was schizoid. Tessa's mother escaped by joining the army as soon as she was old enough. It was there that she met Richard Bulman, Tessa's father, who held the rank of captain in the Royal Engineers. He married her and she went up the social ladder.

★ ★ ★

I had to get on with looking after the children. Luckily, my mother helped a lot, and she had the girls – Bethan was only a baby – for long periods of time. Amazingly, Carol-Ann stuck around, although by this time she'd sold all her drugs. She helped me with the house, my work and the kids. I was still getting plenty of gigs and television work so money was no problem. When we weren't in Caerforiog we stayed at the Sunbury Hotel on Newport Road, Cardiff, conveniently next door but one to the BBC club. The Scottish lady who owned it, Mrs Passmore, was a great character and used to give us our breakfast in the kitchen with the staff. She treated us like family and was very fond of Carol-Ann.

The BBC club in those days was a lively place, situated in a Victorian house with antique staircases. The house had not been altered much, apart from the bars in the basement, and on the ground floor there was a grand old fireplace in the main bar. It's now St Peter's Rugby Club and remains much the same. The club was a members-only club, and it was the place to meet people in broadcasting. Most of the light entertainment, news and current affairs producers and directors were regulars, and in the evenings there was always a bit of a party and some heavy drinking going on.

Carol-Ann got on well with the BBC people, and most of them came to know her quite well. She had become my personal assistant and was very good at her job, typing letters and dealing with bookings in person or on the telephone. We hardly ever went to Caerforiog now. All the other people who used to live there, Emilly Muff, Kevin Westlake and Karen Harvey-Hammer, had gone back to the USA. The house was beginning to look abandoned, a bit like the *Marie Celeste*. My mother had suggested that we give up Caerforiog and leave the children with her until Tessa came out of hospital. The horses had been sold, and only Nofus the black labrador and Bitw the black tomcat remained. Later my mother found homes for them through the RSPCA. The whole affair filled me with gloom, sadness and apprehension. Life would never be the same again; all we'd worked for had gone to ruin, except for the children, who thankfully were too young to understand. I had regular bulletins from Garlands hospital through Dr Gillam. Tessa had begun to respond to treatment, but it would take a long time. And they couldn't say how long.

Eventually Carol-Ann went back to the USA, and I just kept on singing and writing when I could. My heart wasn't in it at all, and I'd started drinking again, though not heavily; I only drank a champagne-like sparkling wine called Kriter and Asti Spumante. I had quite a few drinking mates at the club: Geoff Iverson, who later retired to Cyprus; Gareth Wyn Jones (Napoleon); Rhydderch Jones; Tegwyn Huws; and my old school pal from Solva, Huw Thomas, now gone away fishing. I was friends with many of the artistes too: The Hennessys, Iris Williams, Tony ac Aloma, Hogia'r Wyddfa, Mari Griffith and Hywel Gwynfryn. I also still had many friends in London, although I spent most of my time in Cardiff and Solva.

Something had happened to me during the trauma in Caerforiog. Among other things, I had lost confidence. The vegetarian way of life had been abandoned, and I was losing control in several areas of my life, which had changed so dramatically in such a short time. I would have to be careful, which was easier said than done. I was still in shock, it seemed.

The BBC Club could get quite wild at times. There was too much drinking, and after the bar shut the party crowd would go on to an Indian restaurant, then a night club or casino. We'd spend most of the early hours drinking, dancing or gambling. Some of the club owners would come to the BBC club to solicit customers. Most of us earned good money and could play hard too. There was one guy who looked like Muhammad Ali. His name was Cyril Clark and he owned a couple of clubs down Cardiff docks. Quite a few of the BBC club crowd thought it risqué to drink in the docks, where the people were a bit more colourful – or so they thought. This was bullshit; most of the docks people we met in the nightclubs were hustlers or prostitutes who were just after our money.

I became a really close friend of Hywel Gwynfryn, who hadn't been with the BBC very long and was a fresh, magnanimous and hugely talented guy. I had an extended invitation to stay in his Llandaf flat. He hadn't long been married to Eirianedd Ormond Thomas or Tos, as we called her. Her father was John Ormond Thomas the poet and film maker. She was a charming and beautiful girl, and a good musician too. Hywel helped me a lot at that time. He knew my situation, and he gave me a lot of good advice and support as I tried to reconstruct my life. When Tessa was cured I would have to find a home for us and the children. Hywel took me to some estate agents; he was in the process of buying a large house in Llandaf and thought it a good idea that I do the same.

*Disc a Dawn*, the Welsh version of *Top of the Pops,* went network around that time. This meant that it was broadcast live on all the BBC regional networks, even London. The producer Ruth Price decided to use 'Y Brawd Houdini', one of my songs, as the signature tune, and so my royalties really went up the charts. *Disc a Dawn* had a house band and a musical arranger, Bennie Litchfield, whom I used to meet regularly in the club along with the other musicians. The drummer was a Cardiffian, big John Tyler, an ex-Welsh Guardsman. What a character! John could turn his hand to anything, cheffing, tailoring, even playing the accordion. He lived in Cyril Crescent, right by the club, and his mother was the Hennessys' landlady. I think Ronnie Williams of the comedy duo Ryan and Ronnie was the presenter of *Disc a Dawn* at the time. They also had a network series on BBC1, which wasn't successful, but they were big in Wales. In the end, Ryan went solo, and he later died of a heart attack in America. Ronnie carried on for years as an actor and presenter; apparently he committed suicide by throwing himself into the Teifi estuary in St Dogmael's one Boxing Day. I think booze had a lot to do with the deaths of these great entertainers.

Vincent Kane, the current affairs presenter, was another 'clubber'. Vincent's a Cardiff Irishman who hated all things Welsh. I thought it odd that he worked for BBC Wales, but, I guess every little mouth has to be fed. He was quite open about his dislike of the Welsh, but I never heard him come across with any coherent reason for his dislike of *pobl gwlad y gân*. During an argument in the club, he once told me that he'd fight to the last drop of blood in his body to prevent his children having a 'Welsh education'. I later had the opportunity to make him look totally foolish on his own show *Kane on Friday*, which caused much merriment.

There were a lot of hustlers working at the BBC – people who should really have not been working in the context of creative broadcasting. These individuals were on the gravy train. It's a good job that there were enough talented people there to create some kind of equilibrium – as soon as I realized they were just like civil servants, I understood.

I also worked quite a lot for HTV, the rivals in Pontcanna Fields, but there was no doubt that *Disc a Dawn* was the most popular music show on Welsh television. It typified the Welsh pop music scene, which was largely based on amateur performers. As a result, the quality of the music was not of a very high standard, even though the *Disc a Dawn* team tried their best.

Many of the popular songs were politically inspired. Dafydd Iwan was perhaps the most popular singer, but a lot of people didn't like him because of his politics, which were undisputedly an aggressive form of Welsh nationalism. These were probably Tony ac Aloma fans, who were just as popular with their jingly little tunes and lyrics that meant Sweet Fanny Adams. Tony was another casualty of alcohol and would consume bottle after bottle of sherry every night. He was not a happy man. I liked his simplicity and we got on fine despite our obvious differences. He's alright now and runs a guest house in Blackpool with Aloma.

The Welsh Language Society was very active, attracting more and more members and a huge following. Fred Francis was one of the leading lights, as he is to this day. Even Carol-Ann joined the Welsh Language Society. There were protests practically every weekend, as well as demos, rallies, concerts and festivals. The Welsh Language Society was not only a major promoter of modern Welsh music, it also kept the newsmen and TV film crews busy. Then there was the ongoing daubing campaign – everyone seemed to be painting road signs and the extremists went even further and tore them down. Even those huge signs on motorways were dismantled and chucked on the side of the road!

We had been playing a concert at the Brangwyn Hall in Swansea, and afterwards I asked Huw Jones for a lift home to Cardiff. I must have fallen asleep in the back, and when I awoke the car was stationary in some dark leafy lane. I got out for a pee, but there was no sign of Huw or his mate. We were just off the Jersey Marine near the Briton Ferry bridge. I could hear clanking sounds and so I walked towards the bridge. There was Huw Jones and his mate halfway up a huge road sign and taking it down plate by plate with spanners. I thought it very funny at the time; a bit Robin Hood-ish, but extremely dangerous.

Another time there was a huge demo in Swansea civic centre; hundreds of people bearing stolen road signs converged on the city hall where they dumped the signs on the steps, right under the noses of a large squad of policemen and members of the Special Branch and their cameras. Quite a few members of staff at the BBC were members or sympathizers of the Welsh Language Society; indeed some were openly militant. At that demo in Swansea, Dr Meredydd Evans, Head of Light Entertainment, Gwenlyn Parry of the Drama Department and two ladies from the BBC were seen entering Swansea central police station carrying a large road sign. Merêd was the spokesman.

"We are in possession of stolen property. What are you going to do about it?"

The sergeant looked enquiringly at this band of seemingly respectable middle-aged people, asking "Where is the stolen property?"

"Here it is – this road sign!" as he plonked the sign on the counter.

The Sergeant looked uneasy, but with a faint smile on his face, thinking that they'd had a few drinks. "Wait here, I'll fetch someone."

Soon he was back with an inspector in tow. "Yes, what can I do for you?"

"We are in possession of stolen property, you must arrest us now!"

"I don't see any stolen property!"

By now Merêd was getting angry and he bashed the sign on the counter like a Methodist preacher with the *hwyl*. "This is the stolen property and we stole it!"

It was now clear that the police inspector had recognized Merêd and Gwenlyn. Trying to hide his amusement, he asked, "Well, where did you find it, then?"

"We didn't find it, we fucking stole it! And we demand to be arrested!"

By now, several people in the charge room were pissing themselves with laughter. Also, unbeknown to Merêd and his gang, an HTV film crew had followed them to the cop shop and were waiting outside, camera at the ready.

Eventually, the inspector decided that he'd had enough and that he should get rid of the would be-culprits: "Sergeant, will you take this sign to lost property?"

His words provoked Merêd, Gwenlyn and friends to grab hold of the sign and a tug of war ensued. The police won and Merêd and crew were ejected from the cop shop swearing loudly, caught on film by HTV.

Most of the sign painting and demolition was the work of drunken students. A much-loved girlfriend of mine, Gwenllïan, daughter of Jack Daniel (who was acting president of Plaid Cymru while his friend Saunders Lewis was in jail for arson), was a dauber. One night she got drunk in the Globe pub in Upper Bangor and went round the corner to her parents' house in Menai View terrace to fetch her paint pot and brush. She didn't have a clue where she was, but the result was plain to see for quite a few years – a political slogan daubed in cream paint on her own front wall! Let it be known that her political integrity is beyond doubt – impeccable it could be said.

I'm sure, readers, that many of you had a lot of fun during those days. We all did and it worked beautifully! Praise be the Welsh Language Society.

★ ★ ★

Y Dyniadon Hirfelyn Tesog (the madmen of the long hot yellow) was the name of a group of music students from Cardiff University. A mixture of string quartet and skiffle group, they used to appear in evening dress and were led astray by an eccentric cellist called Gruffydd Miles, a relative of Huw Gruffydd the actor. There was also Y Tebot Piws, also Cardiff students, who pretended to be insane; in fact, one member did go mad but he's fine now. Somehow out of their contrived madness came some of the most beautiful songs of the era, written by Dewi Morris, Emyr Huws Jones and the man who cracked up, Alun 'Sbardun' Huws. Fortunately they're all still alive and kicking; they didn't drink as much as some people I knew.

There was a club within a club at the BBC in Newport Road – the Cardiff Language Society, founded by Big John Tyler. The idea caught on big time, and the Borls and Turns were amazingly funny. All male members wore evening dress and green ties embossed with a golden winkle, while the ladies wore green knickers bearing the same emblem on the crotch. There was an official called the Arch Winkle, as well as an official knickers inspector, who carried a ceremonial broomstick with shaving mirror attached to one end and angled so that he could look up the lady winkles' skirts. People who were unsuitably dressed had to pay a fine, and all proceeds went to charity. Once I had to pay a fine for turning up at the pier ballroom in Penarth dressed as Fidel Castro – I'd been led to believe it was a fancy dress party!

Rhydderch Jones from Aberllefenni, near Corris, was a main man in the club. He used to direct *Disc a Dawn*, and when not drinking at the club he wrote plays and directed short videos for the show at various locations around Wales. I worked with Rhydd, as he was affectionately known, once as Will Hopkin in *Y Ferch o Gefn Ydfa* which was shot in the actual village in the Vale of Glamorgan where the story unfolded and also as Guto Nyth Brân, the famous fell runner of whom it was said that he could catch a bird on the wing or run races against horsemen for bets. This was filmed at Llanwynno in the hills behind Pontypridd. We even filmed in Solva and St David's.

Rhydd liked to have sexy dancing girls on his shows, whether they were relevant or not. He'd invariably bring them back to the club and ply them with drink in hopes of getting off with them. He was a gentle giant of a man, bearded and rather unkempt for an ex-paratrooper.

We actually filmed one of my songs 'Mynd i Bala ar y Cwch Banana' on a Geest banana boat at Barry Docks. As always, Rhydd had hired dancing girls, and they cavorted all over the ship to blaring rock music. Afterwards we were all invited to the cabin of the ship's captain, a Scot. I'd never seen so much booze before, and the only people who walked off that ship were myself and a driver named Reg, carrying Rhydd's personal assistant Glen Forrester between us. The captain gave us a huge stalk of bananas, and Rhydd invited the ship's officers to the club. When they arrived only Reg and I were still standing – all the rest were in bed sleeping it off! Some years later, Rhydderch died in a club near his house in Llanisien – yet another drink-related death. Coincidentally and unbeknown to me it was at the very same club I had my fiftieth birthday party. I hope his ghost enjoyed the *craic*!

Derek Boote from Anglesey was another club stalwart. He was a session bassist and guitarist at the BBC and he played on the records of many of the popular singers of the day: Tony ac Aloma, Iris Williams, The Hennessys, Bryn and Margaret Williams, and Ronnie and Ryan, to name but a few. He also came on tour to the many *nosweithiau llawen* played in rugby clubs and village halls around Wales. We'd have the late Alun Williams as compère and officiating at the pianoforte, and there would be Ryan and Ronnie, supported by myself, Heather Jones, The Hennessys, Iris Williams etc. In the early days, a quiet unassuming young man would sometimes appear. His name was Max Boyce and he came from the Neath Valley. He used to sing straight Welsh folk songs in those days; it was only later that he became world famous for his rugby songs. These live shows were usually on weekends and were always hilarious. Afterwards we'd gravitate to certain hostelries where we'd carry on singing and drinking all night. Then we'd call in Sunday lunch-time at the Skinners in Aberystwyth, or the Red Lion in Dinas Mawddwy, kept respectively by the late Elfed Evans and Danny the Red, two infamous all-night tipplers.

Another interesting character was John Morgan, who was a director of HTV as was his great friend Wynford Vaughan Thomas. John was a political journalist. Originally from Swansea, he became editor of *New Statesman*. He was involved with all sorts of characters on the London showbiz and political scenes and was a big time whisky-drinker. At one time, he had an evening chat show on HTV, *John Morgan at 10.30*, based on a show hosted by David Frost. John's show had a live studio audience, with the front two rows consisting of specially invited people. There was also a panel of experts and celebrities sitting in. John and the celebs would 'chew the fat' over 'burning issues' and public controversies, and I was hired to write a topical song to open each programme. I would be supplied with information by researchers, or would glean my own information.

The producer of the show was Terry De Lacy, who would invite the two front rows to a hospitality room and ply them with drinks. Usually, most of the guests were as pissed as parrots by the time the show went out live at 10.30 on Friday nights. John and the celebs would have been up in the boardroom drinking whisky and champagne. It could have been said that *John Morgan at 10.30* was a party, thinly disguised as a television show!

I remember one night when racism was the topic of the show. There were quite a few Welsh nationalists in the audience, one of whom was Neil Jenkins, a founder member of the Welsh Language Society. Amongst other things, Neil was a notorious drunk, and a very noisy one too. As the floor manager cued me for the opening song, a Big Bill Broonzy number called 'Black Brown and White', Neil got on his feet in the front row, screaming his head off, mainly at Enoch Powell but also at the panel in general. I'm into the first verse "They was takin' them white men's numbers, but they was not taking mine, and if Neil Jenkins doesn't sit down and shut up I'm comin over to beat his fuckin head in!" All went out on the air; John didn't have a bleeper button. Next day, walking through Cardiff I was greeted with handshakes and pats on the back by several passers by who'd seen the show. "Well done, Meic, I'd have smacked him one as well if I'd been there."

Sadly John Morgan died of cancer in his early fifties. His illness was filmed as a documentary, and he left the proceeds to cancer research. He also left behind a lot of sad people, including his wife Mary and son Aled.

John would stay with Terry De Lacy at his house by the river in Taff's Well. They were fond of throwing small house parties after shows and I would frequently be invited. We usually sat around drinking and talking, consuming substantial quantities of wine and whisky. In fact, the distilleries of the Isle of Skye should award John Morgan a posthumous medal for aiding the economy of Scotland!

I was at HTV one day, when up popped Terry De Lacy. "Can you come up the house tonight? John will be down from London and I've got something to show you." I went up on a motor bike that Carol-Ann had bought for my birthday. When I arrived, they were sitting round a coffee table drinking whisky and gin. "Open that," said De Lacy pointing towards what looked like a large date box. Inside the box, wrapped in a doily, was half a kilo of prime Nepalese hash.

"There's another one here as well," said Terry.

"Where did you get this?" I said.

"Some lunatic sent it from India in the fuckin' post. Can you get rid of it?" Terry was really pissed off that some gay friend of his had set him up. There was more than enough hash there to put him in jail if the cops had found it!

"Sure," I said, "no worries. I'll take it away now. How much do you want for it?"

"Just get it out of here, that'll do for me."

That night half of it went to Dave Edmunds, and the rest was doled out to friends and smoked! When the gay guy came back he was absolutely livid and tried to give me a hard time. "Fuck off" is all he got from me. It turned out later that he'd come back from India by air leaving his father to return in a Landrover. The Landrover had got busted at the Turkish border, and as it was loaded to the gunwales with black sharash Dad was thrown in jail.

★ ★ ★

At about this time I met a beautiful girl from Cardigan, and we started going out together. Her Auntie Maj kept a pub called the Stag and Pheasant just outside Carmarthen, an old roadside tavern much frequented by Cayo Evans and the Free Wales Army boys who would arrive in paramilitary uniforms and sing and drink all night. Most of them were non-Welsh speakers from Merthyr, Llanelli and Swansea. They were all great characters. I used to stay at the Stag with Jan, and we'd earn our keep by helping in the pub. I sometimes played in the bar of an evening, but my main job was cooking breakfast. I had a Martin D28, which Carol-Ann had bought for me in California. One night I left it in the bar and went to bed early. The next morning it had all sprung apart at the seams, even the bridge had lifted. The bastards had filled it with piss and beer for a laugh!

These were some very happy times, but my girls were growing up with Betty down in Solva, and Tessa was still up in hospital in Cumbria. I still had a big problem! On a visit to see the kids in Solva I received a letter saying that Tess would soon be discharged; there was no more they could do for her. "Does this mean she's cured?" I thought.

# Chapter 17

# The End of The Sixties

I was in London visiting Gary Farr with whom I still played the occasional gig. We had a great bass player, Andy Lee, who also played with Spooky Tooth, a Birmingham band. On the previous Saturday night, we'd played a gig in a northern art college and were now back in London. Already, Solva was calling again, and on the way the three of us called by at the BBC in Cardiff to record some new songs.

During the recording session, I received a telephone call from my mother. My grandmother Blodwen, who by this time was senile, was on her death bed. Could I go home? Mam was asking for "Meicel bach". We packed up quickly, piled into Gary's Austin estate car and drove like the wind to Solva. When we arrived, we all went up to Mam's bedroom. She was lying in bed propped up in a pile of pillows. She looked weak, pale and close to death, but she was in no pain and seemed to be half asleep. Nevertheless, she recognized me instantly and tried to lift herself up. "Who are these boys with you?" she asked. "They're musicians. We've been playing at the BBC," I said, suddenly realizing that the son of her husband's hero, the boxer Tommy Farr, was against all odds standing in her bedroom.

"Here is Tommy Farr's son Gary," I said.

A strange look crossed her face. "Not Tommy Farr who fought the Black Bomber in the Yankee Stadium?"

"Yes," I said, "that's the one. You can remember?"

Gary moved forward, and she weakly extended her hand which he held gently. Then she smiled and said, "I never thought I would have the pleasure," – pause – "of shaking the hand of Tommy's son. William Henry used to love to see your father fight. He was the greatest." – pause – "I'm very proud to meet you." Gary burst into tears; he was a very emotional man.

At that point, I saw Doctor Gillam arriving in his old black Morris Minor. "The doctor's here, Mam. Me and the boys will have to go now." We all bade farewell, each of us amazed and stunned by this strange and sad meeting.

I never saw her alive again; she died three days later, by which time I was back in London. Once again Gary drove to Solva like a bat out of hell, but we were too late, and she died fifteen minutes before our arrival. My mother was there, as were two of my uncles who were also big fans of Tommy Farr and all agog to meet his son. "I'd do anything for a woman like her," Gary said.

I stayed in Solva for Mam's funeral, again in the tiny chapel, Penuel near where Dada was born. She was buried in the graveyard behind, with William Henry. Mam had been a mother to me – that simple, uneducated woman, who had worked hard all her years, borne seven children and then late in life had the loving kindness to take me on when I was nearly dead, nurse me back to good health, and bring me up as her own. Both she and William Henry were in their sixties by then – she was an angel. My mother told me later that she had died peacefully. "She went to sleep, there was no pain." They buried her with a little silver cross that I'd bought in Petticoat Lane in London and given her on our last meeting.

Shortly after Mam's funeral, a letter came from Tessa's mother. Tessa had been discharged from Garlands and was now staying with her parents at Cumwhinton just outside Carlisle. She wanted to make arrangements for Tessa to come to Solva to be reunited with the children. I arranged to meet Tessa off the Carlisle train in Cardiff a few days later, where I was doing a show for the BBC. I hadn't a clue what to expect, so I booked a double room at the Central Hotel, just a few yards from the station. It was six months since I'd last seen her, but I'd written to her regularly at the hospital and had received a few replies, mostly in the form of grotesque line drawings on sketchpad paper, with nonsensical notes in tiny writing that was practically unreadable. These notes were very similar to an unposted letter I'd found whilst clearing out at Caerforiog. It too was written in miniscule handwriting and was addressed to one of the Milford druggies who used to frequent my house when I was away working. Tessa had obviously been having a sexual affair with him.

I went to Central Station to meet the 4.30 train, waiting on the platform near the stairwell so I wouldn't miss her. I could hardly believe that she was arriving after all these troubled times. The train pulled in and suddenly the platform was teeming. The crowd dispersed, but I still couldn't see Tessa. Then as the train pulled out, I caught sight of someone who looked like a young girl of twelve or so, wearing a tweed overcoat and clutching a small holdall. At first I didn't recognize her, but it was Tessa, looking like a lost child who'd been abandoned and was waiting to be rescued. Immediately I knew that all was not well.

I kissed her and took her holdall. She seemed dazed, confused, so I took her arm and led her to the exit. She barely seemed to recognize me.

"How are you?"

"I'm better, so they say, but I have to take these tablets – tranquilizers."

"How long have you been taking these tablets?"

"Oh, a long time now, and I've had a lot of electric shock treatments too."

By the look of it, she'd really had the stuffing knocked out of her. She was totally cowed and heavily sedated. I cast my mind back to the morning she flipped in Caerforiog, which now seemed an eon ago. I could remember vividly the massive energy she generated. This was a changed girl. Before the schizophrenic attack Tessa was a strongly outspoken, even aggressive person, but the woman walking beside me seemed to have regressed to a meek child-like state. We walked hand in hand to the hotel and went up to the room. I'd already bought some fruit and flowers and one of the hotel staff had put them in bowls around the room. The room looked good, welcoming, and almost lived in.

"Would you like some fruit? Are you hungry?"

She took an apple and ate it slowly as I watched from an armchair on the other side of the room. "Yes, I'm quite hungry." Her voice seemed to come from very far away.

"We'll go to a restaurant," I said.

"No," she replied agitatedly. "I'm not used to people. The train was awful! All those people pushing and shoving. I'd rather stay here. Can we have something here?"

"I'll order some food when the kitchen opens."

"That will be fine," she said.

I turned the television on, and by the time I'd tuned into a programme and looked around, she'd fallen asleep on the bed, still buttoned up in her little-girl coat. She still looked about twelve years old, and I was shaken.

I sat watching her sleep for a half hour or so and then went down to the hotel bar in much need of a drink. Perhaps it was the shock of being in the outside world after such a traumatic experience, then the long journey. They shouldn't have put her on a train on her own. She wasn't ready, she needed to acclimatize. I felt happy that she was out of hospital, but had they released her too soon? The letter from the psychiatrist had definitely stated that her treatment was finished. I wondered whether she was in a fit state to act as a mother again and whether the treatment had failed. It was impossible to know! In those days, after a person had been sectioned under the Mental Health Act (which meant that a doctor had diagnosed a mental illness, that the diagnosis had been verified by a second doctor and that the order to commit the patient to a mental hospital had been signed by both doctors), the next of kin had little or no control of the situation. Backed by the law, the hospital exercised complete control of the situation, including the nature of the treatment given. The next of kin were kept out of things and had to rely on information given by hospital staff regarding the condition and progress of the patient.

I finished my drink and went back upstairs. Tessa was still sleeping, and I was glad of that. She slept for another two hours; it was about 8.30 by the time she woke. She looked around the room and then at me sitting in the chair. There was no recognition. "Tessa, it's me – Meic. We're in Cardiff at the Central Hotel." She muttered that she thought she was still in Cumwhinton and said that she was very hungry. She hadn't eaten all day; she had no money!

"We'll go down to the restaurant," I said.

I didn't have a clue what she could eat; she'd been a macrobiotic veggie when she was admitted to hospital. The hotel restaurant was large and quiet, and we ordered omelettes and a bottle of Chardonnay. Tessa said that she couldn't drink alcohol because of the medication, so she ordered fruit juice, before picking at her omelette, vegetables, boiled spuds and salad. She seemed sedated and wasn't talking much; she didn't even mention the kids.

"We'll go to Solva tomorrow to see Betty and the kids," I said eventually.

"Oh, the children," she said vacantly. "How are they?"

"Looking forward to seeing you," I replied. I was dining with a stranger.

Next morning we were on a train heading on that all-too-familiar journey west. Tessa still wasn't talking, I'd bought her a couple of magazines, and she read quietly with what seemed like little interest. She hardly looked out of the window and made no comment as the journey progressed. I guessed that she'd taken her medication after breakfast; she'd bathed and been in the bathroom for some time.

"My mother says I shouldn't live in Wales any more," she said quietly. "They've sorted out a house for me in Carlisle."

This was the first positive statement she'd made since she arrived the day before. In fact, these were the only important words she'd said to me since she'd flipped six months earlier.

"Will you be happy to live there?" I said.

"Oh, yes. Besides there'll be my parents and Jolyon and the children."

Plans had obviously been made by other people, who had not had the courtesy to consult me at all. Tessa didn't seem a fit person that day to take responsibility for the care of two small girls. It dawned on me that I had been excluded from plans for the immediate future of our children.

"Who is sorting out this house in Carlisle?" I said quietly.

"Oh, Mummy, Dido and Dr Graham," she replied.

With that we were at Haverfordwest station, and I could see old Mrs Lunn's taxi waiting as we crossed the footbridge.

"Hello, Meic. To the farm is it?" Mrs Lunn smiled at Tessa. "Haven't seen you for a long time." But Tessa didn't seem to recognize her.

"It's Mrs Lunn, the taxi lady," I prompted.

"Oh yes, I think I can remember," was the reply, although I don't think she really remembered Mrs Lunn, even though she must have driven Tessa dozens of times.

"No," I said to the taxi lady. "Could you drive us to my mother's in Upper Solva?"

Tessa sat in the back and I in the front – she silent all the way as I chatted to Mrs Lunn. We rolled down Solva hill over the narrow stone bridge and down Main Street, but still there was no reaction from Tessa. I'd have to speak to Dr Gillam.

The taxi dropped us at my mother's house. Betty was expecting us; the front door opened and there they were, Bethan in my mother's arms and Wizzy running towards us with Nofus the labrador beside her. Wizzy leaped into my arms, and the dog jumped all over Tessa, obviously delighted to see her. Tessa reacted with a slow smile, pushing the delighted dog down. She seemed pleased to see her daughters after such a long time, but something was missing. She was still far away.

We sat in the living-room on my mother's old three-piece suite drinking tea. Tessa had Bethan on her lap and was playing quietly with her. Bethan had always been a quiet baby, always happy, never crying much and very easy going. My mother was in the kitchen preparing a meal and prattling nineteen to the dozen through the open door. Tessa hadn't taken off her schoolgirl coat, donated by Mother Superior, which was buttoned up tightly to the throat like chain mail. It seemed to protect her, as if without it she would be vulnerable and might fall apart.

"She's not right," my mother said worriedly, when Tessa had gone upstairs. "What the hell have they done to her? This will never do!"

I'd noticed that Tessa had a deep furrow in her forehead, like a deep cleft between the eyes. I imagined it might have been caused by the electric shock treatment; it had not been there before. Under scrutiny, her face had aged noticeably, but she still had this child-like look about her and even her voice had a shy, childish tone.

It was good to be home again, especially in my mother's house, and I was looking forward to her excellent cooking. Tessa sat quietly in an armchair facing the television. The lounge was a long room running east to west, with an open fire, and large windows at each end. The rear window looked out on a long garden which ran down to Llanunwas woods with its tall trees and noisy rookery. I looked through the window at a loss for words; all I could hear was the ticking of the clock on the mantelpiece and the raucous cawing of hundreds of crows. It was a familiar sound and had a strangely calming effect on me; I drifted away into the sky with the bird wings and clouds.

Tessa had had to give up the macrobiotic diet at the hospital, where she'd been obliged to eat whatever was on the menu. We ate a huge roast dinner, one of Betty's special treats. I remained deep in thought, while my mother, who could talk the hind legs off a donkey, chattered away, filling up space that could easily have become embarrassed silence. Later we went to see Dr Gillam and his family. They were happy to see Tessa of whom they had always been very fond. As usual, Gillam was non-committal, just saying that it would take some time for Tessa to get used to the outside world. He also enquired about her medication and seemed content with the drug therapy; he obviously didn't want to get involved and anyway she was no longer his patient. It looked as if I'd have to go along with this plan to rehouse Tessa and the children in Carlisle. If I argued against it, there would be even more trouble and strife! But first of all I'd have to go up there with her to see exactly what had been arranged.

Tessa's mother, an extremely selfish and self-centred person, had all but washed her hands of her daughter years ago and had never shown much interest in being a mother. Ruth couldn't stand me either, or the Welsh. She had a list, Tessa once told me, of the human race, with the English at the top and the Welsh, Irish and blacks at the bottom; I had no chance with a fascist like her! It was no surprise that Ruth considered me to be the architect of all this trouble.

I always felt apprehensive when I went to Carlisle; I'd never felt welcome there and couldn't wait to get away. Tessa had once felt the same, although she was very fond of her father as he was of her. Unfortunately, his work as an engineer in various parts of Africa meant that he was hardly ever home. Still, we left by train for Carlisle a couple of days later, leaving the children with my mother. We took a taxi from Carlisle station to Tessa's parents' house, which stood beside a country lane in the village of Cumwhinton, about three miles south of Carlisle. The house was a former red-brick barn, now converted into a charming cottage surrounded by a large orchard and a well-kept garden. Gardening was Ruth's hobby and she had green fingers. I was told loftily that Tessa had been allocated a council house on a new estate nearby and that she could move in at any time. Where I was going to live was not mentioned – Ruth had ruthlessly written me out of the script and I was not part of the plan. My main concern, however, was the future of the children who'd spent most of their lives in Solva. I arranged to meet Dr Graham, Tessa's psychiatrist and the only person with the answers, or so I thought!

Dr Graham, a dapper man dressed in country style, wearing tweeds, a discreetly checked Vyella shirt and brown brogue shoes, had known Tessa from childhood. It was clear that he really wanted to help her and believed that the treatment had been successful. He told me that she was a chronic schizophrenic who had been resistant to drug therapy, of which I was already well aware. He went on to say that they had tried some powerful new drugs on her, which didn't make me feel very happy, to say the least. He also said that she had a very strong suicidal tendency. Tessa had never shown any sign of this, apart from falling off horses, and I had always felt that she had an exceedingly strong and well-founded survival instinct. He asked me about the children, where they were and so on, and then stated emphatically that Tessa's future mental stability rested to a large extent on them. I deduced from this very one-sided conversation that if I decided to split with the children from Tessa, it would be detrimental to her future mental health and could lead her to commit suicide. This shook me considerably, especially the suicide angle of which I was totally ignorant.

Next day we went to see Tessa's new home, which was on a pleasant country estate with a profusion of well-established elm, beech and ash trees and a wide but shallow river running around its edge. The house was new – a typically modern two-bedroomed house with a lawn in front and a small walled backyard. The estate itself was a bit far from the centre of Carlisle, but there were shops and a pub on it. All in all, it seemed a peaceful, pastoral place.

I left Tessa with her mother; they planned to move into the house soon. On I went to Cardiff, where I had business to attend to. Later, back in Solva, I discussed the situation with my mother, an ex-nurse of the old school who trusted doctors implicitly. Moreover, she was too old to bring up two children, one of whom was a baby. I appreciated her situation and all the help she'd given me to date. I came to the pessimistic conclusion that it would be better to play along with the Carlisle plan and hope for the best. I knew that the relationship I'd enjoyed with Tessa was most probably over, but I still held a glimmer of hope.

The original Tessa was all but dead, or so it seemed, but things might change! The girl I'd met so recently from that train in Cardiff was a stranger, but yet she had been my lover and she was the natural mother of my children. It was clear that my work and future lay in Cardiff – commuting from Carlisle would have been virtually impossible. So I decided to allow the children to go and live with their mother in Carlisle. This was a momentous decision, and one I would live to regret, God help me!

# Chapter 18

# Balanced in the
# Hands of Time

Thus began what I thought would be the final chapter of my relationship with Tessa. At the time I thought that by handing over the children to her I had sealed the fate of our lives as a family. I was wrong. It didn't happen that way – the hand of fate had dealt me strange cards.

Tessa's father duly arrived at my mother's house in Solva driving his beloved old Daimler coupé. Tessa was with him. She seemed to have improved a great deal, in that her reactions to the children were more normal, and that strange and distant attitude I've tried to describe had disappeared. There was more life in her; she was more positive and focused rather than non-committal and listless. She was obviously making the effort to live in the outside world again.

My mother and I waved them goodbye, and I wondered what I would do next. I had plenty of gigs and other work on the agenda. A little earlier, I had been commissioned by the late Wilbert Lloyd Roberts, then head of Cwmni Theatr Cymru (the Welsh theatre company based in Bangor), to write musical interludes for Y Claf Diglefyd – a Welsh version of Le malade imaginaire – which the company was going to rehearse soon. I was also thrilled by the idea of performing the role of Pulchinello, the lovelorn fool, which was rather apt in my present situation. I travelled by train to Bangor to begin rehearsals.

I had not met Wilbert Lloyd Roberts before; he was an ex-BBC drama producer, whose dream was to establish a Welsh-language national theatre company. Soon after I arrived, I was introduced to members of the cast, most of whom were just out of college, although others such as Meredydd Edwards, Gaynor Morgan Rees and Iona Banks had been treading the boards for a while. I was assigned the task of teaching the young actors, who made up the chorus, to sing the songs in the musical interludes that were always an important part of a Molière comedy. These young actors – Dafydd Hywel, Sharon Morgan, Dyfan Roberts, Marged Esli and others – were dressed like a band of gypsies, and some of them also performed other roles such as doctors. Owen Garmon was also a member of the cast. The wardrobe mistress was the late Mrs Stanley of Old Colwyn. She'd been in the theatre all her life and she was in her late sixties by then. Mrs Stanley was a great character, full of theatrical anecdotes, and outrageous stories. Wilbert had surrounded himself with a huge amount of talent – for example, Nesta Wyn Jones the poet was a production assistant and Alan Cook also worked there. I could write a book on this tour alone. Let it suffice to say that *Y Claf Diglefyd* was a resounding success, and a credit to all who worked on it.

Suddenly, there came a bolt from the blue, in the form of a card from Texas. Carol-Ann Maw, my old rock-'n'-roll girlfriend, would be landing at Heathrow the following day. My mother Bet had never liked her much and was of the opinion that Carol-Ann was a witch. As a result, I always had to play the affair down; if mother had known what was really going on, the shit would have hit the fan big time.

The following evening I was sitting in the club drinking with a few friends from the BBC when a telephone call came through for me; Carol-Ann was in Cyncoed. One of the BBC girls, Helen Pritchard, drove me up in her red Triumph Spitfire, and I found Carol-Ann walking in the rose garden of an old house. Apparently she'd

met the old guy who lived there on the plane and he'd invited her to stay. Nevertheless, she moved into the Sunbury Hotel that night, and the affair started up again, as did the dope circus.

I had always wanted to produce a record of my own and one for Heather Jones. At the time I didn't really know how to go about it, but I had taken a lot in whilst recording in London and at the BBC in Cardiff. We decided to release our records to coincide with the National Eisteddfod at Ammanford and that's what happened. My old mate Gareth Wyn Jones booked free time at a BBC studio in Cardiff, and Bill Lovelady came up from Cardigan to play guitar. Some of the tracks were recorded in Central Sound, London, including 'Mynd i Bala ar y Cwch Banana' with Heather and Geraint Jarman singing backing vocals. These records soon sold out and are hard to find now; if you have one, they are worth around £50 a copy!

Carol-Ann and I travelled down to Ammanford in Ronnie Williams's Jaguar. Ronnie and Ryan had booked a hall for their show, and they asked me to do a spot every night that week. They had booked a backing band, with Noddy Gape and John Tyler as the rhythm section, and I asked these old friends to play with me too. At the time, I had a beautiful Martin D 28, and Carol-Ann, generous as ever, had bought me a second-hand Gibson in a shop in San Francisco. The shows were great, packed out every night. It was like a sauna, and I had to play stripped to the waist. Carol-Ann and I camped next to a huge old army tent which housed Dewi Pws, Y Tebot Piws, and Y Dyniadon Ynfyd Hirfelyn Tesog who, as I've said before, were a serious bunch of drunken loonies. Every night they held an all-night party after the pub; it was madness. One night we found a young guy lying unconscious on the grass outside our tent. He was paralytic drunk, wearing nothing but a T-shirt and jeans, and the loonies had soaked him with beer and cider and even pissed all over him. He was in a state, freezing cold and suffering from exposure. Carol-Ann and I had to warm him up, and so we took him into our small tent and put him in a sleeping bag. His teeth were chattering. Later we became friends, and Gerallt Llywelyn is now a terrific professional photographer and Caernarfon county councillor, as well as a pretty good guitarist.

On the last night of the Ronnie and Ryan show I went out for a breather and to cool off a bit. A girl from Cardigan whom I'd always fancied leaped on me, and by the time Carol-Ann came looking for me we were snogging passionately in a doorway. The next day was the final day of the Eisteddfod, and Carol-Ann and I parted for the last time. I can picture it to this day. She was walking slowly down the road towards Swansea carrying the old Gibson guitar, while the Martin and I headed north towards the A40. I never saw her again, but some years later when I was visiting my mother in Solva she handed me an air mail letter from America.

"I wouldn't answer that," said Bet.

"Why, what's in it?" I replied. I knew she always steamed my letters open; it was a bit of a joke.

"There's an airline ticket in there," she said.

"Who's it from?"

"That American witch!" my mother screamed. "And she's getting married in North Carolina!"

"Great," I said, "Who to?"

"I don't bloody know, but she wants you there!"

"I wonder why," I said, throwing the unopened letter on the fire and watching it slowly burn. That was the end of that; I never heard from her again.

1970 was a hell of a year, both good and bad, and *Y Claf Diglefyd* was probably the highlight.

My relationship with Warner Brothers, to whom I was still legally contracted, was deteriorating rapidly. Sammy had moved to the States and greater, greener pastures and now lived in Sacramento. For my

*Rhydaman Eisteddfod, 1970*

own part, I was much more interested in the Welsh music scene, which was beginning to reveal a lot of future potential, and the gigs rolled in. The 1971 Eisteddfod was to be held in Bangor, and Wilbert Lloyd Roberts asked me to produce a rock show for it. There had never been a professionally produced show like this in Wales before, so it was a bit of a challenge. The show was going to be staged in the large hall of a technical college on Ffriddoedd Road, and I was involved from the start. We decided to book Y Tebot Piws, Y Dyniadon, Y Diliau, Heather Jones and myself. There was also a great band from south Wales called James Hogg – Rob Ashong on bass and slide guitar, Gregg Harries lead guitar and John Lloyd on drums – and I decided to book them as the house band.

During the planning stages of the show, I found myself missing the children more and more. Even though I'd been preparing myself for this, I couldn't stop worrying about them all the time; it was very distracting. I wrote to Tessa regularly, but they all seemed so far away. Then I received a letter from Tessa saying that she'd taken up with a young agricultural worker who had asked her to marry him. This would have distanced me from the children even more, and I decided to travel to Carlisle to see what was going on and to be with the children.

Tessa's house was clean and tidy and the kids went wild when they saw me. Tessa told me about the young guy who wanted to marry her and she said she was in two minds. Basically, she was lonely with only the kids for company; she had no friends in Carlisle. This put me on the spot, and I made yet another rash move by asking her to marry me. She was overjoyed and said she'd always wanted to marry me anyway. So that was that! I told her she'd have to come to Cardiff to live and that I'd find a house for us, to which she readily agreed. She was fed up in Carlisle, where nothing ever happened. Tessa liked entertainment, especially pubs, clubs and dancing, and there was little fun for her up there at that time. After a couple of days, I left for Cardiff to go house-hunting, and I soon found a house to rent at 16 Evansfield Road in Llandaff North. The house was close to the station and a main bus route and within walking distance of the BBC just over the river in Llandaf. And the HTV studios in Pontcanna were just down the road.

Tessa was eager to marry as soon as possible, but the big show in Bangor was only weeks away. Consequently, we decided to get married in Bangor during the Eisteddfod. The Castle Hotel was next to the cathedral, and as I knew the manager quite well we booked in there. I also made arrangements to get married in Bangor registry office. At the time, I was very friendly with Hywel Gwynfryn, but he told me he didn't want to be best man because every one asked him to do that. He felt that I ought to give another friend the chance. So, I phoned Nick Golding in Norwich. "Sure," he said. "Fucking marvellous!" I also phoned my mother who had mixed feelings; she'd been through the mill of Tessa's madness and was wary and unsure.

Both performances of *Sachliain a Lludw* were a sell-out. The rehearsals had gone well, but none of us knew what to expect since no one had produced a live show with lighting rigs and a professional sound system in Wales before. I shouldn't have worried; everyone raved about it. During the finale, the performers could hardly move as the audience invaded the stage, which became home to a frenzy of gyrating dancers and drunks all singing their heads off. This really was a first for Wales! Wilbert was overjoyed at his first foray into the world of rock-'n'-roll, and all of the performers knew that they were part of a ground-breaking production.

The wedding day arrived, and the whole cast of the show were invited along with a host of other friends. The reception was to be held in the ballroom of the Castle Hotel. It was a beautiful sunny day, and we were staying in a suite that had once been occupied by King

George V. There was a bloody great brass plaque screwed to the bed head proclaiming the event!

My mother arrived by car, and we all strolled down to the registry office, while Mrs Wilbert Lloyd Roberts and her daughter looked after the children. Tessa was dressed in a long and elegant dress of beige and silver satin with shoes to match. I wore a black three-piece suit whilst Hywel and Nick Golding wore light grey suits and floral ties. Afterwards we returned to the Castle for a three-course lunch with loads of champagne and red wine. Tessa's parents arrived, a bit amazed at the opulence of the event. The Eisteddfod atmosphere was also a bonus. Hywel drew me aside after the meal and offered to foot the bill for the food in lieu of a wedding present, which was so kind. That's the sort of guy he is.

Later on the bands took to the stage. Y Dyniadon, most of who were classical music students, were first on in their evening dress tail-coats and bow ties. They started with some chamber music, which impressed Tessa's snobbish mother. She didn't have a clue that they were taking the piss until they played 'Eine Kleine Nachtmusik' which gradually picked up tempo until it was being played at breakneck speed. The finale came when one of the fiddlers threw down his violin and produced a washboard from under his seat and started battering it with an umbrella. The rest of the band then started shouting and screaming, throwing their instruments in the air and dancing like a bunch of dervishes.

By now, a crowd of people were watching through the big glass double doors, so I told the landlord to let them in. It was going to be a party! Soon the place was packed: everyone was there, even Sir T. H. Parry-Williams and Lady Amy. It was a bit too much for Tessa's parents who left early driving straight back to Carlisle as the party raved on. Suddenly, Tegwyn Huws, the manager of the hotel, dressed in his loud check suit and boasting huge mutton-chop sideburns, leaped to the microphone shouting, "The champagne is on the house!" That reception didn't cost me a penny! When the booze started to get low, Huw Ceredig just took an ice bucket round and collected a pile of money, and the next thing they were dragging cases of beer into the ballroom, piling them in the middle of the dance floor. Anyone who could sing or knock out a tune got on stage; it was one of the best and most spontaneous of parties ever seen. Poor old Hywel Gwynfryn tried his best to officiate as some kind of compère, but by then everyone was drunk and enjoying themselves too much to care about decorum. Nick Golding, the best man, got annoyed because everyone was speaking Welsh and he drove off in a huff. I found out later that he'd always fancied Tessa and had asked her during the reception to elope with him. "Can't do that, Nick," said Tessa. "I've only just got married but I'll certainly keep the offer in mind!"

Later that night a beautiful thing happened. The dregs of the party were still drinking in the residents' lounge. It was closing time and Bangor bars had no extension after 10.30 p.m. The police enforced this restriction rigidly, so the narrow street in Lower Bangor opposite the cathedral was thronged with drunks who had been thrown out of the pubs but wanted more booze. Fights and scuffles started, accompanied by the sound of breaking glass. The police were losing control of the situation. Heather, Tessa and I were watching from an upstairs window of the hotel. "Let's go down and sing for them," Heather suggested. This was a brilliant idea, and so we got our guitars and went out into the crowd. We stood on the low wall that surrounds the cathedral and sang and played to the crowd for an hour. It was terrific! The drunks went quiet as we sang with no microphones and just two acoustic guitars. We got a huge ovation, and the chief of police came and thanked us afterwards.

When I woke up in the morning in George V's bed, Tessa was convulsed by pain in her abdomen. I phoned an ambulance, which took her to hospital. She had peritonitis and was operated on immediately. By now, most of the eisteddfodwyr had left town and Bangor had fallen strangely quiet. My mother had driven home after the party, so I was alone with the children. I thought that I would just have to stay there with the children until their mother was well enough to travel back to Carlisle. I phoned my mother to tell her what was happening, and she offered to travel to Bangor to pick Wizzy and Bethan and take them home to Solva. Meanwhile I moved to a cheaper room in an annexe of the hotel.

The operation was successful; we had got her to hospital before the septicaemia had time to spread. She was discharged in a week and came back to the hotel, but she wouldn't be fit to travel for at least another week, which screwed up our summer holiday honeymoon. She was still in quite a lot of pain for which pain killers and sleeping tablets had been prescribed. For most of the next week Tessa rested in the hotel. She seemed to be recovering quickly, that is until one night when I woke up at around 3.30 a.m. We were sleeping in twin beds, and there was a dim neon tube above the wash basin in the room. I noticed straightaway that Tessa's bed was empty, the sheets and blankets thrown back. She was standing in her dressing gown by the wash basin with her back to me. "Are you alright?" I asked quietly. There was no answer, as if she hadn't heard my voice. Then I heard something rattle, and I got out of bed to see what she was doing. The rattle was the sound of the sleeping pills that she was swallowing by the handful. An empty bottle of painkillers lay in the washbasin, and the bottle I took from her hand was half empty. I was surprised that she was still on her feet. I walked her across the yard to the phone in the foyer; I'd heard that you had to keep people who overdose on the move and awake, and so while the ambulance was on its way I walked her round the hotel, shouting in her ear and shaking her. She was sagging and nearly asleep when it arrived. I was in a state of shock and the nurses in the hospital were really annoyed; they don't think much of people who overdose on pills. They took her away, pumped her stomach out and told me to come back in the morning as they had to keep her in under observation.

Next day, it was a very worried man who arrived at the hospital. Tessa was sitting on her bed crying hysterically. When she saw me she begged me to get her out of there. A nurse and a doctor were trying to calm her down, but with no success at all. The Pakistani doctor told me that she could be suffering from post-operative depression and that they were expecting a psychiatrist to arrive any minute. I knew that if they found out about her treatment at Carmarthen and Garlands mental hospitals she'd be back inside again, so I had her discharged into my custody and duly signed the forms.

We took a cab back to the hotel, where I put her to bed. She began to calm down and begged my forgiveness, while thanking me for saving her life. I asked her why she'd taken all those pills. She said she didn't know, because she couldn't remember doing it! It was as if she'd been sleep walking or in some kind of trance. The next day a doctor came to examine her, pronounced her unharmed and said the stitches from the abdominal operation could soon come out. I decided to take her down to Cardiff where she could convalesce at the Sunbury Hotel, and I phoned my mother to ask her to hang on to the children.

# Chapter 19

# *Domesticity*

Tessa recovered quickly; she had always been physically strong due to being brought up in fresh country air and her lifelong love of riding horses. The children stayed in Solva with my mother, and Tessa travelled by train to Carlisle to settle her affairs there and to get ready for the move to Cardiff. I hired a box van and driver, and we drove up to Carlisle to fetch Tessa and her belongings.

The house in Evansfield Road was small: a single-fronted, bay-windowed house, it had three downstairs rooms, a back kitchen, and a long garden leading to a back lane and the railway station. Upstairs there was a large room in the front of the house, well-lit by two large bay windows. Behind leading off a long landing lay two more bedrooms and a small bathroom and toilet. The downstairs hallway was quite long, leading to the kitchen. There was an outside loo. The house had not been modernized. A few doors up were some shops, a chemist and a bookmakers' shop with a Barclays bank opposite and a pub, the Railway Hotel, just over the road. It was a convenient, comfortable place to live and was only a fifteen-minute bus ride from the city centre, less on the trains which ran every half hour, or we could walk to town from Llandaff North along a tow-path beside the River Taff. It's a splendid scenic walk that leads through Pontcanna fields and Sophia Gardens into the heart of the city.

When the furniture arrived, there wasn't much of it. I think the only large piece was a very old leather sofa donated by Tessa's parents, which Tessa could remember since childhood. As it happened, Big John Tyler had got divorced again for the umpteenth time, and his ex-wife, who worked at the BBC and was a regular at the club, sold me some beds. There were two fireplaces on the ground floor, one in the front room and the other in the dining room; we both loved an open fire. The children came up from Solva with my mother, who was eager to see our new old house, which was very light and airy. I was really contented. Soon I set to and made a dining table and two benches; I just bought some pine and some tools and they were finished in three days. I made the middle room into a study-cum-workroom, where there was a desk, a reel-to-reel Akai tape recorder and a stereo. There were lots of book shelves in the alcoves and a French window leading to the garden. This was the first home we'd lived in since those happy Caerforiog days. John Morgan called and booked me to do another series of *John Morgan at 10.30* for HTV; I'd already done one series with no problems. Soon Wizzy was old enough to go to school, and she went to a Welsh-language school, one of the first in south Wales, Ysgol Bryntaf in Gabalfa, just down the road. Everything seemed to be falling into place.

An old friend of mine, Charles Oliver Bethel, one of the old Moulders Arms' crowd, had just returned from a long stay in Majorca where he'd been running a bar with two American hippies, Charlie Sprague and Larry Tahune, from Maine and Boston respectively. Both of them came from very wealthy backgrounds, but their lifestyle and behaviour had displeased their families and they had been sent to cool down on generous allowances in Europe. Sprague was nicknamed Charlie the Whore, and Tahune was nicknamed Borracho, Spanish slang for drunk. Charlie 'Puta' spent most of his time in the whorehouse above one of their favourite bars in Palma. On one occasion by the time their allowances arrived they'd run up such a massive bar bill that Tahune said, "Fuck me, man, that's big bread. How much is the bar worth?" It was peanuts to them, so Charlie – who had also inherited a lot of money after his father died – sent home for money, and the small bar and the whorehouse above were soon under new management. This didn't last long, however; the local cops didn't like their style and they eventually closed them down at gun point and issued a twelve-hour deportation order. Charlie Bethel came back to Cardiff and bought a club in St Mary's Street called Les Connoisseurs, commonly known as Good-time Charlie's Elephants' Graveyard.

The Chapter Arts Centre had just opened in an old school in Canton, and all the freaks – many of whom were hippies and hairies – used to congregate there. There were some four or five folk clubs in Cardiff at the time, as well as a poetry club run by Pete Finch and called No Walls. Cardiff was very much alive in those days, even though it was still old fashioned and dilapidated, especially down the docks and in areas on the periphery of the city centre such as Grangetown, Canton, Adamsdown, Pontcanna and Roath. The city hadn't changed much by the beginning of the 1970s and it was still much as I remembered it from my student days. The old open air market on Mill Lane was still in full swing, as was the New Moon Club, which must have been the best R & B club in Wales if not in Britain. The Moon was something else!

Bara Menyn got together once again for a TV show in Dublin. We flew out of Cardiff airport and were soon in the Abbey guest house on Mary Street behind the O'Connell Street post office. The house band on the show was The Chieftains. It was one of those 'homely' shows; the set resembled a tea room in rural England with tables, farmhouse furniture and red and white checked gingham tablecloths. While I was there I met a ballad singer named Al O'Donnell who also worked as a designer for Telefís Éireann. He took me to Slattery's bar in Cable Street where he was singing and playing guitar in a cellar folk club. I asked about the 'real' music, i.e. traditional Irish music, which at the time was totally instrumental, and he said he'd introduce me to some musicians who'd take me to the Pipers' Club. The Pipers' Club is an esoteric gathering of some of the best fiddlers, pipers and accordion players in Ireland, and it was then held in a semi-derelict building up a narrow alley in north Dublin. No guitars were allowed – they were considered to be untraditional and had no place in proper Irish folk music – and so I discreetly left mine at the hotel. There was no alcohol permitted either, and I just sat on a box by a big log fire listening to various fiddlers while a group of around fifteen or twenty players of multifarious musical instruments knocked out jigs and reels all night in another room. The people who'd taken me there in a black Morris Minor, all carrying mysterious black boxes (containing musical instruments) had vanished into the ceildh room. When I emerged from the building at dawn, I had no idea where I was. I've only ever met two non-Irish people who've been to the Pipers' Club.

Soon after the Dublin trip I was invited to play in Voss, a ski resort in central Norway. I sailed from Newcastle to Bergen, where the organizer, a young guy called Arild Vernasse, met me and we travelled by train into the mountains. It was March, and the weather was bad; there were high mountains, huge lakes and lots of snow. The gig itself was in a jazz club, but I often ended up playing in people's houses. The Norwegian kids were most enthusiastic about the outside world. Nothing much seemed to be happening in Voss: the weather was so bad that no one was skiing even.

After three days I flew back to work on the *John Morgan at 10.30* series. The plane took off from the mountain-surrounded airport at Bergen, which was a bit hair raising. It then landed at Stavanger, where we had to change planes. We were invited into the duty-free shed,

*In front of the Cambrian Hotel in Solva, 1972*

*Me, Tessa and Bethan in Evansfield Road, Cardiff in 1972*

where I purchased some champagne and a bottle of Old Crow whisky for John Morgan. I also bought myself a beautiful hand-knitted Norwegian jersey. Back in London, I met Endaf Emlyn, who was working as an announcer at that time at HTV. I was rushing through Paddington and there he was. So we travelled to Cardiff together where a car was waiting to take me to the HTV studio. I just made the show. That was the first of two trips I made to Norway. The second was like a working holiday and I took Tessa and the girls along. We stayed in a ski lodge high in the mountains, but again the weather was bad and I still haven't had the chance to ski down a Norwegian mountain!

Back in Cardiff an equitation centre had opened near the HTV studios in Pontcanna, so we joined and used to go riding there twice a week. Tessa seemed to have returned to normal and didn't show any signs of flipping out again. She had always been a great clothes designer and good with a sewing machine. The wardrobe lady at HTV, the late Dorothy Hodge, needed another assistant, and so Tessa got the job. Everything seemed fine; by now the girls were both in Ysgol Bryntaf, and the house was comfortable and well furnished, Tessa and I were still more or less veggies, and cauliflower cheese was a favourite dish. We bought bicycles and would cycle down the tow-path to the studios in Pontcanna.

We used to drink in the Old Arcade and the Horse and Groom in Womanby Street, which was then an Irish pub run by a friend of mine, Vaughne Davies, who was a big gambler; in fact, everyone in that pub seemed to be a punter and there was a betting shop right opposite. Charlie Bethel would hold court at the Horse and Groom after he'd surfaced after a night in Les Connoisseurs. Much heavy drinking was going on, and most of the BBC club people would also go to Charlie's club after the bar had closed at the BBC club. Charlie's was open till 2 a.m. and anything went; it was a pretty wild place and

Charlie used to hire strippers from an agency in Bristol. Hippies also began to frequent the place, and there was a lot of dope around.

The Conway pub in Pontcanna was another favoured meeting place. A lot of Welsh people would go there, quite a few media types, poets and artists. At that time Conway Road was very dilapidated; many of the bigger houses had been converted into bedsits and there was a community of original Cardiffians living in the smaller ones. Children would play ball games or skip in the streets, and there was a very natural and homely atmosphere. The area around the Conway had once been the orchard of the marquess of Bute, which is why there are so many old fruit trees growing in the gardens. Many now have gone as the area has become overdeveloped. I still have a few friends who live there, and it's now an upmarket suburb.

Wizzy acquired a guinea pig on a trip to London. I was in the Warner Brothers office in New Oxford Street, and Tessa, Wizzy and Bethan went with my old college friend Angela Morgan to a school fête in Hampstead. They returned with a hairy guinea pig in a wooden box, and just a week later back in Cardiff, Louli, as Wizzy called her, gave birth to six more. This went on for a couple of years, and I used to have to take them down to the pet stall in the central market where they were sold into slavery for half a crown each. Wizzy has always been mad about animals, especially horses. She now breeds show ponies and Weimaraner dogs.

I had decided to record my first album of new songs, and so I booked Central Sound in Denmark Street, London. I found two musicians through Peter Swales, who was still working at the Rolling Stones' office in Maddox Street. The drummer was called Gordon Smith, but I can't remember the bassist's name. Pete played singing saw on one track, and the whole album was recorded in two days. I called it *Gwymon* (seaweed). One of the songs, 'Merch o'r ffatri wlân', was a song that I'd written in English for the John Morgan show.

Around this time I began to experiment with songs, by translating them from English to Welsh and vice versa. It was a prolific time for my songwriting. I also wrote an elegy for my Uncle Syd, who had worked in St David's Cathedral as a carpenter.

Tom Davies, a journalist who'd worked on *The Times* and *The Observer,* had come back to live in Cardiff. He had recently signed a contract with a major publishing house to write novels, but he also had his own weekly arts show on HTV called *Nails.* The long elegiac poem I wrote for my uncle was commissioned by the producer of the show, none other than my old friend Gareth Wyn Jones. The piece was called 'The Dewsland Rake'. John Tripp, a Cardiff poet and member of Yr Academi Gymreig, who was a friend of mine at that time and a mighty boozer and raconteur also contributed to the show.

The late Ray Smith the actor, who lived in Dinas Powys, was another member of our drinking club. Ray worked mainly in London, but he'd often go on tour with various theatre companies. I saw him once playing Henry II, with Iona Banks as his queen, at the Grand Theatre in Swansea. He was a very talented actor and had an amazing voice very similar to Richard Burton's.

Rhydderch Jones had bought a house in Heol Hir, Llanisien, and his home always seemed to be full of north Walian actors who'd descended on Cardiff seeking fame and fortune on television. Rhydderch too was a prominent member of the boozing club, which was itinerant and moved between the BBC club, the Horse and Groom, the Conway, Charlie's club and Cyril Clark's clubs in the docks. Quite often, and especially after a show, Rhydd would invite everyone to his house for impromptu parties, where everyone would have to do a turn, a song or maybe read a bit of poetry or tell a story. The whole scene was extremely creative, fuelled mainly by gallons of booze and platefuls of Vindaloo curry! We had some good times.

*Gwymon* was finished and released on the Dryw label, and the album became famous. Quite a few of the tracks were dance music and were very handy for Rhydderch who, as producer of BBC TV's *Disc a Dawn*, had changed the format of the show to make it more like *Top of the Pops*. He still had a thing about dancing girls in mini skirts! As it happened *Gwymon* was the last album I was to record for some years. Unbeknown to me, a big change was on the way.

Les Connoisseurs was situated on the first floor above and to the right of the Castle arcade in High Street. A door on the landing to the left opened on to a small vestibule, then a dark red baize door led to the club, which was basically one large room with a long bar to the right and a small wooden postage-stamp of a dance floor. The large windows, which overlooked the street, were always obscured by floor-length dark red velvet curtains. The carpet was of the same colour; the place was dark and dimly lit. There was a side room, originally intended to be a dressing room for the strippers but now full of junk. The music was supplied by a twin-deck record player. Charlie's club opened at 12 noon until three, then again at 10.00 p.m. until 2.00 a.m., or until the last drunks left. In the afternoon Charlie served businessmen's lunches of steak or plaice and chips, and strippers would perform as the punters ate. A lot of the city centre drinking crowd would also frequent the place. At night time it was different, anything went and anyone could go. Consequently, Charlie's customers were a mixed bunch of hippies, businessmen, journalists, TV types, actors, poets, artists and hustlers. There were no rules to speak of; people's behaviour was unmonitored, and there were a few minotaurs lurking around the dark and dusty alcoves. Charlie's club was a big distraction, and I shouldn't have spent so much time and money there; it had become a bad habit.

Tessa's behaviour during this time was back to normal, or so I thought and she was doing well in her job as a dresser at HTV. She used to go on location quite frequently working as a wardrobe dresser

*Filming for* John Morgan at 10.30 *in 1972*

*Filming on the Gribyn in Solva for a documentary during Haverforwest eisteddfod, 1972*

262

on TV dramas. This is when things started to change for the worse, and this is when the philandering must have begun; to say that a lot of philandering going went on amongst the TV crowd would be a gross understatement. Tessa was working on one of the soaps and she'd gone to north Wales for a shoot. The crew were staying in a good hotel in Shrewsbury that I knew quite well. While she was there it was her birthday and I decided to pay her a surprise visit, take her to dinner and give her some flowers and a present. A rather angry "What the fuck are you doing here?" was the only welcome I got. Immediately, I recognized the insanity in her face, but I stayed for dinner and it was a bewildered and anxious man who caught the last train back to Cardiff. She was obviously having another affair.

From that point, life at Evansfield Road began to deteriorate. Tessa would be absent a lot of the time, and I had to spend more and more time looking after the children. Quite often if we were out at Charlie's club or another late-night watering hole she would refuse to come home with me and make a huge scene if I objected. Tessa could make a lot of noise for a five foot nothing chick wearing size three shoes! I would just go on home to bed; sometimes she wouldn't arrive home until four or five in the morning, sometimes not at all. I knew that under this kind of pressure it wouldn't take long for her to flip. This was a dangerous situation work-wise for both of us. I don't know to this day who her lovers were – I only knew they were media types, probably HTV people, most of whom were married men. There was definitely more than one man involved in the fun and games, probably three or four. What worried me was that television is a cut-throat business, boat rockers are frowned upon and don't last long. Having a well-known artist – such as I was at that time – wandering around asking embarrassing questions whilst trying to locate his wife was an embarrassment to the management among others and soon Tessa got the sack. Dorothy Hodges, the head of wardrobe who was a good friend of mine, didn't want to lose Tessa, but she knew as an old hand in television that I would understand. None of the people at HTV knew that Tessa was a certified chronic schizophrenic. She wouldn't have got the job otherwise, I could only wait for the inevitable. I would do nothing for this lemming, who was racing at speed for the big drop.

My work was suffering, and in television there is always quite a long queue of people waiting for a chance to jump into the front man's shoes, if they think they can get away with it. The fact that she'd been sacked from her job didn't alter her lifestyle; she still hung around with the TV crowd and went drinking and clubbing with the showbiz set. She had introduced me to a young girl who she said was coming to live in our spare room. The plan was that Pat would help out with the kids. In practice, this meant that Tessa could disappear more often and for longer periods of time, which is exactly what happened. I didn't know where she was half the time, and this girl would just hang around the house drinking coffee and playing records. Often the 'babysitter' and Tessa would disappear together, leaving me on my own with the children. All this was affecting much more than my social life; it was hitting my work, my writing, my painting and my composing.

One Sunday evening, Tessa announced they were going to the folk club at the Chapter Arts Centre in Canton, and that I would have to baby sit. Tessa and this girl were now some kind of item, or so it seemed to me, but I don't think they were lesbians; they were more interested in pulling men. The girl was a bit of an amateur folk singer, and she had a nice voice, a bit like Joan Baez. There were a lot of Joanies and Bobbys around in those days! I played my part in this ridiculous situation, but I was tired, angry and frustrated all the time.

One night Pat arrived home late minus Tessa and I cracked. This had been going on for over a year and I'd had enough of it. Reluctantly the girl told me where Tessa was. She'd gone home with a young student who sang at the folk club. I got the address out of her and went down in a cab telling the taxi driver, who knew me, that something weird was about to happen!

The house was in King's Road, Canton and I told the cabbie to wait. I broke in by smashing a window and then crept to the top of the second flight of stairs where the student's room was, opened the door and turned on the light. There were Tessa and Romeo bullock-naked in bed. Tessa leaped at me screaming and spitting, trying to inflict as much damage as she could, but I threw her aside and grabbed the terrified kid by the throat. Tessa was now on my back, biting and punching. I could easily have thrown the student through the top floor window which was wide open. Instead, I threw him back onto the bed, grabbed Tessa, threw her over my shoulder and charged down stairs. She was making a lot of noise and the house was waking up. What the grinning cabbie saw was an angry man carrying an even angrier woman, hysterical and naked over his shoulder. He opened the door and I threw her into the back of the taxi. "Home, James!" I panted, still trying to restrain my biting, spitting, foul-mouthed wife.

When we got home, I went straight to bed, leaving Tessa and the lodger in the lounge. I must have fallen asleep soundly; getting rid of all that tense frustration without killing or badly hurting someone had felt great and well worthwhile. But when I awoke, the bedroom was filled with choking smoke – Tessa had set fire to the bedclothes as I slept. I was very lucky to leap out in time to put out the fire. The madness had returned, the lodger hurriedly left and things looked grim. I phoned my mother and took the children down to Solva.

★ ★ ★

At the time I was working at the time on a historical drama series, a sort of Robin Hood-type adventure series, produced by Patrick Dromgoole for HTV and being filmed on location in Somerset. It was called *Arthur of the Britons*, and a special set had been constructed in the heart of a West Country forest, in the form of an Iron Age village of thatched huts encircled by a palisade of wooden stakes. It looked very authentic. Celts versus Saxons and Norsemen was the name of the game, and some well-known actors were taking part: Brian Blessed, Hillary Dwyer and Oliver Tobias, to name but a few. It was the first time for me to act in a television drama series, and I even had lines, I quite enjoyed dressing up as a Celtic warrior and being King Arthur's court musician. I was also commissioned to design and build a prehistoric stringed instrument based on a Welsh *crwth*. The series kept me busy and away from home most of the week, the pay was good and the bills were being paid. We all stayed in a posh hotel in Bristol called the Unicorn. Nevertheless, I found it difficult to concentrate; my own domestic drama was distracting to say the least.

Hillary Dwyer was terrific and a great comfort to me. She had recently broken up with her husband and we were able to compare notes in the corner of a soggy Somerset field while I gave her singing lessons. We also did quite a bit of boozing, drowning our sorrows, let's say. She was a great girl and a brilliant actress.

One night I was fed up of the hotel, so I took a taxi in torrential rain to Charlie's club in Cardiff. When I walked through the door, there was a gang-bang in progress involving a good-looking dark-haired Irish girl, who was lying in the middle of the dance floor, and some quite well-known poets, actors and BBC types. From the safety of his bastion behind the bar, Charlie thought it was a huge laugh. I sat on a bar stool, my back to the orgy and drank a few bottles of German beer while Charlie's guests exhausted themselves in Ireland.

ning for John Morgan
10.30

I went home to an empty house; at least the children were safe in Solva. Tess wouldn't fuck with my mother; for some reason she had always been shit scared of Bet. Later the next morning I went to the Horse and Groom where the gang-bang was the main topic of conversation amongst the bar flies and gamblers. Suddenly the door flew open and in walked the pretty Irish girl who'd entertained them so well the night before. She was dressed in a smart green velvet suit, sheer green stockings and green leather high-heeled shoes. An embarrassed hush fell on the room as the girl went from man to man, quietly tapping each of them for a large Jamesons. It was quite surreal; no one refused her and after a while she was gone through the door in a trice. This type of debauchery was commonplace at Charlie's. Although he seemed to be a genteel and well-educated man, at heart he was no more than an uncouth rugby centre. His honour, integrity and credibility as a businessman and club owner were dubious to say the least.

By this time the psychiatrists had caught up with Tessa, who from the maelstrom of her madness had admitted herself to Whitchurch mental hospital, just up the road from our home in Evansfield road. The girls were still in Solva, and the house had become a crash pad for some of the homeless reprobates from Charlie's club – Larry Tahune, one of Charlie's mates from Majorca, Charlie Sprague, who was a quiet but dangerous player, Roger, Charlie's driver (dubbed 'the minister of transport') and Tom the Nutter all used the place as an extension to Charlie's club, the betting shop and the Horse and Groom. I suppose that they had to live somewhere. International bohemian debris, infamous alcoholic druggies, pimps, prostitutes, perverts and poets, they all pitched up at Evansfield Road as my family life fell around my ears like the ashes of Dresden. There were quadrophonic sounds in every room, naked nymphos cavorting everywhere, Mexican ponchos, Texan boots, peote, acid, amyl nitrate, speed, sacks of marijuana, as well as hundreds of gallons of wine, rum, whisky and gin.

Tessa was let out of hospital after what felt like years, although it was only a period of some three or four months. I had been going to group therapy sessions at the hospital, which entailed a psychiatrist, the patient (Tessa) and me, in a room talking about 'the problem'. Tessa was back on heavy medication, and the doctor told me that they were trying to find a drug that would stabilize her. I told them it was definitely not alcohol, which does it for me up to a point! None of this was getting anybody anywhere, but at least Tessa was secure in Whitchurch and the kids were safe in Solva with my mother. I too was reasonably safe as long as Tessa was locked up, and so I did my best to ignore the party that went on morning, noon and night in my house. I was weak, confused and vulnerable, but I had to find a way out of this fucking mess! What could I do under these crazy circumstances – no one seemed to give a shit. It seemed as if I were surrounded by maniacs. Was I crazy too?

# Chapter 20

# Saved

I went to see the doctor in Church Road, Whitchurch, the one who'd had Tessa sectioned. He also happened to be our family GP, and I had quite a long chat with him that morning. I told him that I thought I was losing it – my nerves were shattered. He asked me if I had many friends and I said that I had but that they didn't come around much any more, probably because all the trouble I'd been having in my life. He didn't want to prescribe Valium and said it would be wiser just to go out with some friends and have a few drinks. I didn't tell him about Charlie's club and the Horse and Groom, or the lunatics who'd been dosing at my house. Fortunately, the crazy gang had all decided to move the party to sunnier climes, to southern Spain, where Larry Tahune had a yacht in Torremolinos. The house was empty except for me, the quadraphonic sound systems silent. I still visited the hospital regularly, and the psychiatrist told me that Tessa would soon be stable enough to come home on weekends.

It was on one of these weekend visits that I awoke once again to find it hard to breathe. For the second time, the bedroom was filled with thick black smoke, this time emanating from a bonfire which Tessa had lit in the middle of the floor. She had started to perform the evening before – hysterical, shouting abusively, and threatening violence. After failing to get in touch with the doctor I just went to bed. I later found out that she'd collected all my favourite clothes, my hat and boots and the sweater I'd bought in Norway, and had ignited the fire with the aid of combustibles such as eau de cologne and perfume. I went across to the public telephone by the Railway Hotel and phoned first the fire brigade, then the doctor. By the time I got back to the house, a neighbour was trying to douse the flames with buckets of water, while Tessa screamed, raved and laughed hysterically on the landing. The doctor and firemen arrived almost simultaneously and while the doctor carted Tessa, still raving, up the road to the hospital in his red Triumph Spitfire, the firemen, big heavy men in bulky firefighting clothes, put out the fire. The bedroom and the landing were totally destroyed. So was I.

I must have been lying on the green tweed carpet in the downstairs front room where, in more peaceful times, Nansi Richards (Telynores Maldwyn) and her friend Edith Evans (Telynores Eryri) had played with my children. For a week, or maybe a fortnight, I'd lost all sense of time and could only remember the odd lurch to the back kitchen for a drink of water and a pee in the outside loo. I couldn't remember the last time I'd eaten – there had been no food in the house for ages, and I hadn't been in a fit state to go shopping. The phone, gas and electricity had all been turned off; I couldn't say for how long. One day I just lay down on the floor of the downstairs lounge; my bedroom on the first floor had been destroyed. I couldn't get myself together, and nothing mattered anymore. This sudden descent into darkness had knocked me flat. There was no day or night, and no light in my life. I had fallen into a deep dark abyss out of which I could not climb. Occasionally I would hear the mailbox rattle, but I just couldn't respond. I certainly didn't hear the doorknocker, a brass sailing ship I had fixed to the door when we moved into the house. Later some friends told me that they had called, but when they received no response to their repeated knocking and could see the house in darkness behind closed blinds they'd gone away thinking that I'd probably gone to Spain with the others.

The regular work I'd been lucky to get from the BBC and HTV had long since dried up, and I had become a prisoner of circumstances. In reality, all I had to do was open the front door and walk out into a summer's day, but even such a simple act was beyond me. It was all I could do to drag myself off the floor and creep along the wall to take a drink of water and a piss. Sometimes I would sit on the toilet, I knew not how long, in some kind of trance or dream state, some weird unreality. I felt no emotion, even the basic survival instinct had long gone. I felt neither warmth nor cold, I felt nothing. There were no lights or heating in the house and I was too far gone to care, and meanwhile outside life went on without me.

I must have fallen on one of my visits to pee or drink. I had no idea when; I just woke up with a pain in my head and the taste of blood in my mouth. I must have fallen heavily and cut my face on the red tiled floor of the hallway or kitchen. Still, at least I was feeling something, the first feeling in a long time. I fingered the wound on my forehead; there was a lot of congealed blood on my face. Then I heard the brass sailing ship; someone was at the door. I lay where I was on the carpet, waiting for whoever it was to go away, but the knocking continued and I heard a voice calling through the letter-box. It was a woman's voice; I felt afraid and didn't want to be found in this state.

To this day I don't know how I dragged myself to the front door, where I found myself standing on a pile of letters and circulars. I could see the distorted shapes of two persons through the frosted glass pane in the door. "*Meic, Meic, agorwch y drws,*" ("Meic, open the door") someone shouted through the letter-box. I reluctantly shot the bolt and turned the brass knob of the Yale lock. Blinding sunlight flooded the hallway, and I saw two dark silhouettes framed in the open doorway.

The next thing I remember was finding myself sitting on the sofa in the lounge. Someone had opened the heavy curtains, the room was filled with light and there were two girls speaking to me. I couldn't take it all in; I just wanted to crawl away and hide. Suddenly one of the girls was on her knees by my side, her hand was on my arm. I thought she was asking me what had happened and whether I was alright. I couldn't answer. I felt far away; out of reach somehow. I must have been a terrible mess; I must have stunk to high heaven and looked dreadful, with weeks of facial hair, a wild animal. It turned out that these girls were helping put together a concert at the Sherman Theatre in Cardiff, which was being organized by Meredydd Evans of the BBC. It was a Sunday afternoon and one of the performers had dropped out at the last minute. No one had seen me for a long time and my phone was kaput, so Merêd had sent these girls to my house to see if I could sing in the show that evening. Everyone else was already at the theatre rehearsing.

I heard my faraway voice trying to tell them that it was impossible for me to perform but thanks for the invitation. But they were insistent that I go with them to the Sherman, and they left saying that they'd be back in an hour. My head was spinning. Was this a dream? Had somebody been here? The curtains were drawn – had I done that? I could smell Golden Virginia smoke in the air and recalled that one of the girls had rolled a cigarette, and there was an ashtray on the floor with two or three fag ends in it. Somehow their arrival had jolted me out of the black hole I'd been inhabiting for God knows how long. Shakily, I went into the kitchen and washed my face. The cut on my forehead wasn't serious but it had bled quite a bit. I found a razor and some soap and began to shave. Thankfully, what I saw in the mirror was the face of a human being. I moved upstairs, found a towel in the airing cupboard, went into the unburned bathroom, stripped off my filthy clothes and stood in the bath with both taps full on washing myself with soap and a flannel. Then I went into the undamaged front bedroom to find a clean shirt, jeans, socks and shoes. In the kitchen cupboard I found a can of beans which I opened and ate cold. The house was a slum, and I suddenly felt like drawing the curtains and resuming my hibernation. But the brass ship knocked again, an emphatic, loud, rat, tat, tat, and I knew somehow it would not stop until I opened up.

The same two girls stood there staring at me and smiling. They acted quite normally, and I was amazed that they hadn't commented on my disgusting appearance, now radically transformed. "What's their game?" I thought timorously. Was I still dreaming?

"Get your guitar. We'll have to go now. They're waiting for you at the Sherman." I didn't have a guitar; it had been sold long ago like everything else of any value.

"I haven't got a guitar here," I said.

"You can borrow one at the theatre. There are plenty down there," said one of my saviours. "Get in the car."

Siân, for that was the name of the shorter of the two girls, then drove us to the Sherman. Gwenllïan, the other girl, also sat in the front, and I stayed in the back. I felt like a pop star in the back of a limo. It was a long time since I'd seen the streets of Cardiff, and I enjoyed this surreal drive through Llandaf and Pontcanna, the sunlit fields stretching seemingly for miles down to the distant River Taf, and the tall trees in the park covered in bright green and copper coloured leaves. It was good that it was Sunday; in those days the city was quiet on Sunday with hardly any traffic and few pedestrians. If it had been a weekday I might well have had an anxiety attack like I used to have when addicted to Valium. I was experiencing a mild sense of agoraphobia, but not that bad. I felt as if I'd taken an acid trip half an hour before and couldn't tell if it was going to turn out as a nasty hallucination or a beautiful clear trip.

I'd played the Sherman before and knew the layout of the building. We found our way to the green room where I got a huge welcome from Merêd, always magnanimous, gracious and friendly. He offered me a drink which I declined. God knows what alcohol would have done to my fragile constitution. I ordered an orange juice and a sandwich, which went down well. I can't remember everyone who was there; my head was somewhere else that day. Luckily, Siân and Gwenllïan had opted to stay with me as minders, which gave me some confidence. Someone brought me a guitar, and I retired to a corner to see if I could still play it. I hadn't touched a guitar for months, but I could still pick out a tune. A few people came over for a chat, asking how I was and where I'd been. I felt embarrassed.

The rehearsal went reasonably well; I sang three songs accompanying myself on the guitar. Merêd was in the stalls applauding loudly and shouting encouragement, but I felt rather deflated as it must have been a weak performance. They seemed to understand that I'd been through some troubling experience and handled me with care. Later, though, in the green room which was now rapidly filling with other performers, I suffered from an attack of stage fright, a feeling which is very foreign to me. Brother James's air, 'Yea Though I Walk…', went through my mind, along with faint memories of being a choir boy at St Aidan's long ago, of Harbour House, and of Blodwen and William Henry going up the hill to church on a Sunday night on the pillion of Uncle Hayden's terrifying BSA 500 motorcycle. So what is fear and what am I frightened of? I silently thanked those beautiful girls who had unknowingly hauled me out of the pit of darkness. Suddenly here I was, back in the land of the living. After the concert, my Samaritans drove me home and I slept in a bed the first time for months. Early next morning I got up and began to clean the house. I felt like an evil spell had been broken.

Next day I took the 24 bus into town, alighted by the castle, and crossed the road to the Horse and Groom. Pushing the stained glass door open I saw that nothing had changed; the usual crowd was refreshing itself at the bar. I may have changed, but none of them noticed. I felt reassured, ordered a pint of bitter and picked up *The Sporting Life*. Early in the flat racing season, the odds are good on two and three years olds. I sketched out a Yankee – six doubles, three trebles and an accumulator. By4.30 p.m. I'd won £2,500 and I was back in the game, listening dreamlike to the same old bullshit from the city centre n'er-do-wells, hustlers, and con artists. "What's real, me or them?" crossed my mind. Later I went to the station and took a train to Haverfordwest. I had some debts to pay to my mother and my children. I'd been out of the game too long, and I had to make things right.

Back to sunny Solva, before the stink of tourism arrived. Betty was fine, and so were the girls. I'd have to return to Cardiff and repair the fire damage before they could come home and restart school, and, of course, Tessa was still locked up in Whitchurch Hospital and that had to be dealt with as well. Back in Cardiff, I got hold of some Irish builders who used to frequent the Horse and Groom. They came up straight away to clear up the fire damage; within a week the house was back to normal and the debris carted away. I had the phone, electricity and gas reconnected and still had a tidy sum of money left. I resumed my visits to Tessa, who was now responding to treatment in hospital. The doctors told me that when the children were back from Solva, she would probably be ready to come home and that having the children with her again would be therapeutic – I lived in hope, but I doubted everything they said regarding Tessa.

Nevertheless, she was discharged from Whitchurch quite soon after I brought the children back to Cardiff at the end of the summer holidays. I could see that all was not well and probably never ever would be. Fortunately, the children were oblivious to their mother's problem and were quite happy going to school every day. She was on medication prescribed by the hospital and as far as I knew she was taking it. I felt like a nurse and a nanny, but I continued with the gigs etc. Tessa started going out to her usual haunts, and sometimes we'd go out together. However, I did feel that I was just going through the motions; the thrill had gone as had the desire to help her. I no longer needed Tessa in my life. It would be better to go our separate ways. But what about the kids?

I came home late at night from doing a gig in north Wales. The house was in darkness and unusually quiet. When I went upstairs, the children's beds were cold and empty as was Tessa's bed. By now we slept in separate rooms. I was very tired and began to panic, but there was nothing much that I could do at 1.30 a.m., so I got into bed and went to sleep. In the morning the telephone remained silent – there was no word from Tessa. I phoned the GP who told me that to his knowledge Tessa was still an out patient. He told me that he'd check the hospital out, and later he phoned me back to say that as far as they were concerned she'd been discharged and should have been at home. I phoned the school to find that the girls were not there, and then some friends but they hadn't seen Tessa either. Eventually, I phoned the police and reported them missing. Two police officers came to the house and asked the usual questions. Had there been a row? No. Could she have gone to stay with friends? Not that I knew of. There was no note, nothing. The police told me to sit tight and they'd try to find them. My heart was sinking fast and I was getting angry! All I could do was sit in the house waiting for the phone to ring – SHIT!

On the morning of the third day, there was a knock at the door. On the doorstep stood a middle-aged hippy lady wearing a long embroidered kaftan, lots of beads and an Afro hairdo. I'd seen her before at the Chapter Arts Centre folk club and at Charlie's club, but I'd never been in her company. She always had a gang of bohemian arty types, usually very drunk, hanging out with her, and she used to drive them around from pub to club to party in a white Morris

Traveller van. They always seemed to be on the booze around town, and I'd always wondered what their relationship could be. She was a lot older than the company she kept.

The lady's name was Pat Newman. She said that she knew Tessa, and that Tessa had told her in the folk club the previous Sunday that she could no longer live with me. As a result she'd offered Tessa and the kids 'sanctuary' in the large house which was her home in Albany Road. I got angry and soon found out that this do-gooder was totally ignorant of the true nature of the situation and of Tessa's mental health problem. Tessa had spun her a yarn, from which she deduced that my rocky relationship with Tessa was due to the sort of matrimonial problem that could be ironed out by a marriage guidance councillor and some social workers. The woman also told me that Tessa had told her that she didn't want me anywhere near her and the children, and that if I came round her house she'd have to call the police. Then she got in her car and drove off. I had to phone the police to call off the hunt for my family. I was extremely angry, and when I phoned my mother in Solva she reacted in the same way too.

"Cool down, and box clever, Meic" – that was the only way to deal with this problem, I had almost convinced myself that Tessa was a lost cause and that we'd have to go our separate ways. I just couldn't take any more of her, and I'd probably have to let the kids go as well. I knew that this was a stupid idea, but at least I was thinking in a fairly logical way, which would have been impossible a month earlier.

I decided to infiltrate Pat Newman's entourage of bohemian drunks and try to get some inside information. This was easy because they frequented the same dens of iniquity as I had before the shit hit the fan. Eventually I got the information I was after. As I'd thought, Pat Newman was a middle-aged hippy. She was married in her early teens to a ship's cook, who was now a window cleaner, and they had three teenage children. The straight life that she and her husband led was not good enough for her, and she was trying to organize a divorce by running around the pubs, clubs and other 'more interesting' places with her gang of pet loonies. She had recently purchased a shack in a field at Broadhaven on the coast of St Brides Bay. A community of hippy types was squatting there in the old chalets and caravans that English drop-outs had erected between the wars. Broadhaven must have felt like the end of the earth at that time, a good place to feel free in. It's much the same now but much more touristy. This latest community of modern drop-outs predated the New Age travellers by some twenty years and was a static group of like-minded people who lived on social security, stealing and dope dealing. Ninety per cent of them were drop-outs from cities in England, and a lot of them had done time in jail.

Pat Newman and her children, accompanied by Tessa and my children, ended up living there. In one way it was a good thing for me because I had a lot of family and friends in the area and they could relay information back to me. In fact an uncle of mine on my grandfather's side of the family owned the field. He never got paid any rent, and so he was trying to evict the squatters. I knew this would be a short-term arrangement, which was a hopeful thought. One day, I decided to take a trip to Solva; the music scene had gone flat and I wasn't playing much, which was boring and not good for the bank balance. I went fishing with a friend of mine from Solva and we would often drift across the bay in a 14 ft dinghy powered by oars and an outboard motor. Sometimes we'd land in Little Haven, whose inhabitants have a long-standing relationship with Solvaites. We would take our musical instruments and stay at the Castle Hotel for a couple of days or more, drinking and entertaining the locals.

We caught a lot of mackerel that day, more than three hundred, and I suggested we take them to the hippy field and feed the five thousand. This was how I got to see the children. Most of the people there had small kids, who would run around naked, playing and having a good time in the sunshine, whilst their parents lounged around smoking hashish or tripping on LSD. That's the way they lived, and the locals took little notice of them tucked away in their field behind the trees. I only managed to see Tessa, who was living in a caravan with a heavily tattooed jailbird from Milford Haven; the kids were up in Pat Newman's chalet most of the time I was there. Al, my boat mate, and I left after four days. The situation was beyond my control anyway, for Tessa had obtained a custody order for the children behind my back. God knows what she told the magistrates about me!

So I went back to Cardiff to lick my wounds and try to plan some kind of future, which I couldn't picture without the children. One Saturday afternoon I was sitting in the old BBC club in Newport road, having a few drinks with Rhydderch Jones, when suddenly my saviours, Siân and Gwenllïan, crashed through the door. They'd had a few drinks by the look of them.

"Having fun, girls?" says Rhydd, smiling.

They'd been out on the town the night before and a hair of the dog led to a few more. Siân had crashed her mini and they'd been pulled by the cops, who had carted them off to the central police station.

"This is a drag," said Siân. "We've been arrested again."

"No way," says Gwenlli. "We haven't had enough to drink yet!"

"Let's do a runner. When we get through the front door I'll run right, you go left, and we'll meet at the BBC Club in Newport Road." (Sanctuary!)

We spent the rest of the day drinking, then went to a restaurant before ending up at Cyril Clark's club in the docks.

"Meic, man, will you do somethin' about your friends?!'

"What's happening, Cyril?"

"Man, they too much! Fuckin' on my furniture and spewing on

de carpet!" I'd never noticed this kind of behaviour; it was much too dark in Cyril's club and I couldn't recognize anyone across the width of the room even! But I tried to console him more than once. "It's that Selwyn man, he de culprit!" A lot of singing, dancing and cavorting was the order of the night, and we got very pissed. I woke up in the morning to blinding sunlight streaming in through the bedroom windows and a strange girl fast asleep alongside me. I went down to make some coffee. The girl in the bed was Gwenllïan.

Gwenllïan shared a small attic flat with Siân in Rawden Place near the Canton bridge quite near the city centre. She'd come to Cardiff looking for work after graduating in history from Bangor University a couple of years earlier. We got on like a house on fire and enjoyed each other's company tremendously. Soon I was in love again! Gwenllïan was a terrific girl and made the best *cawl* I'd tasted since my grandmother died, and that's saying something. She had relatives from Solva, the descendants of an old Captain Prance, a well-respected mariner who had lived in Solva years ago.

We talked a lot about travelling, especially to Brittany, a place she knew well. I'd thought about going to live and play music there for some time; she said that she'd be interested in coming along. After a while we agreed that this was a natural move to make. I sold off anything of any value in the house at Evansfield Road – by now, the Americans, Sprague and Tahune, had returned from Spain and the party had resumed. Charlie had gone bankrupt and was squatting in the club. He'd nailed the door up to prevent bailiffs re-possessing the place, but here was a secret entrance through which the hippies and other friends would bring him food and booze. Evansfield Road was no longer the place to be, so I gave them the keys and went to stay in Rawden Place with Gwenlli and Siân. I booked tickets from Plymouth to Roscoff and on the eve of our departure to Brittany, we went shopping in town for some necessary items: a small tent and some camping equipment including two clasp knives with bottle openers and corkscrews. *The Western Mail* had published an article on me that day with a picture of me sitting outside their office and a caption 'Fed Up and Off to Brittany'.

Later that night during a farewell meal at Angelo's restaurant in West Bute Street, we were pulled by two uniformed cops: "Somebody wants to see you at the station." I couldn't understand this intrusion. We were simply waiting for our meal to be served in Angelo's, where we were quite well known as regular customers.

"I'm not going to Central. We haven't done anything. What's it about?"

"Oh no," said cop one, "just round the corner in James Street Nick."

Foolishly we went with them in a police car; they had no right to detain us, it was a con. As soon as we walked through the door of the nick I spotted the reception committee, a plug ugly six foot odd sergeant, a lesbian WPC and two other uniforms. They waded into me without warning, as did the two cops from the car. I fought them as best I could, while Gwenlli fended off the WPC who fell on the floor. Then she kicked the bull sergeant in the balls. I managed to break free and ran out of the police station, sprinting down James Street. It was around midnight, I was tired and I wanted to go to bed!

"Fuck, this is ridiculous. Where's Gwenlli?" I asked myself, so I stopped running only to be pounced on by a pack of angry coppers and dragged back to the cop shop in handcuffs. The cops threw me into a cell, ripped all my clothes off and beat shit out of me – four to one, the arseholes! I could hear Gwenllïan in the next cell screaming insults at the cops and kicking shit out of the door. She'd been arrested a few times on Welsh Nationalist demos and bore no love or respect for the police!

Later we were taken to the dungeon cells under the central police

*Outside the* Western Mail's *offices in Cardiff during my last week in Wales before leaving for Brittany in 1974*

*Wizz, Bethan and Bet in Solva around 1974*

station adjacent to the magistrates' court, where we were locked up for the night separately. By now I'd made a phone call to my solicitor at Hallinans, and by six in the morning Ray Vidler, Martin Prowel and John Curran were looking at me bemusedly through the bars.

"What the fuck are you doing here? I thought you'd gone to Brittany?"

"The cops had other ideas," I replied.

The police charged us with being in possession of offensive weapons, the small knives we'd bought the previous day. They also charged us with resisting arrest and assaulting the police in the execution of their duty. We went before the magistrates at 10.30 a.m. John Blackburn Gittings (Lincoln Hallinan's protégé) represented me, and all charges against me were dismissed; they even returned the confiscated knife. Gwenllïan, who was represented by her brother Huw, was somehow found guilty on the grounds that she'd taken the shopping home to her flat and hadn't left the knife there. She'd simply forgotten that it was wrapped up in a paper bag in her pocket. So much for British justice I said as we walked out of the court and dived into the nearest pub. My mouth always gets very dry in court. I guess it's the adrenalin.

Some hours later we boarded a Brittany Ferries ship in Millbay docks, Plymouth, and sailed off into the night bound for Roscoff and freedom.

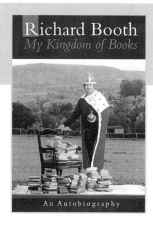

# My Kingdom of Books

## Richard Booth

The candid, anarchic autobiography of the colourful, eccentric second-hand book trader. Richard Booth recalls a lifetime searching the world for books, and his work in developing Hay-on-Wye as the second-hand book capital of the world.

£14.95    ISBN: 0 86243 495 5

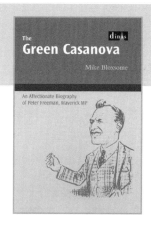

# The Green Casanova

## Mike Bloxsome

Peter Freeman the Newport MP was a vegetarian, animal rights activist, sports star, green campaigner and philanderer to boot. His parliamentary bill to ban fox hunting was introduced in 1929! He had a reputation as a man with many 'women companions', yet this is a love story as unexpected as everything else about him.

*"Peter Freeman emerges from this remarkable book as a brilliant humanitarian and devolutionist."*
Rhodri Morgan, First Minister of the Welsh Assembly

£6.95    ISBN 0 86243 741 5

# Years on Air

# TELERI BEVAN

## Teleri Bevan

*Years on Air* traces Teleri Bevan's long and successful career with the BBC in Wales from producer, editor and manager to senior administrator. Teleri candidly recounts the difficulties of balancing marriage and motherhood with her developing career, providing us with an important document of the cultural, political and economic implications of broadcasting in a Welsh context.

It contains a revealing insight into the BBC's history in Wales, describing the cultural ignorance and arrogance of the London hegemony. An endearing and personal account, it highlights the dominance of language politics and features many anecdotes about Carwyn James, Stuart Burrows and Wynford Vaughan Thomas and others.

This is a unique account of the BBC from a female perspective, and a personal account of one of the most interesting and influential developments in 20th century Wales.

£9.95     ISBN 0 86243 717 2

For a full list of our books, please
request your free copy of our
catalogue, or browse through our
website and order online:

**www.ylolfa.com**

Talybont Ceredigion Cymru SY24 5AP
*e-mail*   ylolfa@ylolfa.com
*phone*   (01970) 832 304
*fax*   832 782

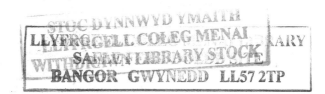